THE POTENTIAL EFFECTS OF INCOME REDISTRIBUTION ON SELECTED GROWTH CONSTRAINTS

A Case Study of Kenya

Osman Sheikh Ahmed

UNIVERSITY
PRESS OF
AMERICA

TO MY PARENTS

TABLE OF CONTENTS

PREFACE

There is growing evidence that the fruits of economic growth in most developing countries have not been shared by the poorest segments of the population of these countries. This has led to a re-examination of the objectives of economic development. It is now well-accepted by most development economists and policymakers that a successful development policy must aim not only at achieving a self-sustained growth in per capita income but also an acceptable level of equality in the distribution of income. As a result, interest in income distributions in the LDCs has increased recently as evidenced by the voluminous literature on the subject.

The literature on income distribution in the LDCs deals with two fundamental questions: Are there systematic forces in the process of economic growth that lead to concentration? What are the effects of redistributive policies on economic growth? The present study deals with the latter question. To limit the scope of the study, however, no formal link between income redistribution and economic growth is established. Instead the effect of various redistributive policies on selected growth-related variables is investigated.

Six transfer schemes are used by themselves and in conjunction with other policies like redistribution of factoral income, import substitution and increased rural productivity. The selected variables affected by these policies are: output (total and sectoral), demand composition, employment (broken down into four skill categories), capital requirements, imports (final, intermediate, and capital), savings (personal, business, and government), and the final pattern of the size distribution of income.

As a result of over fifty simulation experiments, it has been found that output, employment, imports, and capital requirements rise while aggregate savings decline under all experiments. As expected, the incomes of the lower income groups increase while that for upper income groups decline. However, this is mostly due to the transfer itself. The second effects resulting from the initial transfers are small and in most cases work in a direction opposite to the transfer, thus leading to a "trickle-up."

These results are generally in accord with those obtained by similar studies and no startling evidence has been unearthed. However, the present study has augmented the pool of empirical evidence on the effects of income redistribution. Most of the previous studies have been on Asian and Latin American countries and no such study has been done on an African country. Moreover, the model used incorporates numerous methodological improvements and is flexible enough to be used for investigating a number of development and distribution issues.

ACKNOWLEDGEMENTS

This study would not have been possible without the support and constant guidance of a number of people. First, Dr. Alfred Field of the University of North Carolina at Chapel Hill. His patience and constant advice were invaluable. Lots of thanks are also due to Drs. Robert Gallman, Denis Appleyard, Steven Rosefield and Ann Witte - also of the University of North Carolina - for their valuable advice. Many thanks also to Ms. Haley Goris of the World Bank's East Africa Department for sharing with me some of the published data in her possession. Finally, I wish to thank Ms. Ernestine Bland who patiently typed and retyped the entire manuscript from sometimes indecipherable notes.

LIST OF TABLES

CHAPTER 6
The Small-Farm Sector

Informal-Urban Sector

Formal Sector

CHAPTER 8

The main part of the study on which this book is based was undertaken during 1977-1978. It does not, therefore, take into account studies done after that period.

INTRODUCTION

Interest in income distribution in the less developed countries (LDCs) has increased recently as evidenced by the voluminous literature on the subject. During the 1950's and 60's the
main concern of development economists was growth. Equity was
presumed to follow as such development-related factors like
industrialization and improvements in education take place. This,
however, has not happened. The limited evidence in hand indicates
that inequality has increased with growth. This helped strengthen
the suspicion that economic growth by itself may not solve the
problem of inequity within a "reasonable" time. In fact, it is
argued that the very factors that promote economic growth also
lead to increased concentration of income and that attempts to
redistribute income more equitably would lower growth.

The literature on distribution in the LDCs deals with two
fundamental questions: Are there systematic forces in the process
of economic growth that lead to concentration? What are the effects
of redistributive policies on economic growth? The proposed study
will deal with the latter question. Since concern about equity is
mainly a concern for the plight of the poor in the LDCs, absolute
rather than relative income should be considered the major social
welfare variable, hence the importance of growth. To limit the

scope of the study, I will not attempt to establish a formal link between redistribution of income and economic growth. Instead I will analyze the effect of a successful redistributive policy on several important growth constraints like savings, foreign exchange, and labor absorption.

There is a wide range of policy instruments that could be used to redistribute income: income transfers, factor and product market intervention, asset redistribution, redirecting government expenditures to certain target groups, and subsidies for specific goods and services like foodstuffs, mass transportation, public health and education, to mention but a few. These policies differ in their ease of implementation -- some require institutional change while others do not -- their impact on economic growth, and their effectiveness in terms of final impact on the lower income groups. The choice between them is made difficult by the existence of strong complementaries that require simultaneous implementation, and by the problem of identifying the variables most responsible for concentration.

A full discussion of the pros and cons of the various policy instruments is outside the scope of this paper. My objective is to simulate the effects of a redistributive policy, however implemented. But since policies differ in their initial, and possibly final, impact the policy itself should be brought to the fore. For purposes of this study, direct income transfer from the rich to the poor will be the instrument used. The amount transferred will be varied and the results compared. The effect of other policies like factoral redistribution of income, increased rural productivity, and import substitution will also be investigated.

The study is divided into four parts. Part I (Chs. 1-2) is essentially a review of the literature on growth and development.

Chapter 1 deals with the size distribution of income in the LDCs, its "natural" evolution during the development process, and major determinants. Chapter 2 deals with the theoretical relationship between the pattern of income distribution and various growth constraints. The potential effect of income redistribution on economic growth and the differential effectiveness of different policy instruments are discussed.

Part II (Chs. 3-4) is concerned with the development of the basic model that will be used in this study (Ch. 3) and an overview of the existing pattern of income distribution in Kenya (Ch. 4). The theoretical model depicts the structural and technical relationship between the pattern of income distribution and various economic variables. The assumptions made in constructing the model and the methods of estimating the major endogenous variables are discussed in Chapter 3.

Part III is an analysis of the data on the size distribution of income (Ch. 5), employment and income formation (Ch. 6), and consumption and production relationships (Ch. 7). There is a dearth of such data on Kenya and whatever data are available are usually highly aggregative and sometimes contradictory. A major thrust of Part III is to reconcile data from the various sources and attempt to fill the gaps.

Part IV is a discussion of the results of simulation experiments involving various income redistribution plans.

PART I

LITERATURE REVIEW

CHAPTER 1

THE SIZE DISTRIBUTION OF INCOME IN THE LDCs

A. Introduction

There is growing evidence that economic growth in most developing countries has not been equitably shared between regions, urban-rural areas, and socioeconomic groups [Adelman-Morris (4), Adelman-Robinson(5), Ahluwalia (7), Fishlow (28), Weiskoff (89) and ILO (40), among others]. Growth has mostly benefited the already well-off. There is even some evidence [Adelman-Morris (4), for example] that the absolute income of the poor might have fallen with growth. During the 1950's and 60's it was well accepted that the rate of economic growth in the LDCs essentially hinged on the expansion of the "dynamic" modern sector [dual-sector models a la Lewis (64), Fei-Ranis (26)] and that everybody would benefit as the pie grows (the trickle-down hypothesis). It has been shown, however, that the "trickle-down" does not work and might in fact turn into a "trickle-up" in some cases [Adelman-Morris (4), p. 180], that distribution usually gets worse with development in the initial stages [Kuznets (60)], and that therefore growth might not benefit the poorest half of the population in the initial, and possibly later, stages of development. The issue of "distributional justice" had to be explicitly considered. This has led to a reexamination of the goals and objectives of development policy.

It is now well accepted [see, for example, Seers (77), Adelman (3), Chenery et al. (20)] that a successful development policy must aim not only at achieving "a self-sustained growth in per capita GDP and the modernization of the supporting socio-economic structure" [Meier (48), p.   ], but also an acceptable level of equality in the distribution of income.

Until recently, development planning models usually neglected distributional aspects [see Chenery et al. (20), especially chapters 2, 9, 10, and 11]. Chenery-Ahluwalia in [20] argue that growth and distribution should be combined in a single social welfare index which takes into account the distribution of growth. This index is a weighted sum of growth of all income groups:

$$G = \sum w_i \, g_i$$

where G = index of the growth of social welfare, g_i = growth of income of the ith group, and w_i = weight assigned to group i. The weights for each income class reflect the social premium on generating growth at each income level.[1] The conventional use of growth in national income as a measure of economic performance is tantamount to giving each income group a weight equal to its share in national income. Thus if the top 20% gets 70% of the

---

[1] P. 39.

income, then economic performance mostly measures the growth of that group's income without regard as to what happens to the rest of the population and especially the bottom half. Alternatively weights could be assigned according to each group's proportion in the population (equal-weights index) or the weight of the poorest group could be made unity while that for all other groups is set at zero (poverty-weighted index). In the latter, the exclusive concern is to raise the income of the lowest group.

Whatever the weights used, development must aim at improving the material lot of the whole population. Adelman goes even further. She stresses not only material equity but also the removal of social, political and spiritual deprivation for the majority of the population. The latter will in turn ensure the creation of conditions conducive to continuing improvements in equity. [2]

But equity, however defined, without growth might just mean spreading poverty around. Since concern about equality reflects concern about the "absolute poverty" of the poor, absolute rather than relative level of income should be considered the major social welfare variable. Therefore, growth cannot be neglected in search of equality of income unless the two are positively and monotonically related. In cases where they are not so related, emphasis should be on neither growth nor equity but on "equitable growth"

---

[2] P. 306. Equity encompasses more than just equality in income. It implies also equality in opportunities to further one's personal aspirations.

(defined possibly along the lines of the Chenery-Ahluwalia weighted index).

Until recently conventional wisdom was that there is a trade-off between growth and equality in the distribution of income and that while "an advanced country can afford to sacrifice some growth for the sake of social justice, the cost of greater equality may be too great for a country at a low level of economic development."[3] W. A. Lewis [65] also states that:

> "The LDCs cannot ride two horses simultaneously -- the horse of economic equity and the horse of economic development. The USSR has found that [out] ... and has therefore abandoned one of them"[p. 379].

These views imply several assumptions:

a) The rate of capital accumulation is the most important determinant (a la Harrod-Domar models) of economic growth.

b) The rate of capital accumulation is determined by the availability of investment funds.

c) Private savings are a major source of investible funds.

d) The marginal propensity to save of the rich is higher than that of the poor.

So attempts to redistribute income in favor of the poor might reduce savings, the rate of capital accumulation and thereby the rate of economic growth. On the other hand, it is contended that there are inherent forces within the system which would tend to reduce inequality as development occurs.

---

[3]H. Johnson [41], p.

The development process is characterized by capital deepening (increase in the capital-labor ratio) which with an elasticity of substitution of less than unity [4] would lead to an increase in the relative share of labor in the national income. Insofar as non-wage income is more concentrated than wage income, an increase in the relative share of the latter would lead to a reduction in the concentration of the size distribution of income. The above reasoning has important implications for policy. If redistribution would hurt growth and if inequality would automatically be reduced by forces inherent in the market system, the implication is to do nothing. The potential effects of redistribution on economic growth is the subject of the next chapter. The rest of this chapter will deal with the natural evolution of the pattern of income distribution during the development process. Are there inherent forces within the system that increase or decrease the concentration of income? If so, what are these factors?

B. The Distribution of Income in the LDCs: Functional and Personal

As mentioned above, the experience of the LDCs points out that neoclassical results of increasing equality do not hold. This raises several issues:

1. The relevance of neoclassical analysis to problems of distribution and development.

2. The degree of congruence between functional and personal distribution. Does an increase in the share of labor necessarily reduce inequality in personal distribution?

---

[4]This is supported by many studies. See, for example, Arrow-Chenery-Minhas-Solow [11].

3. An attempt to formulate theories of the size (or personal) distribution as opposed to functional distribution of income.

1. <u>The Relevance of Neoclassical Analysis</u>: The neoclassical assumptions of perfectly equilibrating markets and continuous substitutability of factors do not usually hold in DC economies, let alone LDCs. The range of available techniques are usually very limited and at times inappropriate for LDC's factor endowments, and factor markets might be imperfect. Either of these might prevent the functional distribution of income from improving.

a. Inappropriate Technology -

There is no evidence that the share of labor rises in the course of development even for DCs. The share of capital in the US has been constant during the 19th century [Abramovitz and David (2)] and has increased in some LDCs [see Hodd (36), for example]. Abramovitz and David argue that increasing capital-intensity of new investments makes "effective" capital scarce relative to labor, in spite of capital accumulation. Most of the current technology, whether capital-embodied or disembodied, is produced in the DCs and therefore reflects the DC factor endowments and might be inappropriate for LDCs [Eckaus (25)]. In the labor abundant and capital and skill scarce economies of the LDCs, capital-intensive techniques would lead to "technological" unemployment even if there are no factor price distortions. So with capital accumulation, labor share might tend to fall.

Recently there has been a lot of work done on the need for

adopting "appropriate" technology. Appropriate technology may be defined as the set of techniques which makes optimal use of available resources. Fei-Ranis [27] argue that there is a technological "ladder" containing techniques that have been developed and perfected in the DCs in the past. From this ladder the LDCs could choose the appropriate "step." Once imported, this technology could be "assimilated" into the domestic economic structure. The particular step chosen and the subsequent assimilation depend on the general skill level of the labor force. The main question, however, is whether such a ladder actually exists.

There is no evidence that the technology used in the US in the past (say 1900) still exists but even if it does, imperfect information limiting the number of techniques known to the LDCs, price distortion and entrepreneurial inflexibility might still constrain its adoption. The problems of transfer from the DCs would also remain an obstacle [Baranson (15)].

b. Factor Price Distortions -

It is argued that the relative strength of trade unions in the modern sector and the development of social policies that precede economic growth keep wage rates artificially high in most LDCs. Government industrialization policies also artificially lower the price of capital. The combination of artificially low price of capital and high wage rates lead to the adoption of highly capital-intensive techniques even where factor substitution is possible. Thus capital share might increase with capital accumulation.

c. Failure of the Market Equilibrating Forces -

It is now generally conceded that the equilibrating forces of the neoclassical paradigm do not always work. The presence of externalities, institutional rigidities and imperfect information are among the factors that constrain the smooth adjustment of the market forces. More important, the process of development is not one of uniform and smooth marginal adjustments. It usually involves "leap-frogging" and big "jumps" [a la Big Push and Balanced Growth]. Moreover, development is characterized by continuous disequilibrium processes with intersectoral and inter-regional disparities often increasing rather than decreasing (a la Myrdal's cumulative causation). Rural-urban income differentials have not been reduced with migration, increased unemployment is accompanied by rising wage rates in the modern sector, and dualism has become more widespread with development. The evolution of income distribution cannot, therefore, be studied within the conventional paradigm. Lastly, functional and personal income distribution do not necessarily move in the same direction.

2. The Incongruence Between Functional and Personal or Household Distribution of Income: The assumption that labor income goes to the poor while profits go to upper income groups does not hold in many LDCs. A substantial portion of the poor are self-employed and most wage earners are located in the upper income strata. Most of the poor live in rural areas where they are self-employed in farming. In urban areas, the bulk of the

poor are found in the informal sector where again most are self-employed. The problem, therefore, is not one of ownership but low productivity. Also unemployment and poverty are not synony-mous. Limited surveys relating employment and income level show a weak relationship. [5] Various studies indicate that more than half of the urban unemployed are high income aspirants, especially primary and secondary school leavers. This is not to imply that increased labor absorption would not help the poor. The fact that a high proportion of them are engaged in hardly productive activities might merely reflect the lack of employment opportunities. But it indicates that functional and size distribution of income are not necessarily determined by the same factors and that the latter might become more unequal even though functional distribution is improving. Conversely, policies designed to change functional distribution might have no effect or change personal distribution in the opposite direction.

The distribution of factor income across households depends on which households own which factors. Thus, wage payments to labor of different skills depend on which households supply which skill. An aggregate employment figure obtained by using economy-wide labor-output ratios fails to capture the demand for specific types of labor and other factors and thereby changes in the incomes accruing to different households.

---

[5]Chenery et al. [20], p. 136.

C. Theories on the Size Distribution of Income

     There is no fully developed theory of the size distribution

of income. The search for such a theory involved the following:

     a) Empirical investigation of the "natural evolution" of
         the pattern of income distribution during the develop-
         ment process.

     b) Attempt to isolate factors that are correlated with the
         observed pattern of distribution.

     c) Tentative explanations of the relationships and attempts
         to uncover underlying structural changes that could account
         for the observed relationship.

     1. The Evolution of the Pattern of Income Distribution During

         the Development Process: Kuznets [60] was probably the first

to observe that the secular pattern of income distribution during the

course of economic development follows an inverted v-shaped path.

He noted that for the presently developed countries (DCs) inequality

first increased but later declined with growth. In a cross-sectional

study,Morgan [51] also observed that inequality is usually higher in

LDCs than in DCs.

     Various empirical studies undertaken since then [Adelman-Morris

(4), Adelman-Robinson (5), Ahluwalia (7,8), Fishlow (28), Weiskoff

(89), among others] tend to support Kuznet's worsening-then-improving

hypothesis. Some of these studies [e.g., Adelman-Morris (4)] show

that the relative and sometimes the absolute income of the poor falls

in the initial stages of development. The position of the poor im-

proves as an intermediate level of development is attained but the im-

provement is not automatic as shown by Brazil [see Fishlow (28), p. 399]

and Argentina, Puerto Rico and Mexico [see Weiskoff (89)]. So explicit policies designed to benefit the poor are required if the absolute and relative incomes of the latter are to improve. A better understanding of the factors that determine the size distribution of income is needed in order to delimit the appropriate areas of intervention and the variables that should be altered.

2. <u>The Search for "Explanatory" Variables</u>: Using the multiple regression method, Ahluwalia [7] estimated the cross-country relationship between inequality as measured by income shares of the various percentile groups and selected variables reflecting different aspects of development.[6] The income share of the lowest 40 or 60% of the population is found to decline and then rises with increases in per capita GNP while the share of the top 20% follows the opposite pattern. No evidence of an independent relationship between the rate of growth of per capita income and the level of inequality was observed. This would suggest that a country with a higher growth rate might shorten the growing-inequality phase of development without generating greater inequality than structurally expected.[7] Ahluwalia also found that education, the rate of population growth, the share of agricultural production in total output, the degree of urbanization, and the ideological orientation of the country concerned also affect the pattern of the size distribution of income.

Education is positively related to equality in terms of the income share of the lowest and middle 40% of the population.

---

[6]Ahluwalia [7], p. 129.

[7]p. 128.

Primary schooling is more significant in explaining variations
in the income share of the lowest 40% while secondary schooling
is more important in explaining the share of the middle 40%. The
rate of population growth and the share of agricultural production
in the GNP (surrogate for the degree of dualism)are negatively re-
related to equality. The reverse holds for the degree of urbanization. As for the ideological orientation, socialist countries
are found to have the lowest inequality among the group of DCs
and LDCs studied.

Other writers emphasize the degree of integration of a
country's economy into the world market [Best (17)], especially
international capitalism [Frank (30)] and its alliance with the
domestic elite [Baran (14)]. The degree of dualism [Lewis (65),
Adelman-Morris (4)], and the degree of cultural and ethnic
homogeneity [Adelman-Morris, pp. 15-16] are among some of the other
factors mentioned as possible determinants of the pattern of
distribution. There has been very little empirical evidence,
however, partly because of the complexity of the subject. Even
where empirical studies have been performed [e.g., Ahluwalia], the
observed correlation of income distribution with other factors does
not tell us whether there is causation. Both dependent and independent variables might depend on as yet unrevealed variables.

3. Factors Underlying the Relationship Between Income

     Distribution and Economic Development: The inverted U-shaped
relationship between inequality and the level of per capita GNP
reflects the effect of structural changes that occur during the

development process. An explanation of these development-related structural changes and their relationship with income distribution follows.

  a) In a predominantly subsistence economy, the degree of concentration is constrained by the fact that output is only marginally above subsistence levels and so there is very little surplus to accrue to any one group.

  b) Increasing labor differentiation and the appearance of a small group of industrialists employed in the small but growing modern sector leads to an increase in the concentration of income. The high-income modern sector can accommodate only a small proportion of the population and linkages with other sectors are usually weak. This explains the increase in relative inequality.

  c) The absolute incomes of the poor might fall in some instances as segments of the traditional sector are displaced by the modern sector without absorbing the displaced persons [Adelman-Morris, p. 181].

  d) As the modern sector expands it is possible that distribution of income would improve as the per capita income of the traditional sector rises because of the absorption of some of the "redundant" labor by the modern sector.

The political and institutional environment within which development occurs could also be major factors affecting the evolution of inequality. Among them are the following: the extent of public ownership of productive factors and the political orientation of the government, the recency of independence, the degree of political participation and the strength of labor unions [Adelman-Morris (4)]; the distribution of asset ownership across households [Chenery-Ahluwalia in (19) esp. Chapter 11];

the amount of foreign investment and the degree of external de-

pendence [Baran (14)]; the extent of import substitute industrial-

ization [Krueger (59)]; the development of monopolistic elements

in the modern sector, partly resulting from the relative size of

domestic markets; the extent of equality in educational opportuni-

ties [Adelman (3), Tinbergen (87)]; and the rate of growth of

the population [Ahluwalia (7)] and family size [Kuznets (62)].

The above factors were found to be related to the size distribution

of income in the following ways:

  i) Socialist countries where productive factors are publicly-
      owned were found to have the lowest inequality among a
      group of LDCs and DCs considered. This is to be expected
      since in socialist countries profits do not accrue to
      individuals.

  ii) The political orientation of the government in power
      can affect the distribution of income in a variety of
      ways: subsidies for certain commodities, factor and
      product market intervention, fiscal and trade policy,
      redirecting government investment, etc.

      For example, in Brazil, the real minimum wages declined
      by as much as 20% in the period 1964-1967 while per
      capita income rose by 22% in the same period. This re-
      sulted from government measures introduced in 1964.
      Nominal wages were restrained not only to control in-
      flation, but to weaken the urban Proletariat as a
      political threat and to reestablish a political order
      conducive to private capital accumulation [Fishlow,
      p. 400]. Conversely, the distribution of income becomes
      more equal in Argentina under Peron and in Chile under
      Allende as a result of the political orientation of
      the leadership.

  iii) The degree of political participation: Government
      distributive policies usually result from political
      rather than purely economic considerations. In
      general, diffusion of political power would tend to
      lead to a more equal distribution of economic gains.

Some kind of political centralization, however, might be more favorable at earlier stages of development, especially if the political consciousness of the poor is not high and if "revolutionary" measures are needed.

iv) The strength of labor unions and their bargaining power is an important determination of the relative size of factor shares in cases where there are monopolistic elements and where the degree of substitution between capital and labor is low. But in countries where the formal or modern sector is still small the increase in labor share might just acrue to the well-organized workers who were already in the higher stratum of the income distribution. Personal income distribution might not becomes less unequal.

v) The distribution of land is a major determinant of the distribution of agricultural income and land reform is advocated as a means of redistributing rural incomes. The distribution of wage income and profits depend on the distribution of human and physical capital. "Socialization" of physical capital and improved access to educational facilities are some of the policies that could lead to an improvement in the distribution of income. The latter, however, can be effective only if employment opportunities also improve.

Many countries have subsidized higher education to the neglect of primary education thereby creating a skewed distribution of human capital. This is also reinforced by the fact that it is the children of more affluent families who can afford to stay in school longer. [8]

vi) Foreign investment affects income distribution in at least two ways: by increasing the overall capital intensity and having a demonstrative effect on the wage structure of the modern sector.

Theoretically, foreign investment would increase output and employment and so increase per capita income. It could improve the functional distribution of income by reducing the marginal product of capital and raising that of labor as inflow of capital occurs. In reality, however, foreign investment might not involve a net inflow of capital; might displace domestic producers; increase the degree of dualism in the economy and so

---

[8]Cline [23], p. 373.

worsen intersectoral distribution; increase the demand for skilled labor and so worsen the relative distribution of wage income directly and indirectly through "spillover" to domestic industries; and use technology inappropriate for the host country, thus not only raising the overall capital intensity but also possibly having a demonstrative effect on domestic production. In sum, there is reason to believe that relative inequality is increased by foreign investment. It is argued that in some cases even absolute incomes of the poor are lowered [Baran (14), Andre Gunder-Frank (30).

vii) Import substitute industrialization (ISI) worsens the distribution of income in any of the following ways [see Kreuger (59), Balassa (13), among others):

a. It discriminates against agriculture in favor of manufacturing. The bulk of the poor are engaged in agriculture in most LDCs.

b. ISI usually involves import restrictions and foreign exchange controls. The resulting overvalued exchange rates artificially cheapen the price of imported capital relative to labor and so lead to increased capital intensity and thereby reduced employment and worsening functional distribution. Overvalued exchange rates also reduce the profitability of exports as domestic costs rise relative to international prices. Since most LDCs export primary products which employ unskilled labor, reduced exports might worsen the size distribution of income.

c. ISI and the accompanying protection creates monopolistic elements which would contribute to a worsening income distribution. This is especially true in countries with small-sized domestic markets.

Conversely, once a country has attained a high degree of ISI, it might be forced to adopt regressive distributive policies. The reason is that the type of industries built during ISI usually sell to upper income groups and so redistribution would lead to underutilization of capacity and therefore lower industrial growth [Morley-Smith (71), p. 129].

viii) The rate of population growth is another variable that significantly correlates with inequality. The higher the overall rate of population growth, the greater the inequality as measured by the share of the lowest 40 or 60%.

It is estimated that birth rates (and consequently the rate of population growth) are higher in rural than in urban areas, and for poor groups than for the rich in urban areas. This differential birth rate has at least two effects on distribution:

a. The dependency ratio for the poor is higher than for the rich. Since children are consumers but not producers, savings of the lower income classes and consequently their asset accumulation are further reduced.

b. Large-sized families for the poor means that the relative income per household member is even lower than household incomes indicate [Kuznets (62)]. But it could be argued that this is partly compensated for by the fact that larger families need relatively less income because of certain economies of scale in consumption [Fishlow, p. 394].

Families are an important mechanism for redistributing income at a moment of time but also an important source for transmitting inequality into the future. [9] This is because children's earning capacity is influenced by parents' income through investment in human capital.

4. <u>Towards an Improved Methodology</u>: The usual methodology of specifying a simplified theoretical model and then testing it on the basis of scanty and sometimes unreliable data does little to explain the forces behind the observed pattern of income distribution. Income distribution is affected by sociocultural, political as well as a multitude of non-quantifiable economic factors. Moreover, the interaction between these factors and the extent of their presence differs between countries and so weakens the reliability of cross-country results obtained by fitting cross-country data to simple models. In testing the Kuznet inverted-U hypothesis,

---

[9]Fishlow, p. 392.

for example, it is assumed that most LDCs undergoing economic growth display similar characteristics and that long-term changes in the pattern of income distribution can be deduced by comparing the pattern of distributions of countries at different levels of development. The inclusion of more explanatory variables might not have a concrete pay-off because of the presence of non-linear interactions between individual variables and the fact that many are non-quantifiable.

Adelman-Morris [4] employ an overtly empirical approach "since theorizing about the subject to date has produced a variety of equally plausible but poorly validated hypotheses that do not provide an adequate basis for the construction of a priori speci-fied models" [p. 145]. Their study is not intended to provide any definitive answers but to offer tentative insights into the varied interactions affecting income distribution in the LDCs. Because of the importance of this study (it is referred to by most studies on income distribution in the LDCs) and its scope (it in-cludes 43 countries and considers 35 independent variables) I will discuss it at some length. [10]

The independent variables affecting income distribution in-clude not only economic but also sociocultural and political factors. Changes in the pattern of income distribution (the dependent variables) are measured by the income share of the lowest 60%, highest 5% and middle 20% of the population. The independent variables are:

---

[10]Especially chapter 4.

a) economic factors which include:

   i. The extent of factor endowments: resource abundance, adequacy of physical overhead capital, effectiveness of financial institutions, rate of population growth, and improvements in human resources.

   ii. Indicators of sectoral productivity and output compositions like the relative size, productivity and institutional structure of both agriculture and industry; the degree of dualism; and the composition of exports.

   iii. Information on the overall level of development: per capita GNP, rate of growth of the economy, size of the domestic market.

b) Sociocultural factors like the degree of urbanization, importance of the endogenous middle class, the extent of literacy, social mobility, ethnic and cultural homogeneity, and the prevalence of traditional values.

c) Political factors like the extent of political participation, the degree of centralization, relative strength of the different socioeconomic groups, the recency of independence and ideological leanings of the government in power.

Analysis-of-variance technique was used to "explain" variations in the dependent variables in 43 LDCs. The analysis proceeds in the following way: From the set of independent variables is selected the variable that "splits" the parent sample of 43 countries into two subgroups having the smallest possible combined dependent-variable variance. Each subgroup is then treated as a new parent-sample and the analysis again selects the variable that "best" splits the group into two subgroups, each of which is again treated as a new parent-sample and the process is repeated through a series of binary splits.

This technique finds the combination of values of the independent variables that predict the value of the dependent variables with the least error. It is similar to stepwise multiple regression but has the advantage of being able to accommodate non-linear interactions among the independent variables.

Next the results are discussed. For the 43 countries considered, the average income share of the poorest 60% is 26% and ranges from a low of 2% to a high of 38%. The share of this group is best "explained" by the extent of socioeconomic dualism, the level of social and economic modernization, and the expansion of secondary and higher level education [p. 160].

The poorest 60% received the largest share in countries with low levels of income where small-scale subsistence agriculture predominates (most African countries) and in moderately developed countries where widespread improvements in human resources have occurred (e.g., Korea, Taiwan). The income share of this group was lowest in countries where some development had occurred but it was concentrated in a small modern sector dominated by expatriate or externally-oriented domestic elite (e.g., Kenya). The results support the hypothesis that the income of the poorest group may not rise with economic growth in most LDCs.

The average income share of the wealthiest 5% of the population is 30% -- six times more than if income was evenly distributed. It ranges from a low of 15% to a high of 48%.

The relative resource abundance and the extent of government involvement in economic activity are the most significant variables accounting for the income share of the top 5% of the population. The share of this group is higher in resource-rich than in resource-poor countries. Within both group of countries, the degree of government involvement in the economic activity is most important in differentiating countries according to concentration. The share of the richest 5% is smallest in resource-poor countries where the government plays an active role in the economy and conversely for resource-rich countries where government role in the economy is small.

The average share of the middle 20% is 12% ranging from a low of 1% to a high of 17%. The share of this group is the only share that systematically varies with the level of development.

The primary "differentiating" factor is found to be the extent of socioeconomic dualism with countries having a predominantly subsistence sector showing the lowest share for this income group. Within sharply dualistic economies, the variable that best accounts for variations among countries is the institutional structure in agriculture. With the small modern sector mostly preempted by the top 5%, the income of the middle 20% comes from the agricultural sector. Their share in agriculture depends on whether small-scale, owner-operated cash crops or plantation farming and absentee landlordism predominates. The share of the middle group is highest in the former case.

Among relatively more developed, moderately dualistic coun- tries, the structure of foreign trade, the level of socioeconomic development and the degree of political participation are the main differentiating factors. The share of the middle 20% varies in- versely with the level of socioeconomic development. The benefits of development usually accrue to the upper 20%, not to the middle 20% of the population unless development is accompanied by sub- stantial improvements in human resources.

Countries with a diversified trade structure (most of them resource-poor) and direct government role in the economy show a higher than average share for the middle income group as do resource-abundant countries with widespread political partici- pation.

The above analysis supports the view that economic structure rather than level of economic development and the rate of growth of the economy are the primary determi- nants of the pattern of income distribution. Inequality is smallest in predominantly subsistence economies where there is little or no sectoral differentiation. The degree of inequality (as measured by the share of the top 5% or lowest 60%) rises as a narrow-based modern sector expands. This is most marked in

resource-abundant countries where a small expatriat or externally-
oriented elite predominates. As countries become less dualistic,
the share of each income group depends on improvements in human
resources, the degree of political participation and the resource
endowments of a country.

Improvements in human resources and wider political participation favor the middle income group at the expense of the top 5%.
Both the relative and absolute income of the lowest 60% fall as
the share of traditional sector in total output declines with
development and as traditional products are replaced by manufactured goods without absorbing the displaced workers into the
expanding modern sector. The income share of this group might
not improve even at higher levels of development unless there
are explicit government policies to improve the lot of the very
poor [Adelman-Morris (4), p. 181].

5. <u>Limitations of Empirical Studies</u>: Most of the empirical
work on the evolution of the pattern of income distribution during
the development process is based on cross-country data because of
the inavailability of time series data. This poses several
problems:

       a)   The impact of particular factors on the distribution
           of income depends not only on the level of income
           but also on the underlying socioeconomic structure
           in the countries considered. No simple relationship
           valid for all countries could therefore be deduced.
           Results based on time series data may be more reliable
           in that the underlying structure and the quality of
           the data are likely to be more comparable than cross-
           country data but are usually non-existent.

b) The interaction between variables in any theoretical relationship may vary between countries depending on the differences in underlying socioeconomic structure.

c) The highly aggregative nature of cross-country data conceals the factors underlying the observed in-equality. These factors might vary widely between countries yet produce the same overall degree of inequality.[11] The overall pattern of distribution is merely a weighted average of the sub-distributions of which it is composed; focussing on the latter might be more revealing than aggregate measures. For example, in highly dualistic economies it might be more reveal-ing to focus on inter-sectoral differences (i.e., between formal and informal) than on aggregate measures. Since most of the poor are located in the informal sector, reductions in inter-sectoral differences would mean improved relative distribution. Moreover, in order to formulate effective redistributive policies, one must know where the poor are located, the charac-teristics of that sector, and its linkages with other sectors. The distribution of income groups across sectors must also be determined. Two steps are in-volved. First, identify the composition and charac-teristics of different income groups by urban-rural, employment status and ownership and availability of assets. Then determine the source of income for each group by industry and by organizational sector (formal, informal). The first stage is purely diagnostic but this two-stage process might be more revealing than aggregate measures that conceal inter-sectoral differ-ences, and give a distorted picture of sectoral link-ages.

d) Cross-country variations can also result merely from differences in inequality indices used. Measures of inequality are sensitive to the indices used (Gini coefficient, variance of income, percent share, etc.) and cross-country as well as time series comparisons, using different indices, might lead to erroneous con-clusions. For example, Weiskoff [89] used the Gini ratio, the standard deviation of logs of income and coefficient of variation to estimate changes in in-equality. The Gini ratio and the standard deviation of logs of income both rose while coefficient of variation fell. Moreover, conventional indices which provide summary measures of inequality over entire populations are insensitive to the degree of inequality in particular ranges [see Atkinson (12) for example]. Income share data have an obvious advantage in that they shows changes in the income share of each group.

_____

[11]Ahluwalia in Chenery et al. [20], p. 18.

Conclusions

The search for the determinants of income distribution has
not been successful. This is partly because the issue, as addressed,
is intractable. The pattern of income distribution results from
a multitude of social, political, as well as economic forces which
cannot all be considered in a simple theoretical relationship. Moreover, the inclusion of more "explanatory" variables may not have a
concrete payoff as evidenced by some of the more complex models.
Many of these factors are not amenable to quantification and mere
ranking would entail a great deal of subjectivity. Also, there may
be interactions between these variables, the nature and direction
of which depends on yet another as yet undetermined set of factors.
In sum, all the socio-cultural, political, institutional, and
economic forces of a given country play some role in determining
the observed pattern of income distribution.

In addition to the theoretical problems, there is also a
dearth of data and whatever data are available are mostly cross-
sectional rather than time series. This poses several problems.
Results based on cross-country data may be misleading. The impact
of particular factors on the distribution of income depends on the
underlying socioeconomic structure. Thus, no relationship valid
for all countries can be obtained. The pattern of distribition
might be similar in two countries, but may result from totally
different forces and vice versa. Time series data would be more
appropriate in that the underlying structure and the quality of
data tends to be more comparable in a single country over time

than between different countries at a point in time.

At any rate, the main objective of trying to isolate the major factors affecting income distribution is to determine the set of appropriate policies, and an alternative approach could be adopted. Such an approach might involve two stages. First, to identify the composition and characteristics of the target groups and then to determine their sources of income and linkages with other groups. Once this is done, appropriate redistributive policies can be formulated. For example, if most of the poor are unemployed and are located in urban centers a strategy of increasing urban employment, possibly say adopting a more labor-intensive technology, might be appropriate. If, on the other hand, the poor are self-employed farmers, then raising their productivity should be the major policy objective. The instruments used would depend on the factors behind the low productivity and this would most probably vary between countries.

Whatever the basic factors underlying the observed pattern of income distribution, it is now accepted by most development economists that the problem of income inequality will have to be attached directly. But concern about equality mostly reflects concern about the level of absolute income of the poor and so the effect of income redistribution on economic growth should be considered. This is the subject of the next chapter.

CHAPTER 2

THE POTENTIAL EFFECTS OF INCOME
REDISTRIBUTION ON ECONOMIC GROWTH

I. Introduction

The relationship between the pattern of income distribution

and the level of output and employment have received particular

attention in the Keynesian literature [see Lubell (66), for

example]. Concern with these studies was in line with Keynesian

aggregate demand analysis to maintain a high level of con-

sumption. Redistribution of income from groups with low

marginal propensity to consume (MPC) to groups with high MPCs

would increase aggregate demand and thereby the level of output

and employment. The same reasoning does not hold for the LDCs,

however. The main concern in the latter is not the full utili-

zation of available productive capacity as is the case in the DCs,

but the creation of that capacity. A redistribution of income in

favor of the poor would lower savings and therefore the rate of

capital accumulation. Since capital is assumed to be the major

growth constraint it follows that output and employment would

be lowered with redistribution.

In recent years, a new aspect of the relationship between

the pattern of income distribution and output and employment has received attention. Redistribution of income affects not only the level but also the composition of demand. Insofar as there are variations in the factor intensity of goods consumed by different income groups, factor requirements for a given level of output could be altered by income redistribution. In general, goods consumed by the poor tend to be relatively more labor-intensive than those consumed by the rich. A more equitable distribution would increase employment and reduce the amount of capital, and thereby savings, required by a given level of output.

An important source of unemployment is the incompatibility of the pattern of demand with the resource endowments of an economy. Theoretically, foreign trade would eliminate this incompatibility. A country would export goods intensive in the factor it is relatively well endowed with and import goods that use relatively more of its scarce factors (a la Heckscher-Ohlin theorem). Practically, however, the aggregate demand-resource endowment gap might be reduced but never eliminated through trade. [1]

---

[1] The existence of dualism in the domestic economy (trade might be confined to the modern sector and linkages between the modern and traditional sectors might be small) and trade restrictions in international markets are some of the constraining factors. Also through demonstration effect, imports might rise relative to exports and so unemployment not reduced even though exportables are more labor-intensive than importables. Even if optimal allocation of resources could be achieved through trade, other problems arise: risk of specialization resulting from fluctuations in primary export earnings and possible deterioration in the terms of trade; dependence on trading partners especially if relative strengths vary and monopolistic elements prevail; and the fact that resource use in the foreign sector might not reflect opportunity cost of resources.

Redistributing income in favor of consumers of labor-intensive products would reduce unemployment and the stock of capital required for any level of output. The level of imports could also be reduced as a result of redistribution insofar as the marginal propensity to import by lower income classes is lower than that of higher income groups. Thus employment, capital requirements and foreign exchange availabilities -- major growth constraints -- are all affected by income redistribution. Redistribution of income might also have qualitative effects on growth. Entrepreneurial incentives might be lowered and the general health and nutritional status and subsequently productivity of the population might be increased.

Conceptually, then, redistribution of income in favor of the poor might set in motion growth-hindering and growth-fostering forces. The relative strength of each is an empirical matter and would expectedly vary between countries.

1. Forces hindering growth:

    a) Aggregate savings might decline if the MPS of the poor is lower than that of the rich.

    b) The volume of exports might decline because domestic consumption is likely to compete with exports.

    c) The volume of investment is likely to decline as entrepreneurial incentives are lowered.

2. Forces fostering growth:

    a) The income shift to the poorer income classes might change the demand for labor-intensive products, thus increasing employment and improving growth potential of labor-abundant countries. The demand for personal services might, however, fall. Capital requirements for given level of output would also be reduced.

b) Imports may be reduced and therefore foreign exchange availability increased in that

   i.   Imports of final goods would be reduced if the marginal propensity to import by the rich is higher than that of the poor.

   ii. Imports of capital goods may be reduced as overall capital requirements for a given level of output are reduced.

   iii. Imports of intermediate inputs may also be reduced if the goods consumed by the rich have a higher import content than those consumed by the lower income groups.

c) Increases in the level of consumption by the poor might improve their productivity and thereby foster economic growth.

The present study will deal only with the quantitative effects of redistribution. 1(c) and 2(c) will not be discussed. Omitted also will be the effect on exports. The level of exports is more of a function of international demand conditions than the level of competing domestic consumption. An increase in the latter is assumed to raise the level of output to the full extent of the increase in the domestic demand for exportables. The present study will not establish a formal link between redistribution and economic growth. The latter is affected by a host of factors of which those considered above are merely a subset.

II. The Theoretical Relationship Between Redistribution and Growth Constraints

A. Effect on Savings: One of the main arguments against redistribution of income is that total personal savings and therefore capital accumulation would be lowered by transferring income from "the rich who save to the poor who do not."[2] But there is also some evidence that, whatever the validity of this for the developed countries (DCs), the rich classes in the LDCs indulge in conspicuous consumption and emulate their counterparts in the DCs whose income is relatively higher. If this is the case then redistribution might not have a saving-reduction effect. Other writers [Furtado (32)], while not denying the savings-reduction effect of income redistribution, argue that increased consumption, especially by the lower income classes, would increase the production of those mass-consumed goods with potential economies of scale. Still others [Myrdal (72)] hold that increased consumption would raise the health and productivity of the poor. At least part of consumption would then have to be viewed as investment.

The importance of savings on growth can be illustrated by a simple Harrod-Domar growth model:

(1) $Y = F(K/V, L/U)$ where V and U are capital and labor-output ratios. Assuming full capacity utilization

(2) $K = VY$ or $\frac{dK}{dt} = V\frac{dY}{dt}$

For equilibrium

(3) $\frac{dK}{dt} = I = S = sY$, where s is the savings rate.

From (2) and (3) we have

(4) $V\frac{dY}{dt} = sY$

or $\frac{dY/dt}{Y} = \frac{s}{v} = g$, the growth rate that will insure equilibrium and full capacity utilization. From (4) we could see the importance of savings for growth.

---

[2]Cline [22], p. 13.

One way to increase s is to redistribute income from low
savers to high savers. Differential savings rates could be due
to either the level or the source of income. Kaldor [43] postu-
lates that savings from profits are higher than savings from wages
and that policies which redistribute income in favor of capitalists
would increase savings and therefore growth. Conversely, policies
that redistribute income in favor of labor would lower growth. The
basic tenet of dual sector models [Lewis (64), Ranis-Fei (26)] is
also that increasing the capitalist share would increase the rate of
growth on the assumption that the savings rate of capitalists is
higher than that of labor. According to some versions of this
model even a pure inflationary policy would create growth because
wages lag behind prices and thereby profits. [3]   Galenson-Leibenstein
[33] also favor capital-intensive investment because it increases
capital share and therefore the "reinvestment quotient."

The above discussion raises three important issues. First,
the relevance of the simple growth model where growth hinges on
savings. Second, the empirical issue of whether savings from profits are higher than those from wages and the wage earner-poor
classes overlap. Third, the proportion of personal to total savings.
If government, corporate and foreign savings are important, varying
personal savings alone might not have substantial effect.

---

[3]Lewis [64].

1. The Importance of Savings to Growth --

The simple Harrod-Domar or Solow-Swanson growth models
assume that growth of the labor force is given and concentrate
on capital accumulation. The latter depends on the availability
of investable funds and hence the importance of savings. In
pioneering studies Denison [24] and Abramovitz [1] showed that
the proportion of growth accounted for by conventional factor
inputs was small relative to the "residual." Although the
sources-of-growth methodology which Denison and Abramovitz used
was criticized [see Kelly et al. (44)], most economists now agree
 that growth and development entail much more than mere physical
capital augmentation a la Harrod-Domar. But even if capital
scarcity is the major growth constraint, most capital is imported
and the availability of foreign exchange constitutes another constraint. In recognition of this, the two-gap hypothesis has been
advanced. [4]   Growth also entails full utilization of resources
and that means labor absorption in labor surplus economies. Capital
accumulation, even if it proceeds at a rate higher than population
growth, might not be enough if technology becomes increasingly
capital intensive. This problem has been pointed out by Eckaus
 [25] and Fei-Ranis [27].   Skill availability constitutes yet
another constraint, but because of its complexity it has not been
incorporated into formal growth models. The effect of redistribution
on growth will depend on the combined effect on these other factors.
This will be discussed later but let us go back to savings first.

---

[4]See Chenery and Bruno [19], for example.

2. Differential Savings Rate of Different Groups --

The relation of savings rate to the level of income depends upon the type of consumption function used. In the linear Keynesian consumption function the marginal propensity to save (MPS) is constant but the average propensity to save (APS) rises with income. If consumption and income are related curvilinearly both the MPS and APS rise with income. In Friedman's permanent income hypothesis the savings rate is a constant fraction of permanent income. In the Modigliani-Brumberg life cycle model the savings rate mainly depends on the individual's age. Duesenberry's relative income hypothesis makes savings a function of relative (i.e., relative to the average for the relevant socioeconomic group) and not absolute income.

3. The Proportion of Personal to Total Savings --

The third issue concerns the proportion of personal to total savings. Total savings are composed of personal, corporate and government savings, and foreign receipts or

$$S = S_p + S_c + S_g + S_f.$$

There is no reason to expect that S_c and S_f would be altered by income redistribution.* S_g might be altered if taxes are highly progressive, but this might be offset by decreased welfare payments to the poor. The final outcome will depend on the situation but it is not likely to be substantial. The effects of income redistribution on savings will therefore depend on the proportion of

*It is assumed that business confidence is not adversely affected.

personal to total savings and the sensitivity of personal savings to redistribution.

B. <u>Effect on Demand Composition</u>: In addition to savings, redistribution of income could also affect the composition of demand. This could in turn affect growth through:

1. Reducing the demand for imports and therefore increasing foreign exchange availability.

2. Changing the degree of factor utilization.

1. Import Effect --

The role of foreign exchange in growth has been noted by Chenery and Bruno [19] among others. Lacking a well-developed capital goods industry, most LDCs rely on the importation of capital and intermediate goods. Scarcity of foreign exchange, therefore, imposes a constraint on growth in addition to savings.

Private imports of consumption goods also compete with the imports of productive inputs for the available foreign exchange. Income redistribution could reduce imports insofar as:

(a) The marginal propensity to import (MPI) differs between income classes. If MPI of the rich is greater than that of lower income groups equitable redistribution would lower imports of consumption goods.

(b) Domestic industries differ in their dependence on imported inputs. Usually luxury goods have a higher imported content than basic goods. A more equitable redistribution of income would increase the demand for basic goods relative to luxury goods and therefore reduce imported input requirements.

The effects of redistribution through (a) and (b) will depend on
the stage of import substitution attained by a particular country
and the extent to which domestic production can be increased.

Figure 1 [Cline (22), p. 31] illustrates the impact of income
redistribution on the demand for an income elastic (A) and income
inelastic (B) goods. Suppose Δy is transformed from the rich (r)
to the poor (p).

Figure 1

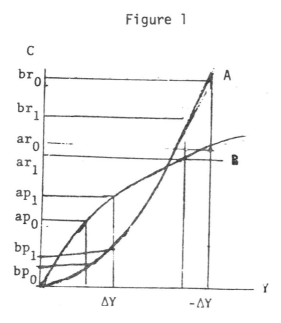

It can be observed that $br_0 - br_1 > bp_1 - bp_0$ and $ap_1 - ap_0 >
ar_0 - ar_1$ which implies that demand has shifted against A and
towards B. The impact on imports will depend on what proportion
of each good is imported. For LDCs that have not attained a high
degree of import substitution, usually more of the income elastic
goods are imported than basic goods. There are, however, exceptions
(e.g., food imports by many LDCs), and the final result can only
be ascertained by empirical analysis.

In cases where both A and B are domestically produced imports of productive inputs would be affected if the two goods differ in their dependence on imported inputs. As mentioned above, we would normally expect that goods that cater to the rich have a higher import content than those consumed by the lower income groups and that redistribution would therefore reduce total imported inputs. But that depends on the stage of import substitution.

During the 1950's and early 60's, many countries adopted import substitution policies in order to save foreign exchange. For those countries that have attained a high degree of import substitution, the import effect of redistribution would not be substantial. In fact, it is possible that once import substitution has occurred these countries might be forced to adopt regressive distributive policies.[5] The reason is that the type of industries built during import substitute industrialization sell to the upper income classes. Redistribution would then lead to under-utilization of capacity, and, therefore, lower industrial growth.

While import substitution might save foreign exchange, it leads to misallocation of resources and could prove costly in terms of domestic resources. Johnson [42] estimates that the equivalent of $4,000 in domestic resources is used to save $1,000 worth of foreign exchange in the Chilean automobile industry. The growth costs of import substitution have been succinctly discussed by Balassa [13] among others.

---

[5]Morley and Smith [71], p. 129.

2.   Effect on Factor Utilization --

Some studies show that total personal savings decline as a result of redistribution. [6]   This would reduce the amount of investable funds and thereby capital accumulation. But as mentioned above, foreign exchange might be a more binding constraint as long as most capital is imported. The possibility of import reduction as a result of redistribution has been discussed above. Another potentially important effect of redistribution is that expenditures might shift from capital-intensive to labor-intensive goods, which would lower capital requirements and at the same time lead to labor absorption.

Before assessing the factor utilization effect of income redistribution, let us turn briefly to the importance of labor absorption in the development of labor surplus developing economies.

It is estimated that unemployment and underemployment amount to 30% of the labor force in many LDCs and that this is rising due to population growth. [7]   It is suggested that the industrial sector must expand by more than the rate of population growth to ultimately absorb the surplus labor. Since the industrial sector represents less than 20% of total employment, that means it must grow at about 15% a year just to absorb increases in the labor force of 3% a year. [8]   The 15% rate, however, assumes that the

[6]See, for example, Chinn [21], Cline [22].

[7]Fei-Ranis [27], p. 75.

[8]Morawetz [69], p. 491.

overall factor use pattern does not change. It will be less if
more labor-intensive techniques are adopted, more if its capital
intensity increases. Evidence shows that the latter has been the
case. [9] One way to increase employment is to adopt techniques
"appropriate" for LDC economies. However, there are technological or
market factors that militate against the adoption of "appropriate
technologies (see pp.8-11).

An alternative way of changing current overall factor use to
a more "appropriate" one is to alter the composition of output if
it is found that factor intensity differs between goods. Note that
if the "appropriate" technology is forthcoming and can be adopted,
changing the composition of output would supplement it; if not, it
could prove to be a substitute. The composition of output is
largely determined by the structure of aggregate demand and the
latter is in turn influenced by income distribution insofar as
different income classes consume different goods. The extent of
the change in factor use will depend on the relationship between
the capital-intensity and income elasticity of goods. This is an
empirical question which will be investigated later.

III. Brief Review of the Literature

In recent years a number of studies simulating the effect of
income redistribution on economic growth have appeared [see, for

---

[9] Ibid., pp. 491, 496.

example, Adelman-Robinson (5), Bardhan (16), Cline (22), Foxley

(29), Paukert-Skolka (74), Soligo (80), Sunman (81), and Tokman

(88), among others]. Before the current spate of simulation models,

the effect of income distribution on savings has received the most

attention in the literature [Kaldor (43), Lewis (64), and Galenson-

Leibenstein (33), among others]. The early emphasis was on func-

tional rather than personal distribution. It was argued that savings

and capital accumulation would be lowered if the share of profits in

relation to wages falls.

To test the hypothesis that savings rates vary with the source

of income, Houthaaker [34] estimated the following equation for 28

countries:

$$S = \alpha_0 + \alpha_1 L + \alpha_2 P$$

where S = total personal savings, L = labor income, P = all other

income. He found that α_2 was twice as high as α_1. But the results

may be biased. If there is a high correlation between entrepreneu-

rial income and upper income level, the results might just be show-

ing that savings rates vary directly with income -- a result that

is not disputed by most economists. In Argentina, entrepreneurs

represent 30% of income recipients but 70% of the upper 10% income

bracket. [10] So what Houthaaker showed could be the relationship

between savings and the level of income without regard to the type

of income.

Friend and Kravis [31] compared the savings rates of entrepreneurs

---

[10]Chenery et al. [19], p. 43.

and non-entrepreneurs at each income level for the U.S. They found that savings ratios for entrepreneurs at low levels of income are lower than that of non-entrepreneurs in the same income bracket, but that this is reversed for higher income groups. The total contribution of each income group, therefore, depends upon the distribution of its members among the various income classes. In the U.S., this distribution is such that the average savings-income ratios for unincorporated businesses is 14% while that for all urban income recipients is only 4%. However, unless there is a high degree of congruence between functional and personal income distribution, the emphasis on functional distribution is misplaced. Available evidence shows that there is no such congruence. More than half of the poor in most LDCs are self-employed and do not enter the wage economy. Most wage earners are already in the middle-income groups, so that policies affecting the distribution between wages and profits concern the upper end of the distribution.

The attention of development economists has now shifted to personal distribution of income. Functional distribution is deemed important only insofar as factor ownership across income recipients differs and therefore affects the size distribution of income. A common feature of these studies is that they combine consumption functions by type of good, savings functions by income class, input-output relations, and factor and import coefficients by industry to determine the effect of income redistribution on savings, capital and labor usage and imports. The primary distinguishing feature between these studies and a possible cause in the differences of the results obtained is whether or not the income generation process is incorporated into the models. The initial redistribution leads to a subsequent change in income through employment and asset ownership. The first genre of these models [Cline (22), Chinn (21), Soligo (80), Sunman (81), Morley-Smith (71), Paukert-Skolka(74), Bardhan (16), for example] usually neglected this income generation process and merely measured the effect of the initial redistribution on various growth constraints. The results are then translated into growth (not by all studies) using Harrod-Domar relationship. The second-genre models which are undertaken mainly under the auspices of the World Bank [Adelman-Robinson (6), Sengupta-Thorbecke (84)] and the ILO [Pyatt-Thorbecke (86), Hopkins et al. (37)] explicitly consider the income generation process. These models reflect the level of sophistication attained in incorporating distributional issues into development models.

A. First-Genre Models: In general, the growth effects as well as effects on growth constraints of redistribution in the first set of models has been small, the actual magnitude, of course, depending on the size of the redistribution and the area concerned. Cline [22] investigated the potential effect of changing the distribution of income in six Latin American countries to the level of equality found in Britain. The results indicated about 6% increase in labor absorption and 3% reduction in capital requirements, between zero (Argentina) and 7.6%

reduction (Mexico) in savings, and virtually no change in imports. The latter probably reflects the fact that most Latin American countries have attained a high level of import substitute industrialization. Morley-Smith (71) concentrate on the effect of redistribution on the growth of industrial sector and find the growth of the dynamic industries such as automobiles and consumer durables is not retarded by equalization.

Chinn [21] obtained similar results for Taiwan and Korea. He found a negligible reduction in savings and no change in imports, and capital and labor requirements. These studies add weight to the growing evidence that the assumed growth-equity tradeoff does not exist and that a country can safely adopt income equalization without sacrificing growth. Oshima [73] even argues that the two might be positively related in some cases. He argues that promoting the growth of the informal sector (urban and rural) where the poor are located would reduce inequality and at the same time increase growth. This militates against the basic premises of the dual-sector models where the development of the formal or modern sector is assumed to be the key to growth and, ultimately, to an improvement in the absolute as well as relative income of the poor as more and more of them are absorbed into the high-income modern sector. Oshima's line of thought has been strengthened by ILO studies on Kenya [40] and Columbia [39].

It is argued that production in the informal sector is not only less capital-intensive than that in larger more modern establishments, but the kind of capital used is usually second-hand

and workers have very little embodied human capital. The informal sector does not therefore compete with the modern sector for the limited capital (especially imported capital) and human resources. Promoting the growth of this sector will not only foster growth of output and employment, but increase the absolute as well as relative incomes of the poor. One way to foster the growth of informal sector is to redistribute income in favor of the poor whose consumption pattern favor informal sector output. But this is still an empirical issue and rests on the still unsettled issue of factor intensity of the consumption patterns of different income classes.

Soligo [80], Sunman [81] and Tokman [88] are among those who made empirical investigations of the factor intensity of the consumption baskets of different income classes. In a study on Pakistan Soligo concludes that the capital intensity of demand increases with income and is greater for urban than rural areas. The implications for the rate of growth of income, employment and redistribution are then investigated. A distribution favoring the poor is found to require lower savings-income ratio or, given a certain level of savings, leads to a higher level of output. The actual magnitude will of course depend on the size of income transferred to the poor. The employment effects vary between the short-run and the long-run, with more favorable results obtained in the long-run.

Sunman [81] reaches similar conclusions for Turkey. Tokman [88] reaches contrary conclusions. In a study on the industrial sector

of Equador he estimates that industries producing non-durable
consumption goods are more capital-intensive than those producing
durable consumption goods. On the assumption that durable consumption goods are more income elastic than non-durable goods, he concludes that redistribution would not lower capital requirements
or increase labor absorption. The Tokman study, however, has
several shortcomings (some of which he himself admits [p. 50])
which could bias the results. First, all establishments employing
less than seven persons are excluded. He justifies this exclusion
on the grounds of unavailability of data. Second, his analysis is
not economy-wide but is limited to the modern industrial sector.
Insofar as output is dominated by few large establishments in a
particular industry, that industry would tend to be capital-
intensive. Third (and this is a problem that confronts most
studies), aggregation might result in distortion since a great
variety of technologies co-exist within each sector. For example,
non-durable consumption goods , tobacco and beverages are highly
capital-intensive while food processing, clothing and furniture
are typically labor-intensive.

The factor intensity will therefore depend on the relative
weight of different industries in each branch and the distribution
of establishments by size within each industry.

It is believed that small-scale, labor-intensive industries
are heavily concentrated in products with low income elasticity
which are regarded as necessities by the poor. [11]   Redistribution

---

[11]See, for example, Oshima [73], p. 170.

of income would therefore increase the demand for small-scale industry products and thereby increase labor absorption. While it is commonly agreed that small-scale industries are concentrated in the production of basic goods, the claim that technology varies with size is disputed.[12]

In the study previously mentioned, Tokman estimates the labor productivity (proxy for capital intensity) of different-sized establishments for shoes, clothing and wood furniture (three branches dominated by small industries and handicrafts). No systematic covariation was observed. Oshima [73], however, disagrees. He points out that in Asian countries the capital intensity of small concerns is one-sixth that of large ones in manufacturing, one-seventh in services, one-half in mining and two-thirds in construction.[13]

The differences in the two studies may reflect the special characteristics of the two areas considered (the Philippines and Equador), difference in data base (Economic Census of the Philippines, 1961; and Manufacturing Census of Equador, 1965), or may result from the very definition of small-scale industrial establishments. Oshima includes the informal sector while Tokman concentrates only on the formal sector. The difference in the results might be due to the sectors considered.

Singh [78] contends that in Kenya (the country of this study)

---

[12] See Tokman [88].

[13] Oshima, p. 170.

the problem of technology does not have to be given as much weight
in industry as in agriculture since a few large establishments account
for almost all industrial production.[14] The ILO Report for Kenya [40]
also finds that technology does not vary with size for industry.[15]
This points out the need for empirical work in other countries.
If technology is found to vary with the size of establishments
even within same modern sector industries, then labor absorption
would be maximized by channeling demand to smaller establishments.
But the relative efficiency of different size establishments would
have to also be considered. If efficiency improves with size there
would be a trade-off between output and employment. Even if employment is given a relatively higher weight, the larger more efficient
firms would just move in as the demand for basic goods increases
with redistribution in the absence of explicit policies to protect
the smaller establishments.

The Indian Planning Commission [Bardhan (16)] investigated
the effect of raising the income of the lowest 30% of income recipients by 60% over the 1974-1978 Five-Year Plan. The per capita
consumption of the top 30% was reduced to finance it. Assuming
that the overall growth rate of the economy would not be affected,
the projected growth of the different sectors was estimated. Of
66 sectors considered, the annual growth rate of 22 of them increased by about 1%. The consumption of food grains and textiles

---

[14]P. 396.

[15]P. 138.

was appreciably increased while that of durables decreased.[16]
Foreign exchange requirements were also reduced. This, however,
hinges on the dubious assumption that increases in demand for
foodstuffs can be met by expanding domestic output. The methodology was analogous to most of the studies mentioned above.

Paukert-Skolka [74] performed comparative static general
equilibrium simulations of alternative income distribution
patterns for the Philippines. The first version of the model
simply assumes that a certain amount of income is taken from the
rich and given to the poor [cf Chinn (21)] by a mechanism that
does not affect preferences between consumption patterns in ways
other than through income elasticities [p. 6]. In a second version,
distribution is affected through changing primary income patterns.
It is assumed that no changes in final demand other than private
consumption occur, that no divergence between savings and investment occurs as a result of redistribution and that prices and wages
are fixed. The results indicate that employment, GDP and personal
income increase, the amount of change depending on the alternative
distribution pattern assumed. The biggest increase is in the
employment level and the smallest in the level of personal imcome
[p. 30]. Employment increases amount to as much as 10% in some
cases. The volume of imports increases but the increase is less
than the increase in GDP so that the ratio of imports to GDP declines. Savings are reduced but public and corporate savings are

---

[16]Cf Soligo [80], Sunman [81], and others.

not. The latter depends on the level of GDP and so rises slightly.
Using data on the ICORs of 64 industries, the effect on capital
requirements are estimated once sectoral value added are deduced
from the changes in the composition of private consumption. A
small change in overall capital requirements is observed. The
reduction in savings and capital requirements is then combined
to estimate the implied rate of growth using average ICORs. The
loss in growth is found to be about one-half of 1% [pp. 38-39].

Almost all of the models mentioned above indicate that the
previously-assumed growth-equity tradeoff does not exist, or is
negligible and that regressive patterns of income redistribution
need not be tolerated. The primary focus of these models was
not the type of policy used to redistribute, although the results
would partly depend on that, but the effect of a redistributive
policy, whatever its nature, on economic growth. Prices and wages
were assumed constant and the nature of the income propagation
process was not discussed.

B. Second Genre Models: The new genre of studies took off
where the old ones left off. The main objective was no longer
to investigate whether a tradeoff exists but the kind of feasible
policy packages that would, in an acceptable time frame, lead to
the satisfaction of the basic needs of the majority of the poor
population, and the effectiveness of different policies. The
process of income generation is considered and many of the variables
like prices and wages that were hitherto assumed exogenously fixed

are endogenously determined. Probably the most important feature of these models is the incorporation of the income generation process. Most of the other features can merely be added onto the previous models.

- The Nature of the Income Generation Process -

There are two-way linkages between the distribution of income across households and the structure of production. The income distribution-structure of production linkage has been discussed. The structure of production also determines the size distribution of income via the distribution of human and non-human capital across households. The pattern of income distribution is embedded in the structure of production so that an initial income redistribution would induce secondary changes in the distribution of income. Income redistribution changes both the level and composition of private demand. The resulting change in output composition leads to a change in factor demand, the degree of which depends on the factor intensity differential of consumer goods. The resulting factoral income can then be mapped into personal or household income according to factor ownership. The resulting change in the size distribution of income leads to a subsequent change in private demand, output, employment and so again a change in the pattern of income distribution. This process would continue until the effect of the initial income redistribution dies out. Convergence can be insured by assuming an MPC of less than unity. The above process is illustrated below:

Change in income → Change in consumption → Change in →
of the kth group   of the kth group   output structure

Change in facto- →   via factor   → Change in income →
ral income   ownership   of vth group

The initial impact of redistribution could also fall on
the structure of production (e.g., changing technology, factor
market intervention, subsidies to the production of certain commo-
dities, etc.). The important point here is that whichever direction of the linkages one starts from, subsequent changes would
affect both the structure of production and the pattern of income
distribution. The sum of these changes would be more than the
direct effect of redistribution [Miyazawa (68)]. This would
probably explain why more marked results are obtained from models
that incorporate the income generation process than ones that do not.

The linkages between the structure of production, employment
and income distribution depend on the degree of dualism and the
sector in which economic activity is taking place.[17] In general,
linkages are greater in the formal sector than in the informal sector,
and least in the non-monetary sector which is a subset of the informal
sector. Therefore, production in each industry is further classified
according to the level of technology and the organizational sector
to allow for the existence of dualism.

Thorbecke-Pyatt [86] define production activities by type of

---

[17]Thorbecke-Pyatt, p. 39.

commodity, form of organization (i.e., formal or informal), technology used, and whether production is for market or own-consumption. A fixed-proportions production function is used to estimate
the derived demand for factors once production levels are known.
Incomes accruing to various households are determined from occupational and skill characteristics and asset ownership of households.
The model is applied to data from Sri Lanka. Its importance lies
not so much on results as in the method used. It is a substantial
improvement on a previous model co-authored by one of the authors
[Sengupta-Thorbecke (84)] where the mapping of factoral income to
households was done in an eclectic method. Using base year data
the authors calculated the ratio of labor and non-labor income to
sectoral value added in non-agricultural activities. Applying
this ratio to given year sectoral value added and dividing the
result by the number of economically active persons (EAP) in that
sector yields sectoral value added per EAP. This was used as a
basis for ranking industries. From this the distribution of labor
income in non-agriculture was derived. Non-labor, non-agricultural
income was allotted to the top 5% of the population. As for the
distribution of agricultural income, the lowest 50% received 20%
while the top 5% received 38% (Table 9, p. 28). The sum of these
components yield the personal distribution of income.

This methodology is based on a set of assumptions, the basis
of which is unclear. The fact that the results approximate the
actual distribution as estimated by others does not validate the
procedure. It may be valid for Columbia, for which it was designed,

but a more general method is needed to perform the mapping in other countries where the same conditions do not hold. Such a method was developed by Thorbecke-Pyatt [86] and Adelman-Robinson [6].

The two methods are similar except that the Adelman-Robinson model is in the neoclassical tradition with some short-term inflexibilities (i.e., factor markets do not respond to prices in the short-run)and is highly disaggregated. About 3000 variables are endogenously determined in a static and intertemporal framework. The model is validated by comparing model solutions for the endogenous variables with actual data and the results are extremely close. The potential impact of a set of policy packages on the relative and absolute incomes of the poor was then investigated. The results were found consistent with those of Thorbecke-Pyatt [86] and Hopkins et al. [37] and strengthens the authors' contention that it is applicable to a wide class ofLDCs. The major interactions between socioeconomic variables and the policy implications seem to be insensitive to a wide variation in parameter values. This would tend to increase the applicability of the results to countries other than Korea (to which the model was applied). Among the results obtained are:

1. It is easier to change functional rather than household distribution of income but the two do not necessarily move in the same direction.

2. It is easier to change the composition of the various socioeconomic groups than it is to change the overall distribution. Thus, it is easier to favor or discriminate against particular groups but difficult to change the relative degrees of wealth and poverty in the economy as a whole. This has implications for the rural-urban imbalance.

3. Single policies are usually ineffective and are quickly dissipated. Policy packages, on the other hand, may have significant impact on distribution because of the interactions between the different policies in the package. The outcomes of the combination of policies are rarely equal to the sum of their components.

4. The short-run and long-run effects of redistribution policies are different. In the short-run distribution is affected through wage and price adjustments while in the long-run quantity adjustments like migration, skill-upgrading and education are important [Robinson (56)].

   Other results of the model include:

   a. Confirmation of the Kuznets U-shaped hypothesis where distribution becomes unequal in the initial stages of development and later becomes more equal.

   b. Low income elasticity of demand for agricultural products by all groups.

   c. Rural households spent a larger share of their incomes on agricultural products as compared to urban households in the same income group.

   d. Price responsiveness of demand is fairly low and is less important in determining demand than income changes.

   e. The supply response to variations in prices are limited by the fact that:

      i) labor is not partially mobile across sector and skill categories in the short- and medium-run.

      ii) technology is fixed in the short-run. [Adelman-Robinson, p. 23.]

The Hopkins et al. [37] model is similar to Adelman-Robinson's and the results are in general the same. The former, however, is a long-run model and includes educational, demographic and migration submodels.[18]

---

[18] I have read Hopkins et al. [37] only through secondary sources, e.g., Robinson [75].

IV. Redistributive Policies

There is a wide range of policies that could be used to
redistribute income: taxation, factor and product market intervention, asset redistribution, improved access to educational
opportunities, consumption transfers, redirection of government
investment being among the most-often mentioned. But there is
no consensus with respect to optimal policies. One reason is
that the effectiveness of any given policy depends on the underlying socioeconomic structure.

The policy chosen will depend on ideology (revolutionary or
evolutionary); the weights attached to the incomes of the different socioeconomic groups; the characteristics and source of
income of the target group, and its linkages with other groups; and
the relative strength of all the affected groups. The success
of a chosen policy mainly depends on the commitment of the government and the relative strength of the different classes, their perception of their interests and their commitment to secure them.
We now turn to a more detailed discussion of these policy instruments.

1. Taxation: The traditional instrument of income redistribution is progressive taxation. But progressive taxation (mostly
income tax) is likely to be ineffective in most LDCs. First,
because of difficulties in collection and enforcement of such
taxes, only a small fraction of tax revenues come from income tax
in most LDCs. An attempt to raise the tax rate might just increase

evasion. Second, in most LDCs the segment of the population at the top is usually small but highly organized. Substantial increases would be resisted and moderate increases might turn out to be insignificant in raising the incomes of the poor once it is spread around. Even in DCs where progressive income taxes account for a large proportion of the tax revenues and where most income recipients are engaged in organized, easily taxable sectors, taxation was found to have minimal redistributive effect. It has been estimated, for example, that the share of the top 5% of the population in the U.S., U.K. and Sweden can be decreased by only 10-20% through progressive taxation [Fishlow, p. 401].

2. <u>Factor Market Intervention</u>: Factor price distortions resulting in an over-statement of the price of labor and under-statement of the price of capital might lead to the adoption of capital-intensive technology in a labor-abundant economy. Factor market interventions aimed at removing the price distortions would lead to greater labor absorption and depending on the elasticity of substitution, to an increased labor share.[19] If profits are more concentrated than wage income, an increase in labor share would lead to an improvement in the size distribution of income, but studies show that elasticity of substitution is less than unity and so a decrease in the relative price of labor would lead to a decrease in labor share.[20] But even here overall income

---

[19] Labor share would increase if the elasticity of substitution is greater than unity.

[20] Arrow-Chenery-Minhas-Solow [11].

distribution might improve as some of the previously unemployed
get jobs.

In the absence of price distortions labor absorption can be increased through tax rebates to employers which would reduce the relative
price of labor to producers. The effectiveness of this policy
again depends on the degree of substitutability. The opportunity
cost of the rebates would have to also be considered.

Some authors [Eckaus (25), for example] argue that unemployment might result from technological factors rather than distorted
factor prices. The range of available techniques might be so
limited that lowering the wage rate will not lead to higher employment. The problem of identifying and then transferring "appropriate"
technology has been the focus of much recent attention.[21] If
such technology exists and can be adopted it would have the effect
of redistributing income by increasing the degree of substitutability
in the relevant range of production.

Policies aimed at raising the price of capital through the
removal of subsidies arising from low interest rates, overvalued
exchange rates and various incentive schemes would have a direct
positive effect on the relative distribution of income. It would
also increase labor absorption without reducing wage rates. The
direct and indirect savings from reducing subsidies to capital
might also benefit the poor. For example, import restrictions
intended to encourage domestic industrialization discriminate

---

[21] Fei-Ranis [27], Morawetz [69].

against primary exports by reducing the profitability of exports as domestic prices rise relative to foreign prices at the over-valued exchange rate. Insofar as the poor are concentrated in primary production, lifting import controls and exchange rate restrictions would improve distribution of income.

3. Commodity Market Intervention: By lowering the prices of agricultural relative to manufactured products, the demand for and output of the former would be increased. The magnitude will depend on the price elasticities of demand and supply. Since most of the poor are engaged in agriculture and consume more agricultural than manufactured goods the relative income of the poor would be raised through the reduced prices of their consumption goods and increased employment and incomes.

4. Asset Redistribution: One of the primary causes of in-equality is the concentration of asset ownership. Redistribution of assets between groups (e.g., land reform), between the private and public sectors (socialization or collectivization) and between domestic and foreign owners (e.g., nationalization) are among the more revolutionary policies which can be used to change the dis-tribution of income. But the benefits to the recipients would have to be weighed against the direct qnd indirect costs to the rest of the economy to determine the net benefit of asset redis-tribution. Some of the possible costs are the compensation to present asset owners and possible loss of output.

Redistribution of land is among the most effective means of equalizing rural incomes in areas where land ownership is highly concentrated. But unless land reform is followed by complementary policies like education through extension services, extension of easy credit to new farm owners, output might not rise. In fact, output might fall, at least in the short-run, because of the general economic dislocation resulting from land redistribution, destruction of property by present land owners especially if they expect not to be adequately compensated, and economies of scale lost by subdividing larger holdings. The latter could be avoided by forming cooperatives. At any rate, economies of scale may not result from large holdings because operating units and property units do not always coincide. Some land may be held for prestige and government policies that tax the product and not the land itself do not encourage full utilization of large holdings. In such cases the break-up may result in more intensive farming and thereby raise rather than lower production. The amount of compensation and the cost of services to the new owners are among other cost elements to be considered.

Nationalization and socialization are other redistributive instruments. However, they might accomplish little unless accompanied by explicit policies to redirect the benefits to the poor. Otherwise, the beneficiaries might be the bureaucrats and organized workers who run the enterprises after the takeover.

5. <u>Redirecting Investment</u>: The pattern of asset accumulation

by different income groups can be changed instead of just redistributing existing assets. If the poorest groups can achieve
above-average asset accumulation their relative income would rise
over time. But since increasing private savings is not usually
possible for the poor, the establishment of credit facilities
favoring the poor and redirecting government investment to sectors
or areas in which the poor are employed might be alternative ways
of accomplishing this.

Rural development programs aimed at directly alleviating rural
poverty have recently attracted attention. With the failure of
the "trickle down" hypothesis and the redefinition of development
as including distributional equity, policies aimed at increasing
rural productivity including redirecting government investment
from the highly visible formal sector to the rural poor have become
an accepted part of the development literature. But no consensus
has so far been reached as to the most effective ways of doing this.

6. Education: Education is another way of creating new
assets (human capital). Improved access to educational facilities
for the poor will increase the latter's rate of human capital formation. But equality in educational opportunities does not mean
equal access to employment opportunities or that these opportunities
exist in the first place. Also, the current emphasis on higher
education in most LDCs might merely change the composition of high
income recipients but will not improve overall distribution or
raise the absolute incomes of the poor.

Other Policies

Direct provisions of, or subsidies for, certain goods like food, low-income housing, public health and water supply might also raise the level of welfare of the poor. The advantage of this type of redistributive policy is that its benefits directly accrue to the target group instead of through the behavioral and technological responses of the system.

Rural-urban and regional imbalance in infrastructure and provision of public goods is another important source of inequality. For welfare purposes, the imputed value of these services should be included in household income. Redirecting these services towards the poor would help raise their level of welfare.

The above discussion focussed on single policies but single policies are usually ineffective and are quickly dissipated [Robinson (75), p.123]. Also the objectives of redistribution are multidimensional and single policies usually have an impact on only part of the distributional problem [Ahluwalia in (20), p. 90]. So packages containing policies that reinforce each other (e.g., land reform accompanied by establishment of extension service centers, provision of easy credit to new landholders, etc.) are usually more effective. Moreover, the target groups might be diverse and a single policy might affect only a segment of that group. For example, the poor consist of the landless, the unemployed, submarginal workers, small farmers and those engaged in informal urban sector activities. So an understanding of the target group --its characteristics, primary sources of income, and linkages with other groups -- is an important prerequisite for policy formulation.

Finally, the success of any policy depends on the commitment of the government, and especially the implementing agency, and the resistance or support of the various interest groups and their relative strengths. Group loyalties are not always formed along income lines but may be based on ethnic, regional, or religious factors. To formulate redistributive policies one must consider these extra-economic factors.

Conclusion

The effect of income redistribution on economic growth will depend on the type of policy instrument used and the country concerned. Empirical studies on the growth effects of redistribution have been done on a number of LDCs and the results indicate that the assumed growth-equity tradeoff either does not exist or is negligible. In the next chapter, I will attempt to formulate a model that incorporates income-generation process. Income transfer from the rich to the poor will be the redistributive instrument used. The model will subsequently be applied to data from Kenya.

PART II

THE MODEL AND COUNTRY BACKGROUND

CHAPTER 3:   THE MODEL

CHAPTER 4:   COUNTRY BACKGROUND

CHAPTER 3

THE BASIC MODEL

Objective

The purpose of this chapter is to build a mathematical model which would provide a laboratory within which the potential effects of several income transfer schemes on economic growth constraints (not growth itself) can be explored. The major objectives/features of this study are:

1. To provide further empirical investigation of the concept of equity-growth tradeoff which until recently held sway in the development literature. Several recent studies [e.g., Cline (22), Chinn (21), Paukert-Skolka (74)] have shown that the presumed tradeoff does not exist. Most of these studies were concerned with Asian or Latin American countries and no such study was ever done in an African country. It could very well be that the results obtained from these studies have universal validity. However, since these results hinge on parameter values which in turn depend on the underlying structural factors of the countries considered, the contrary possibility cannot be ruled out; hence the need to augment the pool of empirical evidence. However, it is the effect on growth on selected growth constraints that is investigated.

   The model is applied to data from Kenya. Kenya has been chosen because:

a) It has one of the highest concentration of income in the world with the highest 20 percent of income recipient getting almost 70 percent of national income.

b) The overall rate of growth of the economy has been around 7 percent a year for over two decades in real terms leading to a doubling of income in every 10 years. The fruits of this growth, however, have been concentrated in the formal, primarily urban, sector and have not benefited the bulk of the rural population [see the ILO (1972) and World Bank (1975) reports] who constitute 90% of the population. But a more equitable redistribution of income might lower the growth rate. Kenya is a good case for investigating this.

c) Compared to most African countries, Kenya has a good data base even though it is still riddled with gaps. But there is sufficient, though scattered, information that could be pieced together to fill these gaps.

2. To integrate the expenditure, employment and income generation processes so as to capture the full feedback effect of the initial income transfer. Many of the models designed to simulate the effect of income redistribution (cf. first-genre models, ch. 2, page 45) consider only the initial impact of redistribution. For example, the effect on employment is estimated but the secondary effects of the latter on income, consumption, output and employment are not taken into account. A new set of models

developed mainly under the auspices of the ILO and the World Bank endogenize these secondary effects (cf. second-genre models, ch. 2 p. 52) but their primary focus is not to investigate the nature of growth-equity relationships, but the set of feasible policies or policy packages that would improve the lot of the majority of the population and the relative effectiveness of these different policies. In this study, I will concentrate on income transfer as the redistributive policy and investigate its effects on economic growth, taking into account the employment and income generation processes -- thus combining the primary features of both sets of models. Simulations involving other redistributive policies like factor and product market interventions, asset redistribution, redirecting government expenditures to the poor, subsidies for merit goods, etc., could also be performed. The model is sufficiently disaggregated and the framework developed and the data compiled could be used to capture the effect of these other policies.

3. By appropriate sectoral and income group disaggregation (16 productive sectors further broken down by urban, small-farm and estate, and 11 & 7 income groups), inter- and intrasectoral linkages and so the potential economy-wide effects of changes in any one sector can be investigated. For example, changes in

rural income can, through consumption and production relationship, affect the rest of the economy.

The economy is further subdivided into monetary and non-
monetary sectors. The latter has little spillover to the rest
of the economy and is a subset of the small-farm sector.

The level of disaggregation also helps in better understanding the characteristics, location and source of income
for the different income groups and will prove to be of help in
identifying the target group and suggesting appropriate policies
for affecting their income.

Description

The study will employ a static single-period (1974) highly
disaggregated model using estimated expenditure coefficients, input-
output accounts, the initial pattern of income distribution within
each sector (i.e., distribution within the urban, estate and rural
sectors), sectoral factor use and value added. To translate factoral
income into household income a mapping method is formulated. The
following broad steps are involved:

1. Income is transferred from the rich to the poor. The
   method of transfer is not discussed.

2. The effects on the level as well as composition of total
   consumption are traced.

3. Changes in the composition of demand are mapped into production via interindustry relations.

4. Using incremental capital-output ratios (ICORs) and labor-output coefficients changes in sectoral and overall factor usage are estimated.

5. The resulting changes in factoral incomes are distributed according to the occupational distribution and asset ownership of the different classes. Since such information is not available, alternative methods of mapping factoral to personal income are used.

6. Changes in skill requirements are next estimated by multiplying the proportion of skilled to total sectoral employment with changes in sectoral employment.

7. Changes in intermediate and capital imports are estimated by multiplying intermediate and capital inputs coefficient to change in sectoral output.

8. Imports of consumption goods are easily estimated once overall consumption changes are known. The latter is the sum of exogenous (resulting from the initial income redistribution) and endogenous (resulting from changes in household income as sectoral output changes) components.

9. The model developed below is essentially a short-run one and so the growth-effects of redistribution are not directly investigated. But having obtained the effect on certain growth constraints the impact on growth can be calculated. One method usually followed [see Cline (22), for example]

is through the rate of capital accumulation. Given changes
in savings and capital requirements, and the ICOR values,
the rate of growth is calculated. However, ICORs are
highly unstable and growth depends on a host of factors
other than capital accumulation. Such a method might therefore lead to erroneous conclusions.

10. The final pattern of income distribution is estimated to
    investigate the ultimate impact of the transfer on the
    target groups. Policies designed to help the poor might
    sometimes have the opposite effect depending on intergroup
    linkages.

11. The amount of transfer is then varied and the resulting
    changes in the above factors estimated.

12. Each of these transfer schemes is coupled with complemen-
    tary policies like redistribution of factoral income,
    import substituting and raising rural productivity.

Step 2 provides changes in savings; step 4 changes in factor demand,
and the sum of steps 7 and 8 changes in imports. The final pattern
of income distribution is given by steps 1, 5, and 10.

Since the model deals with the short-run, factor supplies are
assumed given. Thus migration, skill upgrading, and household asset
accumulation are not considered. Also the qualitative aspects of
redistribution (e.g., effects on entrepreneurial incentives, worker

motivation, flow of foreign capital, flight of domestic capital, etc) are not considered. This is not to imply that these factors are not important. The latter, especially, could be pivotal in cases where radical programs are introduced in a short period of time. But their inclusion would extend the study beyond its original objective. At any rate, little could be said about the nature, direction, and actual impact of these factors beyond the descriptive level.

Notation

X_j = gross output of sector j, where: j = 1,...,n

X_{ij} = input of good i into sector j

a_{ij} = input of i per unit of j $\qquad a_{ij} = \dfrac{X_{ij}}{X_j}$

m_j = imported intermediate input per unit of output of j $\quad m_j = m_j^r / X_j$

M^r = total intermediate imports $\quad M^r = \sum\limits_{j} m_j X_j$

M^C = total imports of consumer goods

m_i^C = proportion of i's final demand that is imported $\quad m_i^C = \dfrac{M_i^C}{C_i}$

M^K = total imports of capital goods

$a_{\ell_{\lambda j}}$ = labor input per unit of jth output $\quad a_{\ell_{\lambda j}} = L_{\lambda j} / X_j$, λ refers to skill level

a_{Kj} = capital input per unit of jth output $a_{Kj} = K_j / X_j$

L_j = employment in sector j

K_j = amount of capital utilized by j

Y_k = income received by class k. This is an endogenous element.

t_k = class k's direct tax rate

$Y_k^d = (1 - t_k) Y_k$

t_{kT} = rate of transfer tax applied to richer households

T_k = urban-rural income remittance

Y_{kT} = income transferred to ($\div$) or from (-) class k. This portion of income is exogenous.

Y_T = total transferred income $\qquad Y_T = \sum_k Y_{kT}$

W_j = wage payments of sector j

Π_j = non-wage payments of j

Π_j^h = non-wage payments accruing to households

W_{kj} = wage income of class k from sector j

Π_{kj}^h = non-wage income of k from j

S_{kj}^W = percent share of k in jth wage bill

S_{kj}^{Π} = percent share of k in jth non-wage payments

y_{kj} = k's income per unit of jth output

C_i = total expenditure on good i

C_{ik} = total expenditure on i by k out of earned income

$\bar{C}_{ik}$ = total expenditure on i by k out of transferred income

$c_{ik} = C_{ik}/Y_k$ and is same for both C_{ik} and $\bar{C}_{ik}$

N_k = average household size of class k

H_k = number of households in income group k

r = place of residence -- urban/rural

Sp, Sb, Sg = Personal, Business and Gov't. Savings.

Assumptions

(a) Technology remains unchanged during the period of analysis.
This does not mean that overall factor use will not change as
a result of redistribution. Overall factor use will change if
factor intensity of goods consumed by the various classes differ.

(b) Consumption and value added coefficients (c_{ik}, v_{kj}) remain unchanged.

(c) Households immediately assume the consumption characteristics
of the income class they move to after redistribution.

(d) All the usual input-output assumptions (e.g., prices do not
affect input use, no excess capacity, no economies of scale, etc.)
are retained.

(e) The marginal as well as average propensity to consume is less
than 1 for all income classes. This insures the convergence of
the expenditure part of the model.

(f) The column sum of input coefficients is less than one; i.e.,

$\sum_i a_{ij} \leq 1$ or $v_j > 0$ for at least one sector. Also

all $a_{ij} \geq 0$ - non-negativity constraints

and $1 - a_{ij} > 0$ - Simon-Hawkins Condition.

(g) $\sum_i a_{ij} + v_j \leq 1$. This ensures the convergence of the whole

system [Miyazawa, pp. 16, 21].

(h) Numerous secondary assumptions are made along the way. For

ease of reference, these are mentioned in the context in which

they occur.

The Equations

Three types of redistribution policies are examined.

1. Adopting a minimum level of income and raising households

below it through direct income transfer. Households above

this minimum are taxed to pay for the transfer. The amount

of income transferred to (+) or from (-) each household

$$Y_{kT} = t_{kT} H_k (\bar{Y}_{min} - \bar{Y}_k)$$

where $\bar{Y}_{min}$ = the post-transfer minimum income for each household.

and $t_{kT} = 1$ if $\bar{Y}_{min} > \bar{Y}_k$

$0 < |t_{kT}| < 1$ if $Y_{min} < Y_k$

The total amount transferred

$$Y_T = \sum_k Y_{kT}$$

2. (i) is coupled with other redistribitive policies like factoral income redistribution, raising rural incomes through higher productivity, and import substitution.

3. Changing parametric values to simulate the sensitivity of the results obtained to alternative assumption about values of major parameters.

The first impact of the income transfer to (+) or from (-) class k is on the composition of personal consumption. It is assumed that

(1) $\quad C_i \quad = \quad f_i(Y_{kT}, Y_k, N_k, R_k)$

so

(2) $\quad \Delta C_{ik} = f_i(Y_{kT}, \Delta Y_k)$

and

(3) $\quad \Delta C_i \quad = \quad \sum_k \Delta C_{ik}$

Define

(4) $\quad c_{ik} Y_{kT} \quad = \quad \bar{C}_{ik}$

and

(5) $\quad c_{ik} Y_k \quad = \quad C_{ik}$

and

(6) $\quad C'_{ik} \quad = \quad C_{ik} + \bar{C}_{ik}$.

Since income transferred Y_{kT} is an exogenous element, (5) is also exogenous. Urban and rural consumption are estimated separately and then combined.

Once the change in personal consumption is estimated from equation (2), the effect on the composition of output can be calculated using input-output relations

(7) $\quad \Delta X_i = \sum_j a_{ij} \Delta X_j - m_i \Delta X_i + (1 - m^C) \Delta \bar{C}_i$

Equation (7) indicates that output of i changes as a result of changes in total intermediate and final demand less imports. It is assumed that other components of final demand like government expenditures, investment and exports are not directly affected during the period of analysis. Investment is affected in subsequent periods through changes in savings and capital requirements brought about respectively by changes in consumption and output composition. However, a high proportion of capital goods in the monetary sector [80% in some cases (Stat. Abstracts)] are imported and so changes in investment demand will not appreciably affect domestic output.[1] Expanding, combining, and placing in matrix form, (7) yields

(8) $\quad \Delta X = (1 - A + M)^{-1} \Delta \bar{C}$

$\qquad$ where $M = M^r + M^C$

Changes in output composition lead to changes in sectoral value added. This is then distributed across households after appropriate adjustments for income earned, but not received, or income received, but not earned (Equation 12). The change in personal income in turn leads to secondary set of changes in personal demand, output composition, and further changes in personal income. The distribution of

---

[1] Most capital formation in the rural sector like the construction and huts and water works are in the non-monetary sector.

sectoral value added across income groups depends on (i) the factor requirements of each sector, (ii) occupational and skill characteristics, and (iii) the distribution of asset ownership across households. Given (i) sectoral value added can be translated into factoral income which, given (ii), can then be apportioned to different households. Figure 2 elucidates this process.

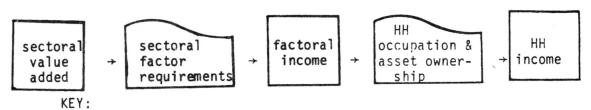

KEY:
    ☐ variables affected
    ⌂ intervening distribution

Using a specified production function, changes in factor usage as sectoral output changes can be ascertained. Factoral income is simply the product of factor prices and factor usage. Factoral income is then distributed to households according to factor ownership. Thus, wage income goes to the household owning labor of different skills and operating surplus (profit, interest and rents) to owners of non-human resources. In order to group households into income classes it could be assumed that household within each income class are homogeneous with respect to factor ownership.

While the method is theoretically attractive, it has numerous shortcomings especially as applied to Kenya. The heterogeneity of asset, the lack of efficient factor markets, the high degree of dualism in the Kenyan economy as well as the unavailability of data, especially on the distribution of asset ownership, all conspire to reduce the relevance of this method. Moreover, a vast majority of the population is self-employed on small farms or in the informal-urban sector, and a significant portion of small-farm activities are for self-consumption, further complicating the link between factoral income distribution and household or personal income distribution.

An alternative method is adopted. Since $\Delta X = \Sigma X^S$ [where s = organizational sector (e.g., formal-informal)], value added is first broken down into formal (agriculture and non-agriculture) and informal (small-farm and informal-urban) sectors. Second, the sectoral location of household income groups and their major sources of income are determined. Third, the share of each income group in sectoral income (both production and organizational), further broken down by production activity, is calculated. The change in income of each class resulting from changes in sectoral output can be calculated once the share of each income group in sectoral income is determined. The latter can be obtained from the available data. The income of the kth group is equal to the product of sectoral value added and the share of that group in the latter.

$$(9) \qquad Y_k^r = \sum_j s_{kj}^r V_j^{hT}$$

$$(10) \qquad S_{kj}^r = S_{kj}^{wr} + S_{kj}^{\Pi r}$$

Equation (10) indicates that S_{kj} is the sum of the kth share in sector j's wage and non-wage income.

(11) $V_j^{hr} = W_j^r + \pi_j^{hr}$

where V_j^{hr}, π_j^{hr} are respectively the amounts of jth value added and non-wage income accruing to households. It is assumed that all wage payments directly accrue to individuals while a portion of operating surplus goes to institutions in the form of business retained earnings, profits of public enterprises, and expatriated profits.

(12) $\pi_j^h = \pi_j - (\pi_j^g + \pi_j^f + \pi_j^d + T_j^i + \delta_j)$

π_j^g = profits of government-owned enterprises

π_j^f = profits repatriated by foreign corporations

π_j^d = undistributed profits

δ_j = depreciation allowance

T^i = indirect taxes

Define $D_j = \pi_j^g + \pi_j^f + \pi_j^d + \delta_j + T_j^i$.

Substituting (12) and (11) in (9)

(13) $Y_k^r = \sum_j [s_{kj}^{wr} W_j^r + s_{kj} \pi r(\pi_j - D_j)$

π_j is obtained from the national accounts and D_j can be estimated by piecing together the fragmentary evidence that is available (see Chapter 5). Equation (13) indicates that the income of group k is the sum of its share in sectoral wage and non-wage incomes, where

$D_j = \pi_j^g + \pi_j^f + \pi_j^d + \delta_j$.

The share of k in jth wage income is the amount of total wages received by all households in that group (W_{kj}) divided by jth wage bill.

$$(14) \quad S_{kj}^{wr} = \frac{W_{kj}^r}{W_j^r}$$

W_{kj} is merely the product of the number of workers of type k in sector j multiplied by their wage rate.

$$(15) \quad W_{kj}^r = W_{kj}^r L_{kj}^r$$

Similarly,

$$(16) \quad S_{kj}^{\Pi r} = \Pi_{kj}^h / \Pi_j^{hr}$$

The distribution of Π_j^h gross households will depend on the household factor ownership. Such information, however, is not available. In the absence of information about factor ownership, Π_{kj} for the formal sector is based on various assumptions which are discussed in more detail in Chapter 5. Formal sector non-wage incomes are a residual obtained by deducting from total operating surplus contained in national accounts the small-farm and informal-urban operating surplus.

For the small-farm sector, the share of each income group in farm and non-farm operating surplus and wages can be obtained from available data. Data on the informal-urban sector can be obtained by piecing together relevant fragmentary information. It is assumed that the income share of each class within the relevant sector does not change as output changes.[2]

---

[2]This is a less stringent assumption than it might seem. It does not mean that the share of each group of the total income of a productive sector remains the same as output changes. The share of estate owners might increase more than small farmers as agricultural output changes. However, if the agricultural sector is first divided into estate and small-farm sectors, there is a far greater chance that each income group would maintain its share within the relevant sector.

Rewrite equation (13) as

$$(17) \quad Y_{kj}^r = s_{kj}^{wr} \frac{W_j^r}{W_j} \cdot W_j + s_{kj}^{\Pi r} \frac{\Pi_j^{hr}}{\Pi_j^h} \cdot \Pi_j^h$$

Let $\quad \dfrac{W_j^r}{W_j} = w_j^r$

and $\quad \Pi_j^{hr}/\Pi_j^h = P_j^r$

where: w_j^r and P_j^r are the share of sector r in sector j's wage and non-wage payments.

Substituting w^r and P^r in (17)

$$(18) \quad Y_{kj}^r = \sum_j s_{kj}^{wr} w_j^r W_j + s_{kj}^{\Pi r} P_j^r \Pi_j^h$$

Omitting r for the time being, define

$$(19) \quad y_{kj}^w = \frac{w_{kj}}{X_j}$$

and

$$(20) \quad y_{kj}^\Pi = \frac{\Pi^h}{X_j}$$

so that as output changes

$$(21) \quad \Delta Y_k = \sum_j y_{kj} \Delta X_j$$

Disposable income,

$$(22) \quad \Delta Y_k^d = \sum_j (1 - t_k) y_{kj} \Delta X_j$$

As disposable income changes so does consumption. But this portion of consumption is endogenous (as distinguished from the portion that results from the initial income transfer).

The effect of this endogenous change in consumption demand on output composition using input-output relations is

$$(23) \qquad \Delta X_1 = \sum_j a_{ij} \Delta X_j - m_i \Delta X_i + \sum_k (1 - m^c) \, C_{ik} \, \Delta Y_k^D$$

Substituting (22) in (23) and then combining it with (4) yields

$$(24) \quad \Delta X_i = \sum_j a_{ij} \Delta X_j - \sum_i m_i \Delta X_i + (1 - m^c) \sum_k [\sum_j (1 - t_k^d - t_k^r) c_{ik} y_k \Delta X_j + \overline{\Delta C_{ik}}]$$

Rearranging (24) becomes

$$(25) \quad \Delta X_i = \sum_i a_{ij} \Delta X_j - \sum_j m_i \Delta X_i + \sum_{kj} (1 - m^c)(1 - t_k) c_{ik} y_k \Delta X_j + \sum_k (1 - m^c) \Delta C_{ik}$$

Expanding, combining and placing (24) in matrix form yields

$$(26) \qquad \Delta X = [1 - A + M^r - (1 - m^c) C y (1 - T)]^{-1} (1 - m^c) \Delta C$$

where $T = T^d + T^r$

and T^d = direct taxes

$\quad T^r$ = urban-rural remittance

Equation (26) shows the enlarged inverse matrix indicating the effect of the first-round changes in final demand (resulting from income transfer) on output via interindustry relationships and induced consumption. However, consumption unlike production, is not technically determined but results from conscious decisions by households. To separate the inverse reflecting production activity from convergence to that of consumption (and thereby making (26) comparable to (8)), we multiply and divide the RHS of (26) by B where $B = (1 - A + M^r)$.

$$(27) \quad \Delta X = B[I - (1-T)(1-m^c) \, CYB]^{-1} (1-m^c) \, \Delta \bar{C}$$

The inverse $[I- (1-T)(1-m^C) CYB]^{-1}$ is referred to as the sub-
joined inverse matrix and reflects the endogenous effect of changes
in each income group's consumption. The initial change in group kth
domestic consumption demands leads to a change in output composition
and factor demand, the degree of which depends on the factor intensity
differential of goods. The resulting change in the functional distribution will, when translated to personal income distribution and
personal taxes deducted, start a secondary chain of changes in demand
and output composition and so again income of another group, say M.
This is shown below.

Change in income of kth group	→	Change in con-sumption of kth group	→	Change in output composition	→	Change in factor demand
ΔY_k		ΔC_{ik}		ΔX_i		$\Delta K, \Delta L$

→	Change in the functional distribution of income	→	Change in income of the mth group	→
	ΔW_j		ΔY_m	

The final pattern of income distribution might therefore differ from
that envisaged by the redistributive policy.

From equation (27) the effect on savings, imports, and factor use
can be estimated. Assuming constant technology, factor input requirements can be calculated given ΔX.

(28) $\quad \Delta L = \sum_L a_{\ell j} \Delta X_j$

For skill-level λ,

(29) $\quad \Delta L_\lambda = \sum_j a_{\ell\lambda} \Delta X_j$, where $\lambda = 1,\ldots, 4$ and $a_{\ell\lambda j}$ = proportion of labor input of skill λ per unit of jth output.

(30) $\Delta K = \sum_i a_{Kj} \Delta X_j$

Changes in total imports and thereby foreign exchange availability is next estimated.

(31) $\Delta M = \sum_j m_j \Delta X_j + \sum m_{ci} \Delta C_i' + m_k \Delta K$

where: $m_j = \dfrac{M^r}{X_j}$; $m_i^c = \dfrac{M_i^C}{C_i}$; $m_k = \dfrac{M^K}{K}$.

M^r, M^C, and M^K have been previously defined.

Substituting (24) and (30) in (31)

(32) $\Delta M = \sum_j m_j \Delta X_j + \sum_{kj} m_{cj} (c_{jk} y_{kj} \Delta X_j + \Delta \bar{C}_j) + \sum_j m_k a_{kj} \Delta X_j$

The effect on savings can be estimated either directly from savings, propensities, or as a residual. Since changes in consumption and income have already been estimated, I will use the latter method.

(33) $\Delta S_p = \sum_k [\Delta Y_{kT} + \Delta Y_k - \sum_i \Delta C_{ik}']$, where S_p is personal savings.

Business and government savings (S_b, S_g) can also change.

(34) $\Delta S_b = \sum_j [\Delta \delta_j + \Delta \Pi_j^d]$

(35) $\Delta S_g = T^d + T^i + \sum_j \Pi_j^g$

(36) $\Delta S = \Delta S_p + \Delta S_b + \Delta S_g$

According to equation (35), government savings are the sum of direct and indirect taxes and profits of government enterprises. It is assumed that current government expenditures do not change, and that changes in government revenues go to savings.

The effect of the initial (policy-induced) income redistribution on savings, imports, and input factor requirements can thus be estimated in a more integrative framework. The feedback from the initial income transfer is captured by endogenizing personal consumption. The resulting inter-group linkages are therefore brought out. This is in contradistinction to many of the studies on income redistribution and economic growth [for example, Cline (22) and Morley and Smith (71)] where consumption is exogenous. These linkages are shown in the diagram below.

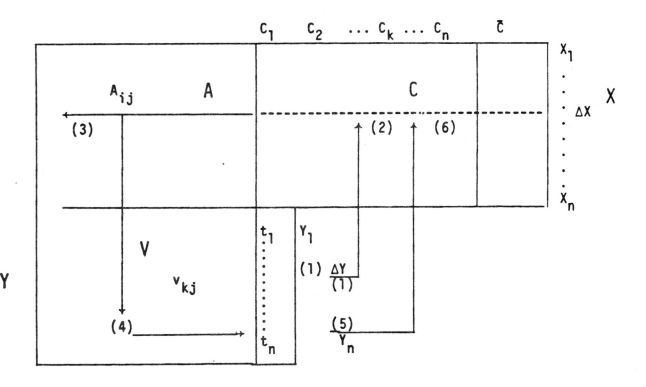

The exogenous change in income (Step 1) leads to a change in consumption (Step 2). This leads to a change in output consumption (Step 3), which in turn results in a change in the value added (Step 4), and thereby a change in income. This new pattern of income distribution (Step 5) results in a new demand composition (Step 6), and the process is repeated again. The assumption that MPC $\leq$ 1 for all k ensures convergence of the system.

Convergence of the Model

The convergence of the whole system has not been discussed. From assumption (f) and (g) on page 10,

$$(37) \qquad \sum_i a_{ij} + v_i \leq 1, \quad \text{and} \quad \sum_i a_{ij} < 1 .$$

Some of the value added (v_j) accrues to households while the rest accrues to non-individual recipients.

$$(38) \qquad \sum v_j' = \sum_k y_{kj} + d_j , \text{ where } d_j = D_j/X_j \text{ refers to the portion}$$
$$\text{accruing to non-individuals.}$$

Putting (38) in (37) gives

$$(39) \qquad \sum_i a_{ij} + \sum_k y_{kj} + d_j \leq 1$$

$$\text{or} \quad \sum a_{ij} - m_j + \sum_k y_{kj} + d_j \leq 1 \text{ for an open economy.}$$

If only the portion of value added that accrues to individuals is considered consumption included,

$$(40) \qquad \sum a_{ij} - m_j + \sum_k c_{ik} y_{kj} < 1 .$$

The existence of a solution is guaranteed by (40) [see Miyazama, p. 17].

Consistency

The model developed above integrates the production, distribution, and expenditure blocks. It does not, however, account for all the income leakages out of the system giving rise to the possibility of inconsistency between output and expenditure. For example, leakages from the distribution block (δ, π^d, π^2, π^f, T^i, equation 12) are not compensated for by any inflow.

To close the model, investment and government expenditures are included.

$$(41) \qquad I + G = S + T$$

$$(42) \qquad S = S_p + S_b + S_g$$

$$S_p = (1-c-t) Y$$

$$S_b = \delta + \pi^d$$

$$S_g = \pi^g + T$$

$$T = T^i + T^d$$

where S_p, S_b, S_g, are respectively personal business and government savings, and T^d and T^i refer to direct and indirect taxes. The other symbols have been defined above (page 14). Exports (E) and government expenditures (G) remain unchanged and M has been accounted for.

From equation (12)

(43) $\delta + \pi^d + \pi^g + \pi^f + T^i = D$

Define $D' = D - \pi^f$

so that

(44) $D' + (1-c-t) y = I + G$.

Since D is a function of output, I will change with output.

Adding (29) to (44), we obtain

(45) $\Delta X_i = \Sigma a_{ij} \Delta X_j - m_i \Delta X_i + \underset{kj}{\Sigma\Sigma}(1-m) c_{ik} y_{kj} (1-t_k) \Delta X_j$

$+ (1-m^k)\left[\underset{kj}{\Sigma\Sigma} d_j \Delta X_{ji} (1-c_k + t_k) y_{kj} \Delta X_j\right] + \underset{k}{\Sigma}(1-m) c_{ik}$

when $d_j = D'_j / X_j$.

While it is theoretically sound to assume that all leakages flow back into the system through investment (Public or private) expenditures, it is highly improbable that this would be the case. Retained earnings might not all be ploughed back into businesses, increased taxes might be used to increase current government expenditures or to reduce existing deficits. Since it is not known what proportion of the leakages translates itself into investment and government demand, in any one year, sensitivity analysis using different values of this ratio will be used. Equation (45) then becomes

$$(46) \quad \Delta X_i = \sum_j a_{ij}\Delta X_j - m_i\Delta X_i + \sum_{kj}(1-m)c_{ik}y_{kj}(1-t_k)\Delta X_j$$

$$+ (1-m^k)[Z\sum_{kj}(1-c_k-t_k)y_{kj} + Zd_j]\Delta X_j + (1-m)\sum c_{ik}$$

where Z is the proportion of the leakages of sector j (i.e. income that does not acrue to households) and private savings that flows back into the system through investment expenditures.

In equations (24-27), no such flow back occurs.

Rearranging and placing in matrix form (46) becomes

$$(47) \quad \Delta X = [I - A + M - (1-m^c)cY(1-T) - (1-m^k)\{1-c+T)Y - D\}Z]^{-1}\overline{\Delta C}$$

With some of the outflow thus accounted for, the production-expenditure multiplier is increased. The portion that does not acrue to individual and well as personal savings flow back to the system as public or private investment.

The time lag between the leakage and reflow of income as well as the amount of income that ultimately reenters the system will depend on the components of the leakage. For example, it is very unlikely that personal savings and taxes will be translated into investment in the same year. Moreover, there is nothing in the system to guarantee that the two are ex ante equal (a la Keynesian arguments). The same does not apply to enterprise (public or private) savings. The amount of earnings retained by a particular enterprise is partly dependent on anticipated investment demand.

Another difference between personal and institutional savings is that it is difficult to determine the distribution of funds from personal savings and taxes across industries. In other words, there is no way of predetermining which industry gets what portion of aggregate personal savings and direct taxes. The same does not apply to enterprise savings since the enterprise is also the investing enterprise. For these reasons, it is assumed that for personal savings and direct tax revenues the value of Z may be zero. Equation (47) then becomes

$$(48) \qquad \Delta X = [I - A + M - (1 - m^C)cy(1 - T) - (1 - m^k)\ ZD']^{-1}\Delta C$$

Equation (26) is the special case where Z = 0. Since there is little information about the value of the coefficient Z alternative values are assumed and the sensitivity of the results to these values observed. It is assumed that Z

$$Z = 0, .3, .5, .8$$

The actual size of this coefficient will depend on the extent of funds, the outflow, and the time lag between the receipt of and investment.

In a closed system, the size of the fraction indicates the proportion of enterprise savings and indirect taxes that are invested in the current year, i.e., the extent of the time lag between enterprise savings and enterprise investment.

Equation (46) replaces equation (26) and Figure 3 changes to Figure 4 below:

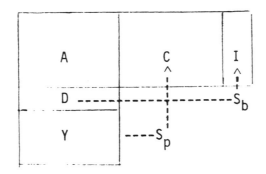

From equation (38) the effect on total savings, imports, and factor use can be estimated, assuming constant technology.

Matrix Dimensions

The above matrices have the following dimensions

$A = M \times n$

$M = 1 \times n$

$Y = K \times n$

M^r, M^C, $M^k = n \times 1$

$C = k \times m$

$T = k \times 1$

$D = 1 \times n$

$a_k = 1 \times n$

$a_\ell = \lambda \times n$

$n = 1, \ldots, 16$

$k = \begin{cases} 1, \ldots, 11 \text{ for urban and estate} \\ 1, \ldots, 7 \text{ for small-farm} \end{cases}$

$\lambda = 1, \ldots, 4.$

Zeros are used for the small-farm sector to make the matrix square. So $Y = 3kn$. The dimensions of m and n are different and will be reconciled.

Diagram 3

Schematic Framework of Model Operation

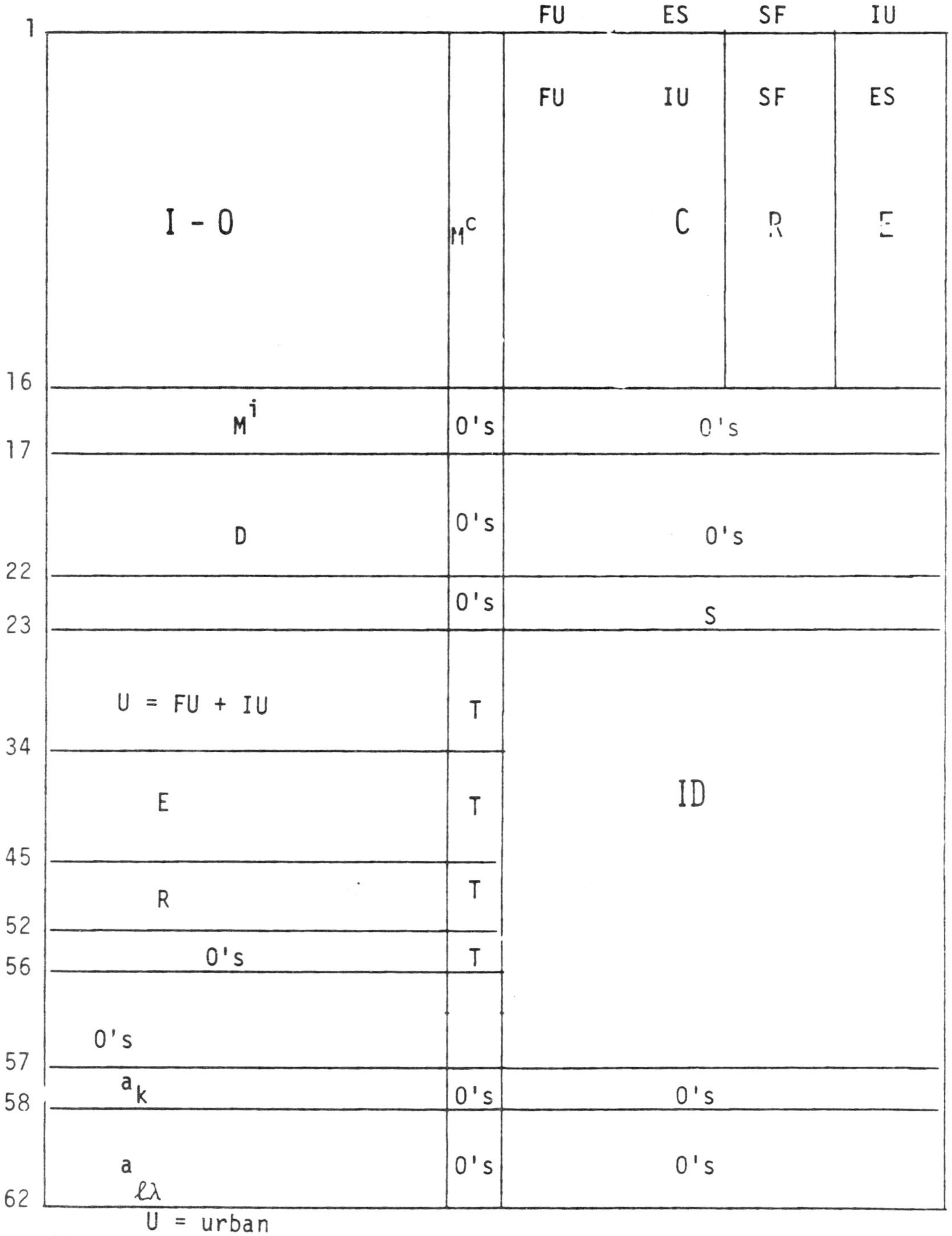

		FU	ES	SF	IU
		FU	IU	SF	ES
I - 0	M^c		C	R	E
M^i	0's		0's		
D	0's		0's		
	0's		S		
U = FU + IU	T				
E	T		ID		
R	T				
0's	T				
0's					
a_k	0's		0's		
$a_{\ell\lambda}$	0's		0's		

Row markers: 1, 16, 17, 22, 23, 34, 45, 52, 56, 57, 58, 62

KEY:
U = urban
FU = formal-urban   E = estate
IU = informal-urban   0's = zeroes
R = rural   ID = identity matrix

94

Diagram 4*

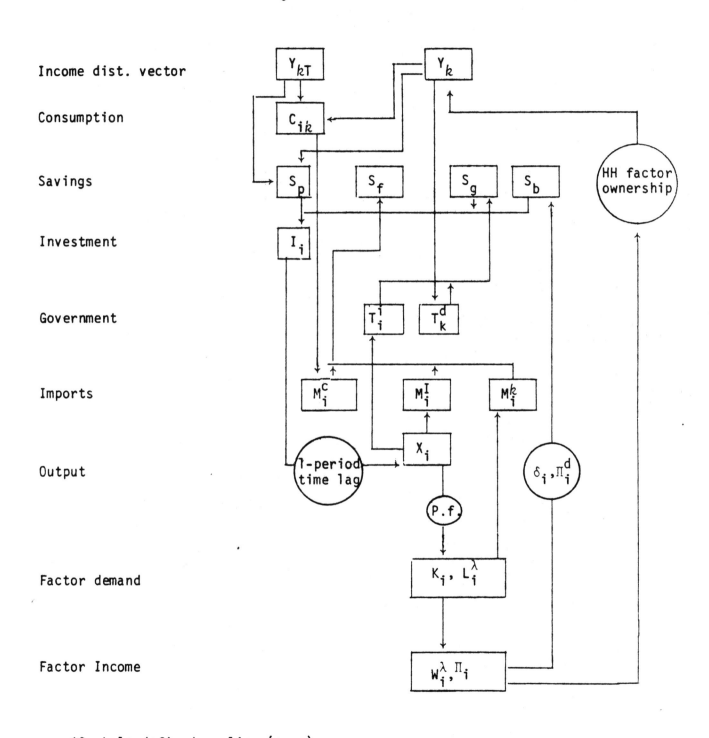

Income dist. vector

Consumption

Savings

Investment

Government

Imports

Output

Factor demand

Factor Income

*Symbols defined earlier (p.   )

Intervening factors.

CHAPTER 4

AN OVERVIEW OF INCOME DISTRIBUTION IN KENYA

I. Introduction

The GDP of Kenya was K£900 million and its population 12.8 million in 1974. The GDP has been growing at the rate of 7 percent per year since independence in 1963. This rate has appreciably fallen in 1974 because of the world economic crisis but has subsequently resumed the normal trend. The population has been growing at 3.3 percent per year -- one of the highest in the world -- and expected to rise even higher as the rate of mortality declines further without a corresponding decline in fertility. At present, the average percapita income is growing at the comfortable rate of 4 percent.

The primary stimulus in the growth of the economy is the small but dynamic modern sector. However, thie sector employs only 15 percent of the labor force, and the fruits of growth have not reached the rural sector where most of the population live.[1]

Approximately 90 percent of the population live in rural areas where 80 percent are self-employed on small farms. The rest are engaged in non-agricultural rural activities. The prevalence of considerable underemployment especially in the dry season and the low levels of

---

[1] About 45 percent of the population of 12.8 are in the labor force.

income both absolutely and in relation to urban areas results in considerable migration to the cities. Since the modern sector cannot absorb the available supply of labor, the informal-urban sector acts as a residual employer. Most of the urban-poor are located in this sector. Earnings in this sector are only a fraction of the average wage in the formal sector and even much lower than the latter's minimum wage. The limited available evidence indicates that the distribution of income has not improved since independence although the composition of the highest income groups has changed (e.g., ILO Report (40)]. At the time of independence most of the top positions in the formal sector were occupied by Europeans or Asians and most of the large farms in high-potential areas were in "Scheduled Areas" (i.e., reserved for Europeans). So most of the income in the formal sector went to non-Africans. With the "Kenyanization" drive which was launched after independence the racial composition of this top group changed, but the high concentration of income remained unaltered. Today Kenya has among the highest inequality of income in the world.

II. Income Distribution

A. General

The available estimates on income distribution show that the top 20 percent of the population receives about 70 percent of the national income while the bottom 40 percent receives only 10 percent. Moreover, this broad grouping conceals the high concentration of income within the top 1 percent or so.

Underlying the inequality in the personal distribution of income are urban-rural imbalance, formal-informal differences and racial inequalities.

1. Urban-rural:

About 87 percent of the population live in rural areas, yet only 30 percent of the national income originates here.[2] The average income in Nairobi, which accounts for about 70 percent of the urban population, is four times that of the country as a whole and almost 15 times that of rural areas.[3]

Within the rural areas, there is a great disparity in incomes even when large farms and plantations are excluded. The highest 12 percent of the households receive almost 44 percent of the small-farm income while the lowest 18 percent receive less than

---

[2]Income of small holdings is K£260 million. Estimated from the Integrated Rural Survey [54], esp. table 8.5, p. 54.

[3]World Bank [90], p. 184.

1.3 percent.[4] The disparity in urban income is just as great. It has been estimated that in Nairobi the top 20 percent of income earners receive almost 60 percent while the bottom 20 percent receive less than 3 percent.[5]

2. Formal-Informal:

Probably the most important factor in the rural-urban as well as the overall inequality is the disparity between earnings in the formal and informal sectors. Roughly, the formal and informal sectors correspond to the modern and traditional sectors (a la dual sector models). The former classification, however, includes both rural and urban. A worker on a plantation or a government office in a rural area is in the formal sector, while an unlicensed street vendor in an urban center is in the informal sector. The main distinguishing feature (at least in Kenya) is whether an employee is covered under the government's Annual Enumeration of Employees and whether a business is formally recognized. Most informal sector businesses are paralegal.

The average income from formal sector employment was about ten times that in the informal sector in 1969 [ILO, p. 77] and there is no reason to believe that this gap has closed. Even the unskilled worker in the formal sector makes several times the average

---

[4] See Table 5.2.

[5] Nairobi City Council estimate cited in the World Bank [90], p. 184.

for the informal-urban. But earnings in the latter are higher than those in rural areas and would represent a second-best to those migrants who could not get into the formal sector.

3. Racial Inequalities:

The vestiges of the hierarchical racial system inherited from the colonial administration have produced great disparities between the incomes of Africans, Asians and Europeans. The average earnings of a European are 13 times that of an African in the formal sector and almost 7 times that of an Asian.[6] The gap is even wider if the overall African average (whether informal or formal) is taken. The best and most fertile land was "scheduled" for Europeans while the Africans were concentrated in the less fertile "African reserves".

The racial differences at present reflect skill differentiation and concentration of factor ownership. Since the Kenyanization drive following independence in 1963, the racial factor has, if anything, favored the Africans who replaced the Europeans in many of the highest paying jobs. Many of the large estates in the former "Scheduled Areas" have been broken up and distributed to Africans. But the racial inequality still persists though some of its ugliest features have been eliminated. At any rate, the concentration of income among the privileged few has not been lessened though the racial composition of this group has changed.

---

[6]Ibid., p. 184.

B. Existing Data

There are no reliable data on income distribution in Kenya but several attempts have been made recently by the ILO [40], and the World Bank [9C]. These estimates differ in coverage (national or urban) and recipient unit (household, individual or income recipient basis) and are not therefore readily comparable.

1. The ILO Estimates:

The ILO estimates are shown below.

TABLE 1

URBAN[1]		Σ% Income		NATIONAL[2]		
Income Group (Sh/mth) more than but less than	Σ% HH	After tax	Before tax	Income Group (£ year)	Σ% HH	Σ% Income
0 - 199	8.51	1.12	1.40	less than 20	14.1	1.3
200 - 299	25.14	5.95	5.93	20 - 60	62.8	19.2
300 - 399	38.46	11.22	11.17	60 - 120	76.9	28.4
400 - 499	47.51	15.83	15.8	120 - 200	87.2	40.6
500 - 699	61.05	25.09	25.02	200 - 600	96.6	67.9
700 - 999	70.93	34.58	34.57	600 - 1000	98.6	80.5
1000 - 1399	80.79	48.88	48.00	over 1000	100.0	100.0
1400 - 1999	90.07	66.67	65.89			
over 2000	100.00	100.00	100.00			

Source: 1. ILO report [40], pp. 352-353.

2. Ibid., p. 74.

The first estimate in Table 1 is based on an unpublished urban household
budget survey conducted in 1968-1969. It is the consolidated
distribution for Nairobi, Mombasa and Kisumu which together accounts
for 90 percent of the urban population.

The second estimate is not directly shown but can be obtained
from p. 74 of the ILO report and summarized in table 2 below:

TABLE 2

Bracket (K£/year)	Average Income* £/year	Number of HHs	Income for Group (000's)	% HH	% Income
Over 1000	1500	30	45	1.3	14.1
600 - 1000	800	50	40	2.1	13.0
200 - 600	400	220	88	9.4	28.6
120 - 200	160	240	41.8	10.3	13.6
60 - 120	90	330	29.7	14.0	9.6
20 - 60	40	1140	45.6	48.7	14.8
Less than 20	16	330	5.3	14.1	1.7
		2340	307.4		

*The average income for highest bracket is assumed to be 50 percent
over lower bound, that of the lowest bracket is assumed to be 80
percent of the upper limit. For the rest the midpoint is taken as
the average.

Source: ILO report, p. 74.

These estimates in table 2 are dificient in two main respects. First,
the total number of households is overstated. The census data
shows that in 1969 the number of households was 1,938,000 instead
of the 2,340,000 the ILO figures show. Second, total personal
income is understated. The latter is only £ 307 million according
to Table 2. But private consumption alone amounted to £330 million
in 1969 [Statistical Abstracts (56), 1974, Table 46a].

The understatement of total personal income and the overstatement
of the number of households in each group would lead to marked
understatement of the absolute incomes of some, if not all, of the
income groups. Although there is no reason to believe that the
relative distribution is affected by these stated deficiencies, it
would tend to cast doubt on its reliability.

An attractive feature of this estimate is that distribution
is shown by type of economic activity as well as income size.
For example, the highest income group which averages over £1000
and includes only 1.3 percent of the households consists mostly
of high professionals and owners of large farms and modern sector
industries [See Appendix 13]. This is still too broad a classification
for discerning the location of the target groups for policy purposes and
for understanding intergroup linkages [See Ch.2], but is a start
in the right direction.

2. · IBRD/Jain Estimates:

Shail Jain [40a] of the World Bank compiled income
distribution statistics for 81 countries. The distribution for
Kenya is shown in Table 3.

TABLE 3

| % POPULATION | % INCOME | |
	National, IR[1]	Urban, HH[2]
0 - 10	1.8	1.5
10 - 20	2.1	2.4
20 - 30	2.5	3.4
30 - 40	3.1	4.4
40 - 50	3.9	5.7
50 - 60	4.9	7.4
60 - 70	6.4	9.6
70 - 80	8.4	13.0
80 - 90	12.0	18.7
90 - 100	54.9	33.9
95 - 100	46.2	20.2

IR = Income recipient
HH = Household

Source: 1. Christian Morrisson, "Income Distribution in Kenya."
Unpublished memorandum of the Income Distribution
Division of the World Bank, 1969, p. 30.

2. ILO report, p. 72.

Jain points out that the figures he compiled do not represent
a set of officially accepted estimates of the distribution of
income and are merely approximations of the underlying distribution that is being measured [p. xi]. He cautions the reader that
this data "is not in any way presented as 'reliable' or even
'best estimates'."

In light of this frank admission of its shortcomings, one
should not put too much stock in these figures. Together with

other estimates, however, they could be used as indicative of the underlying pattern of distribution.

An obvious mistake in Jain's estimates is that the urban household distribution is not contained in the cited source (i.e., ILO report, p. 72). The same, however, could be found in pages 352-4 of the ILO report (Table 52). Table 3 above can be obtained by converting ILO distribution to a decile basis.

CONCLUSIONS:

The above estimates vary in detail but show a comparable picture. The income share of the lowest 10 percent is 2 percent or less while that of the highest 10 percent is between 56 and 68 percent. Each has certain shortcomings and all are rough estimates involving a lot of guesswork, partly because of the dearth of data. In the following chapter I will attempt to make my own estimates. I will do this for three reasons:

a) New data has become available since these studies were made. Little was known about the rural sector where about 90 percent of the population lives until 1977 when the Integrated Rural Survey [54] was published.

b) The overall distribution of income is merely a weighted average of the underlying subdistributions. The latter might be more revealing than aggregate measures that conceal differences within and between sectors.

c) For purposes of this study, I need to know the source of income by sector (productive and organizational) for each income group so as to be able to map sectoral to personal or household income. As the level and compositions of output changes, the factoral income changes. To map this to personal income one must know either (i) the factor demand by sector and the distribution of factor ownership, or (ii) the source of income by industry for each group. The former data are usually non-existent.

In Chapter 5, I will estimate the pattern of income distribution within the formal sector, small-scale farmers,[7] and urban-informal sector. In Chapter 6, I will disaggregate the income of each group by industry and by wage and non-wage income to find out how much of the income of each group comes from a particular industry. Since the purpose of this study is to estimate the potential effects of income redistribution, the consumption pattern of each income class and the structure of production, including interindustry relations, will also be discussed in Chapter 7.

---

[7]This category comprises all rural households except those engaged in large-scale farming and pastoralism.

Appendix to Chapter 4

Some Basic Information on Kenya

1. Demographic:

	Urban	% Rural	Total
Population	13.	87	
Male:female	57:43	48:52	49:51
Under 15	39.5	63.7	51%
Rate of population growth			3.3

2. Social and Economic: (1974)

GDP	£ 908 million
Monetary	732 million
Non-monetary	176 million
Rate of growth	7%
Share of:	
Agriculture, forestry, fishing & mining	34%
Manufacturing & construction, electricity and water	18%
Services (private)	24%
Public services	24%
Wages	£ 405 million
Operating surplus	£ 503 million

3. Employment:

	Wage Employment		Self-employed	
	# in 000's	Income £000	# in 000's	Income £000
Formal-urban	386	199	98	48
Formal-rural				
Agr.(big farms)	261	30	21	2.5
Non-agriculture	179	38	0	0
Informal-urban	48	2.6	72	4.7
Informal-rural				
(mostly small-farm)	626	29	5,500	196

4. Income Distribution:

Income class	% Recipients	% of Income
1. Richest	20	67.0
2.	40	23.5
3. Poorest	40	9.5

5. Other Information:

Area: 582,647 Sq. Km.

      60% semi-desert

      10% suitable for agriculture

Currency:

K£1 = Sh. 20

Sh1 = 100 cents

Sh7 = US $ 1.00

Sources:
1. Demographic Baseline Survey Report, 1973 [49].
2. Economic Survey, 1976, Table 2.3
3. Formal sector (except self-employed): Statistical Abstract (56), 1976, Tables 237, 240, 250.
   Employment and Earning in the Modern Sector, 1974 [52], pp. 19-22.
   Informal-urban: Table 5.3.
   Informal-rural: IRS, various tables.
4. Jain Shail [40a], Table 43.

PART III

THE DATA

CHAPTER 5: INCOME DISTRIBUTION

CHAPTER 6: SECTORAL LOCATION OF INCOME GROUPS
AND SOURCES OF THEIR INCOME

CHAPTER 7: PRODUCTION AND CONSUMPTION ANALYSIS

I. INTRODUCTION

Kenya has a much better data base, in both quantity and quality, than most African countries, but it is still deficient in several respects. Data from different sources are usually inconsistent and sometimes contradictory. Comparability is reduced by differences in scope (formal-informal, urban-rural, monetary-nonmonetary, and small- and large-scale farming), dates covered, and level of aggregation. At times the required data simply do not exist and have to be constructed by piecing together information from various sources. Existing data are also usually riddled with gaps.

The bulk of Part II consists of reconciling data from different sources and with different dates and levels of aggregation, constructing the required data when it does not exist, and filling the gaps of existing data sets. The procedures used and the assumptions made will be discussed in the relevant sections of the text. The 1974 calendar year is taken as the period of analysis because several of the surveys on which this study is based were undertaken in that year and because that is the latest year for which some of the rest of the data is available. Data from earlier dates are projected to 1974.

Chapter 5 deals with the size distribution of income. Its purpose is to piece together relevant data and derive the existing pattern of income distribution. The method used is in part dictated by intended end-use of the data. Since the main objective of this study is to simulate the effect of income redistribution on economic growth constraints, income distribution is estimated from the source rather than recipient viewpoint. Given the source of income by industry for each income

group the effect of changes in production and employment resulting
from exogenous income redistribution on the income of each group can
be calculated. The consumption, production and income generation
processes can therefore be integrated. Such a method is in contradistinction to estimates that concentrate only on the income shares of
each group without regard to their source. Chapter 6 deals with the
source of income by sector/industry for households in the urban, small-
farm and estate sectors.

Chapter 7 is concerned with the production structure (labor and
capital coefficients, inter-industry relations, etc.) and the consumption characteristics of households.

DEFINITIONS:

1. Sector: A group of economic units that are homogeneous with
respect to the activity being investigated [Kendrick (17), p. 51].
In production, sector refers to a group of firms producing similar
products. Conceptually, it is the similar to an industry. However,
sector refers to the type of market that the industry serves. Several
industries could constitute a sector.

A sector could also refer to a group of economic entities that
are homogeneous with respect to their organizational structure (formal-
informal, modern-traditional).

2. Formal and informal sectors: Formal-informal sectoring roughly
corresponds to the modern-traditional concept (ala dual-sector models).
But the latter is in general used as synonymous to the urban-rural
sectoring while the former encompasses both urban and rural. For

example, there is highly mechanized large-scale farming in rural areas, and "petty" traders and others engaged in unregistered secondary activities in urban areas. The terms formal-informal have been popularized by the ILO report [40].

The two sectors are characterized by [ILO, p. 6]:

informal	formal
a) ease of entry	difficulty of entry
b) reliance on endogenous resources	reliance on overseas resources
c) family ownership of enterprises	corporate ownership
d) small-scale operations	large-scale operations
e) labor-intensive, adopted technology	capital-intensive, imported technology
f) skill acquired outside formal school system	formally-acquired skills, often expatriate
g) unregulated and competitive markets	protected markets (through tariffs, quotas and licenses)

Informal sector activities are, in general, paralegal as they are not recognized by government and so workers in this sector are not included in the "Annual Enumeration of Employees" conducted annually by the government to determine the level of employment. Operationally, inclusion of this annual survey demarcates formal from informal in Kenya.

Most of the "working poor" are located in the informal sector. The informal-urban sector acts as the residual employer of urban-migrants who could not be absorbed by the formal sector. It is therefore an important source of income for a large number of urban residents. The informal-rural sector covers practically all small-farm households. A large part of the latter is non-monetized.

3. <u>Monetary and non-monetary sectors</u>: The non-monetary part of the economy roughly corresponds to the subsistence sector. Output is own-consumed and there is little linkage with the rest of the economy. In official publications on Kenya, the word "non-monetary" has recently been changed to "semi-monetary".

4. <u>Urban</u>: Population centers with 2,000 or more inhabitants.

5. <u>Large and small farms</u>: Large farms (or estates) are mostly located in the former "Scheduled Areas" which were reserved for Europeans. The average farm size is 700 hectares. Small farms include all other areas of arable land and average between .2 and 12 hectares.

6. <u>Gross Operating Surplus</u>: Total income less wages. It includes depreciation, indirect taxes, retained earnings, repatriated profits, profits of government-owned enterprises as well as dividends and interest payments. Thus, only a portion of operating surplus accrues to individuals. It is to be distinguished from both non-wage incomes and profits.

7. <u>Non-wage Income</u>: Refers to the portion of operating surplus received by individuals or households, i.e., gross operating surplus less the portion received by non-persons.

8. <u>Gross Profits</u>: Gross operating surplus less indirect taxes.

CHAPTER 5

INCOME DISTRIBUTION WITHIN THE URBAN,
SMALL-FARM, AND ESTATE SECTORS

I.1. THE APPROACH

The economy is first divided into formal (including large-scale
farming), small-farm, and informal-urban sectors. This is preferable
to the formal-informal or urban-rural classification. Large-scale
farming is very dissimilar to the rest of the rural sector and there
are substantial differences between informal-urban and the small-farm
sector to lump them under the informal sector. But the main reason
for this classification is because available data are classified in
this fashion. Official data (especially on distribution) exist for
the formal and small-farm sectors but not for the informal-urban sector.
Data on the latter are obtained by piecing together relevant information from various sources. At any rate, this sector is insignificant
in terms of its share in GDP (about .4%) or share in labor force (.2%).

Income distribution within the informal-urban and non-agricultural
formal sector (after deducting formal-sector employment, especially
government jobs, in rural areas) are combined to obtain income distribution within the urban areas. The small-farm and large-farm (or
estate) sectors are also classified separately. Thus, there are three sectors:

urban, small-farm (rural), and estate.

While there are ample data on employment income in the formal sector, there are no data on either formal sector operating surplus (gross value added less wages) or its distribution across households. The latter is obtained by subtracting from the operating surplus of the monetary sector the small-farm and informal-urban operating surplus. Only the monetary portion of the small-farm operating surplus is included. Before the formal sector operating surplus so estimated is apportioned across households, the following items are deducted: depreciation, profits remitted by foreign corporations, undistributed profits, and profits of government enterprises. There is no information available on any of these items except depreciation. The latter can be obtained from the input-output tables for Kenya. The rest are calculated by piecing together relevant fragmentary evidence. The remaining portion of formal-sector operating surplus accrues to households or individuals as non-wage income and includes the imputed labor income of the self-employed and compensation to property owners (rental income).

The imputed wage rate of the self-employed individuals is assumed to be equal to the overall sectoral wage rate. Rental income is distributed across households under three different sets of assumptions. Next households are distributed across the three sectors and the within-sector size distributions of income are determined. A summary of the required data, the main sources of existing data, and procedures for estimating unavailable data are shown in Table 1.

TABLE 1

Summary of the major sources of information and
procedures of estimating income distribution within the
formal, small-farm, and informal-urban sectors

SECTOR	REQUIRED DATA	MAIN DATA SOURCE	PROCEDURES/COMMENTS
1. Small-scale farming	1. a) operating surplus; farm and non-farm	Integrated Rural Survey, 1977	
	b) Employment income	Integrated Rural Survey, 1977	
	c) Other income	Integrated Rural Survey, 1977	
	2. Distribution of income by household	Integrated Rural Survey, 1977	
	3. Monetary and non-monetary output	IRS and national accounts.	The non-monetary sector is the amount of output which is own-consumed (IRS). Reconciled with non-monetary income in National Accounts.
2. Formal	1. a) Employment income by sector	Statistical Abstracts, Annual Economic Survey	--------------
	b) Operating surplus by sector	Not available	Total monetary sectoral operating surplus which is obtained from The Economic Survey is subtracted from monetary portion of small-farm and informal-urban operating surplus.
	2. a) Distribution of labor income across income recipient	Statistical Abstracts	--------------
	b) Distribution of operating surplus:		
	(i) Income from self-employment	Employment & Earnings In the Modern Sector, Ministry of Planning, Kenya 1974	It is assumed that wage rates of the self-employed are equal to average sectoral wage rates. Also assumed that the size distribution follows the overall distribution of income from wage employment.
	(ii) Rental income	Not available	Only a small proportion of (ii) acrues to individuals. Depreciation, indirect taxes, undistributed profits, profits remitted by foreign corporations and profits of government enterprises are deducted. The remainder distributed by using simplifying assumptions (see pp. 29-36).
3. Informal-urban	1. a) Employment income	ILO (1969), IBRD (1971)	Projected to 1974 and cross-checked with other estimates. It is assumed that (a) goes to hired labor and (b) to the self-employed.
	b) Operating Surplus		
	2. Size distribution of income	Not available	Within-sector variance is very small. Most persons fall in lowest income groups. So it is assumed there are only two classes: the self-employed and the hired labor, with the former forming the upper group.

I.2. INCOME DISTRIBUTION WITHIN THE SMALL-FARM SECTOR

The Integrated Rural Survey (IRS) [54] is an excellent source
of data for rural areas. Such information has hitherto been very
scanty, or non-existent. The IRS provides a broad baseline descrip-
tion of the socioeconomic profile of the small-scale agricultural
households in Kenya. It contains highly disaggregated data on the
consumption, production, and income distribution patterns for the
1.48 million households which comprise the small-scale agricultural
community. Information on large-scale agriculture is included in
the formal sector for which ample data exist.

The total income of small farms is about K £287 million and
includes £ 96 million in consumption of own-products. The distribution of income within the small-farm households is not explicitly
shown in the IRS, but can be easily estimated from the available data
and is shown in Table 2.

The distribution of income shown in Table 2 is on household
rather than personal basis. In rural areas the family works as a
unit on the farm or other family-owned small-scale non-agricultural
enterprises. Approximately 80% of the heads of rural households
are self-employed. In urban areas and large farms, on the other
hand, wage employment predominates and income is at first distributed
on a personal basis and then later converted into households. However,
differences in household size must be taken into consideration when
making inter-group welfare comparisons. A small household with a
small income might be better off than one with a higher income, but
with a proportionately larger number of members. So it is usually

TABLE 2

Distribution of Income Within
Rural Households[a]

Income Bracket (in Shs/year)	Avg. hh Income (in £/year)	#hhs [c] (000's)	Income for [c] Bracket (in 000's of £)	% of hhs		% Income	
0 - 999[b]	27	274	7,398	18.4		2.6	
1,000 - 1,999	74	333	24,628	22.5 } 54.7		8.6 } 20.1	
2,000 - 2,999	125	205	25,625	13.8		8.9	
3,000 - 3,999	173	174	30,102	11.7		10.5	
4,000 - 5,999	241	201	48,200	13.6		16.8	
6,000 - 7,999	348	118	41,064	8.0 } 20.0		14.3 } 52.7	
over 8,000	616	180	110,264	12.0		38.4	
		1,483	287,281				

% Cumulative hhs	% Cumulative Income
18.4	2.3
40.9	10.0
54.7	19.0
66.4	29.6
80.0	46.6
88.0	61.1
100.0	100.0

[a]Excludes large-scale farmers and pastoralists.

[b]The lowest income group showed an income of -2,840
Shs because of losses during 1974-1975 draught season
when the survey was conducted. It is assumed here
that average income of this class during normal seasons
is equal to that of the income class above it (i.e.,
0 - 999 Sh).

[c]Small errors due to rounding.

Source: Integrated Rural Survey [54], Table 8.5, p. 54.

better to convert household income to personal income rather than the other way around. But this is different from distribution on an income-recipient basis since the latter excludes non-working family members. The distribution of income from employment (both wage and non-wage) might tend to do this. Also, families consume as a unit and there might be some economies of scale in consumption. These problems could be avoided by distributing income on a household basis but also noting differences in family size when such data are available.

One of the primary sources of inequality within small-scale agriculture is the quantity and quality of landholdings. Distribution of farm size by income group is shown in Appendix 2. The quality of land also varies greatly between regions and this may be an important cause of income differential within small-farms. Most of the high quality land was formerly reserved for Europeans ("Scheduled Areas"). After independence some of these large farms were purchased by the government and then distributed among Africans after considerable subdivision ("settlement schemes"). Farmers on settlement schemes therefore tend to be in the upper brackets of rural income distribution.

The upper income group accounts for 53% of the income, but only 20% of the population. In absolute terms, the income of the highest 12% of households is over £600 per year or about 25 times as high as that of the poorest 20% of the farmers. Below this group are about a quarter of small holders whose income share corresponds to that which would have obtained had income been very evenly distributed. These households have been able to commercialize their operations but for a variety of reasons -- insufficient or poor land, lack of knowledge

or capital, unavailability of credit, etc. -- have not been able to
raise their incomes. They hire seasonal labor but usually not on a
permanent basis.

The majority of small holders numbering about 800,000 households
have not been able to raise the productivity of their farms and live
in extreme poverty. A high proportion of their meager incomes come
from remittances of relatives employed mostly in urban areas, or from
casual employment (see Appendix 2).

At the bottom (not shown in Table 2) are a small group of landless households or squatters on land they do not own, and pastoralists,
who live in arid areas under very precarious conditions. A high proportion of their livestock have been killed off by recurrent draughts in
recent years.

In sum, there is a high degree of relative inequality in rural
Kenya even when large commercial farms are excluded.

1.3. INFORMAL-URBAN SECTOR

Only rough figures are available for the informal-urban sector.
The best estimates come from the ILO [40] and World Bank [91] reports,
and these pertain to 1969 and 1971 respectively. To estimate the 1974
employment and earnings for this sector, the 1969-1971 figures are projected using modified modern sector growth rate. Alternative estimates
of informal-urban employment are also made as described later.

Employment in the modern sector grew from 627,200 to 826,300 between 1969 and 1974 or a growth rate of 5.6 percent. Total earnings rose by 56 percent over the five-year period. I will assume that informal-urban employment rose by more in formal-urban, but that the per capita earning in the former rose by less than that of the formal sector. The effect of these two differential increases is assumed to equalize the overall growth in the earnings of the two sectors. The reasoning behind these assumptions is based on the following observations:

a. The informal sector is characterized by ease of entry, un-regulated and competitive markets, reliance on indigenous (mostly family-owned) resources, and small-scale operations. The formal sector, on the other hand, is characterized by difficulty of entry, protected markets, reliance on imported technology, and large-scale operations.[2] The number of workers in the informal sector would therefore tend to grow faster than formal sector.

b. The informal sector acts as a residual employer for all those who could not get employment in the small and protected formal sector. The high rural-urban migration and the increasing capital intensity of the formal sector increases pressure on the informal-urban sector. Moreover, the rate of urban-rural migration has increased since the 1973 draught which devastated much of the rural areas. This would tend to keep down growth

---

[2]ILO Report, Page 6.

in average earnings of the informal sector.

The net effect of (a) and (b) is that supply pressures on the relatively competitive informal sector would tend to keep increases in wage rates below that of the modern sector even though the former starts from a much lower base.[3] I will assume that this is compensated for by the differential increase in numbers employed. This results in equivalent increases in the earnings of the two sectors. The results are shown below:

Table 3a

Informal Sector
Employment and Earnings
1969 and 1974

	1969	1974[c]
Employment in 000's	96[a]	123
Total earnings in K 000's	4,800[b]	7,488

[a] Includes self-employment.

[b] Based on average earnings of £50 in 1969. ILO, p. 77, Table 27.

[c] Based on formal-sector growth rate.

Source: World Bank, Page 54, Table 5.

---

[3] Average incomes in the formal sector are about ten times that of the informal sector. See ILO Report, Table 27, Page 77.

I.3.1. Distribution Within the Informal-Urban Sector

Income variance within this sector is small since everybody is poor. The highest income recipients in this sector earn much less than the minimum wages in the formal sector. Within-sector variations are usually influenced by location (Nairobi or other town) or employment status (wage-employment or self-employed). Generally, average earnings in Nairobi are higher than those in smaller towns and the average earnings of squatter settlements around Nairobi are smaller than those inside the city. Also, adult males earn more than females or juveniles, and the self-employed fare better than the wage-employed. But whatever variation exists in this sector takes place within the lowest socioeconomic groups.

The average earnings for Nairobi are brought down by the low earnings in the squatter settlements. Also for welfare purposes one has to consider the differential cost of living between Nairobi and other small towns. I will assume that within informal-urban income variance is determined by whether somebody is self-employed or wage-employed and whether one is primary (adult male) or secondary (adult female and juveniles) breadwinner.

In Nairobi, 45 percent of those engaged in informal activities are self-employed.[4] In smaller urban centers, however, the proportion of self-employed is usually higher resulting in a higher overall proportion of self-employment. It is assumed that the overall self-employment to wage employment in the sector is 60:40 and that average earnings in the former are about 20 percent higher than those in the latter. Informal earnings are thus apportioned 1.8:1 between the self-employment and wage-employment. Distibution within informal-urban would then look like this.

---

[4] ILO Report, p. 54, n 1.

TABLE 3

Distribution of Informal-Urban Income

	Projected World Bank ILO Estimates		Alternative Estimates	
	Income (K£000's)	Average Per Worker	Income (K£000's)	Average Per Worker
Lowest 40%	2,698	54.84	2,570	53.67
Highest 60%	4,790	64.91	4,630	64.30

Source: Table 3a and the text on pp. 14-15.

I.4. FORMAL SECTOR

There is ample data on formal sector employment for estimating the distribution of wage income. The distribution of non-wage income (profits, rent, interest, etc.) is, however, difficult. The latter requires knowledge about the distribution of asset ownership across income groups and returns to different types of assets. Such information is unavailable and the distribution of non-wage income is estimated indirectly. But first, I will discuss the distribution of wage income.

1.4.1. The Distribution of Wage Income

Formal sector employment in 1974 was 826,000, including 261,000 employed in large-scale agriculture. Total earnings amount to K£274 million or an average of £332 per worker (see Appendix 3). If agriculture is excluded, the average wage rate rises to £411 ranging from £180 for unskilled workers to over £5,000 for managers of large corporations.

Wage income is distributed according to Table 8 in the Appendix. Total number of workers in each income group is obtained by column summation. The average income for each class (except open-ended classes) is assumed to be its midpoint. For the lowest income group the mean is assumed to equal .65 of its upper bound while for the highest the average is assumed to be .35 above the lower bound.[5] The income share of each class is given as a product of the class average wage rate and the number of workers in that class. This is shown in Table 4.

---

[5] For more discussion of the methods used in estimating the mean of grouped data, see Richard J. Szaal [82].

TABLE 4

The Distribution of
Formal Wage Income*

Income Bracket (Sh/month)	Average Wage Sh/month	Average Wage £/year	# Workers	Income for Bracket (in£000)	Percent Workers	Percent Income
Under 100	75	45	47,039	2,117	6.71	.88
100 - 149	125	75	102,630	7,697	14.63	3.20
150 - 199	175	105	66,741	7,008	9.51	2.30
200 - 399	300	180	179,790	32,362	25.63	13.68
400 - 599	500	300	121,929	36,579	17.38	15.46
600 - 799	700	420	59,869	25,145	8.53	10.63
800 - 999	900	540	38,731	20,915	5.52	8.84
1000 - 1499	1250	750	36,167	27,125	5.16	11.46
1500 - 1999	1750	1050	19,150	20,108	2.73	8.50
2000 - 2999	2500	1500	15,177	22,766	2.16	9.62
3000 & over	4500	2700	14,297	34,742	2.04	14.68
			701,551	240,484	100.00	99.25

*Excludes casual employment.

Source: Appendix 7.

125

Formal sector employment is further disaggregated by urban and estate (or large-scale agriculture) and their respective distributions derived. Distribution of employment income from formal, non-agriculture is then combined, after deducting that of formal-rural, with that of the informal-urban sector (see Table 3) to obtain distribution of wage income in urban areas. Thus the sub-distributions within urban, small-farm, and estate sectors are derived.

In combining the distribution of wage income from the non-agricultural formal sector with that of the informal-urban, it is estimated that all individuals engaged in informal sector activities earn incomes below 75 per year. In Table 3 it has been estimated that the average income of hired labor is about £54 while that of the self-employed is £64. Thus, these two groups fall within the lowest (under £ 60/year) and second lowest (£60 -£90/year) income groups in the formal sector (Table 4). The number of hired and self-employed persons in this sector is multiplied by their average earnings and the product added to Table 4 to obtain Table 6.

Table 6 indicates that the highest 7.1% of income recipients receive 33.4% of urban wage income. This conforms to estimates that the ILO made from urban household budget studies for the period 1968-1969 (see Appendix 10). But the latter refers to all urban income, while Table 6 considers only labor income. Since the inclusion of profit and interest incomes from formal sector would lead to a higher concentration of income, the estimates in Table 6 and that of the ILO might not be as comparable. Two possibilities arise.

TABLE 5

Distribution of Formal Wage Income by Income Group:
Agricultural (A) and Non-agricultural (NA), 1974

Income Bracket	Average Wage £/year	No. of Workers		Income for Bracket (in £ 000)		% Workers		% Income	
		NA	A	NA	A	NA	A	NA	A
Under 100	45	9,926	37,143	447	1,670	1.9	20.2	.2	7.0
100-149	75	11,377	91,254	853	6,844	2.2	49.5	.4	28.7
150-199	105	46,637	20,104	4,897	2,111	9.0	10.9	2.3	8.8
200-399	180	159,761	20,029	28,757	3,605	30.9	10.9	13.5	15.1
400-599	300	114,798	7,131	34,439	2,140	22.2	3.9	16.2	9.0
600-799	420	56,795	3,074	23,854	1,291	11.0	1.7	11.2	5.4
800-999	540	37,378	1,353	20,184	731	7.2	.7	9.5	3.1
1000-1499	750	34,589	1,478	26,016	1,109	6.7	.8	12.2	4.6
1500-1999	1050	18,205	945	19,115	993	3.5	.5	9.0	4.2
2000-2999	1500	14,156	1,021	21,234	1,532	2.7	.6	10.0	6.4
3000 & over	2430	13,534	763	32,888	1,854	2.6	.4	15.5	7.8
		517,256	184,295	212,684	23,880				

Source: Table 4.

TABLE 6

Distribution of Wage Income Within Urban Areas*

Income Class	# of Workers	Income for Bracket £000's	% Workers	% Income
1	60,577	3,147	9.5	1.4
2	83,726	5,643	13.1	2.6
3	46,637	4,897	7.3	2.2
4	159,761	28,757	25.0	13.1
5	114,798	34,439	17.9	15.7
6	56,795	23,854	8.9	10.8
7	37,378	20,184	5.8	9.2
8	34,689	26,016	5.4	11.8
9	18,205	19,115	2.8	8.7
10	14,156	21,234	2.2	9.7
11	13,534	32,888	2.1	15.0
	640,256	220,174		

*Includes imputed wage income of the self-employed in informal-urban sector.

Source: Tables 5 and 3.

1. The distribution of urban income is more concentrated in 1974
    than in 1968-1969.

2. Families tend to under report or conceal certain incomes,
    especially from family-operated businesses and rental of
    property. Since the ILO estimates are based on household
    budget surveys performed by the Ministry of Planning, it
    is likely that non-labor incomes were under-reported or con-
    cealed.

It is possible that both factors are operative and that the
inclusion of property income and the imputed value of those self-
employed in the formal sector would make the distribution of income
more unequal than indicated in Table 6. To an investigation of the
distribution of non-wage income I now turn.

I.4.2. The Distribution of Formal-Sector Operating Surplus

Non-wage income consists of profits, rent, and interest. In
the national accounts the sum of these items, plus depreciation and
indirect taxes, is called "operating surplus." To obtain formal
sector operating surplus, the monetary portion of the small-farm
and informal-urban operating surplus are subtracted from the economy-
wide monetary operating surplus. Before the results are apportioned
across households or individuals, the following deductions are made:
depreciation, undistributed profits of corporations, profits remitted by foreign-owned businesses, the profits of government enterprises, and indirect taxes (less subsidies).[6]

---

[6]The figures for operating surplus obtained from the national accounts
are net of indirect taxes and so the latter need not be estimated.

The operating surplus of the small-farm and informal-urban sectors are shown in Tables 2 and 3. The other items are estimated below.

I.4.2.1. Depreciation

The average ratio of depreciation to value added is obtained from the I-0 tables for Kenya. This ratio is estimated to be 6.77%. Current-year (1974) depreciation is the product of the depreciation ratio and a GDP at factor cost of £725.11 million which comes to £49.118.

I.4.2.2. Profit of Government Enterprises

The product of public share in sectoral value added (outside of services) and sectoral profits gives the amount of profits that accrue to government enterprises (see Table 25, Chp. 6). Summing over sectors, the public share of total profits is estimated to be £33.19 million. It is assumed that profits do not result from the provision of government services.

1.4.2.3. Indirect Taxes

The ratio of indirect taxes to gross value added can be obtained from the I-0 tables. The product of this ratio and the GDP gives a total indirect tax of £41,986,000 in 1974. However, the GDP as shown in the National Accounts is already net of indirect taxes and so this item need not be deducted from the operating surplus.

I.4.2.4. <u>Undistributed Profits</u>

Undistributed profits (π^d) have been calculated by the World Bank for 1964-1971. Current-year (i.e., 1974) total π^d is not available and is estimated with the help of the 1964-1971 "trend".

TABLE 7

Undistribution Profits in Kenya, 1964-1971

Year	Amount (£ million)	As Percent of Total Savings
1964	13.5	19.9
1965	6.7	13.2
1966	12.0	16.4
1967	6.9	9.3
1968	3.6	4.5
1969	10.6	10.2
1970	12.0	10.6
1971	13.1	11.8

Source: Ministry of Finance, Kenya, cited in IBRD, p. 375.

It could be seen that undistributed profits do not show a consistent pattern but that it tends to stabilize, with a slight upward trend, in the late 1960's. I will assume that total π^d is £14.0 million in 1974.

I.4.2.5. <u>Profit Repatriation</u>

Data on profit and interest repatriation are not directly available. However, there is an item called "net international investment income" in the National Accounts which amounts to £36.1

million in 1974 [Economic Survey, 1977, Table 3.1]. This item is assumed to correspond to the net profits of foreign-owned businesses. The ILO estimates that 43.5% of such profits have been repatriated in 1967-1970.[7] Assuming that this percent continues to hold in 1974, the total amount of repatriated profits amounts to £15.7 million.

I.4.3. Operating Surplus Received by Individuals (Non-wage Income)

The portion of operating surplus that accrues to households or individuals in the formal sector is estimated as shown in Table 8. This is then distributed across households in the form of imputed wage of the self-employed and rental income.

I.4.3.1. Self-Employment in the Modern Sector

In addition to the total employment shown in Table 4, there are also 120,000 self-employed individuals in formal sector activities whose earnings are included in operating surplus. They are mostly owners of small establishments with no hired labor. They are concen-- trated in trade which accounts for 50% of the modern sector self- employment. Within trade more than half are involved in the retailing of food, drinks and tobacco. Another 18% are in agriculture. Assuming the average net earning of the self-employed in each sector is equal to the sectoral average wage rate, the imputed labor income of those self-employed in modern sector activities can be calculated.[8]

---

[7]ILO, p. 136. This does not consider the amount of surplus transferred as a result of the practice of over-invoicing of import and under-invoicing of exports. The ILO estimates that this accounts for over 50% of total foreign exchange leakages.

[8]This assumption is based on generally accepted practice. See Kendrik [58a, p. 37].

TABLE 8

Breakdown of Monetary Sector Operating Surplus
1974, in K£ million

Total Monetary Operating Surplus:		330.44
Less: Depreciation	49.12	
Profit of government enterprises	33.19	
Interest paid to institutions	15.00	
Undistributed profits	14.00	
Profit remittances	15.70	
		127.01
Operating Surplus that Acrues to Households:		203.03
Less: Small-farm operating surplus (monetary)		
Farm	70.83	
Non-farm	9.42	
Informal-urban O.S.	4.71	
		84.96
Formal sector		118.08
Imputed labor of the self-employed*		47.83
Rental income & imputed wages of unpaid directors		70.24

Source: Economic Survey, 1975, Table 2.5.

*See Table 9.

TABLE 9

Self-Employment in The Modern Sector, 1974

Sector	Self-Employed (000's)	Avg. Sectoral Wage Rate (£/year)	Total Earnings (£000's year)
Agriculture	21.85	115	2,512.75
Mining & quarrying	.13	365	47.45
Manufacturing	12.76	437	5,576.12
Building & Const.	1.00	350	350.00
Electricity & water	---	---	---
Transportation & communication	5.71	322	1,838.62
Wholesale & retail trade	61.35	485	29,754.75
Finance, insurance, real estate, & business services	2.58	873	2,252.34
Services	15.01	366	5,493.66
	120.39		47,825.69

Source: <u>Employment and Earnings in the Modern Sector</u>, Ministry of Finance and Economic Planning, Nairobi, Kenya, 1974, pp. 19-22.

It is assumed that the distribution of income from self-employment is the same as that of formal-sector wage employment. This is partly necessitated by lack of data. But also, the average sectoral wage rate for self-employment is the same as that of the rest of the formal sector. The percent distribution of income in Table 4 would therefore not be affected although the absolute figures would be. The balance of the "residual" operating surplus, amounting to $\pm$ 70 million, goes to property owners as rental income and as compensation to unpaid directors. It is distributed by income group under three experiments using different sets of assumptions.

I.4.3.2. Distribution of Rental Income: Experiment with Alternative Assumptions

Experiment I: In order to distribute the "residual" operating surplus or rental income across income groups, it is assumed that:

1. The rental income of large firms employing more than 50 workers goes to the top two income groups (i.e., 2000-3000, and 3000+ Shs/month) which are composed of managers of large corporations and high-level professionals.[9] The share of each group is assumed to correspond to its relative share in formal sector wage income. It should be remembered that the recipients of rental income are households and not individuals. The rent-generating assets have resulted from past household savings.

2. The rental income of small and intermediate sized firms (1-50 workers) goes to the next two income groups (i.e., 1000-1499 and 1500-1999 Shs/month).

---

[9]This does not mean a paid manager is also the recipient of rental income but that both individuals belong to the same income group.

Before apportioning sectoral income across households, it is first
distributed across firms by size of establishment. The share in sectoral
rental income of each set of firms is assumed to be equal to its share in
total sectoral employment.[10] Having estimated the profit share by firm
size, sectoral rental income is then distributed by income group using
assumptions 1 and 2.

Justification for These Assumptions

These assumptions are broadly in line with ILO guesstimates [ILO Report,
Table 25, reproduced in the Stat. Appendix, Table 13]. According to this
report, most of the owners of medium-sized to large non-agricultural enterprises in the formal sector, big farmers, "rentiers", self-employed
professionals and holders of high-level jobs in the formal sector belong
to the top 30,000 households. Owners of medium-sized non-agricultural
enterprises in the formal sector and less prosperous big farmers belong to
the next 50,000 households. The ILO distribution is a rough estimate, the
basis of which has not been made clear. But it nevertheless points out the
concentration of formal sector profits in the top-most income brackets.

Using the assumption that the average number of workers per household
is 2.0 (see p. 147 for underlying reasons), the number of households in each
of the four income groups mentioned above can be calculated from Table 4.
The total number of households in the highest two income groups is about
16,000 while that for the next two income groups is 32,000. This is

---

[10]This is a realistic assumption in the Kenyan context. Technology does
not vary with firm size (once the owner-operated ones are excluded) and
so the level of output and profits depends on the number of workers
[see Singh (78), Chapter 2].

slightly less than the ILO figures (Appendix, Table 13), but then the ILO over-estimated the total number of households: 2.34 million in 1969 instead of the 1.9 million shown in the census for the same year.

To calculate the proportion of rental income that accures to individuals according to the assumptions mentioned, the following procedure is followed:

1. Rental income is apportioned according to firm size. It is assumed that the profit share of each type of firm is proportional to its share in modern sector employment.

2. The figures obtained in (1) are distributed across households using assumptions (1) and (2).

Apportioning Rental Income to Firms by Size Category

It has been assumed that the share of each type of firm in rental income and thereby profits corresponds to its relative share in formal sector and employment (see Table 4). Implicit in this assumption is that technology and therefore labor productivity is the same for different sized establishments. While this might not hold in general, it has been shown [Tokman [88] for Equadore and Singh [78] for Kenya] to be valid in many LDCs where few large firms dominate modern sector industrial production. The same might not hold if the informal sector is included.

As shown in the Stat. Appendix, Table 7, 80% of formal sector employment is accounted for by large (i.e., over 50 employees) establishments. Under the above assumption, these firms account for 80 percent of rental income. With a total rental income of £70 million; this comes to £56 million. The rest (£14 million) is accounted for by small and medium sized establishments.

TABLE 10

Distribution of Rental Income by Size of Establishment
1974

Size of Establishment (Number of Employees)	Total Rental Income (RI) (£ million)
1 - 49	14.05
50 and over	56.19
Total	70.24

Source: Table 8 and the text preceding this table.

Distribution of Rental Income by Income Group

By assumption (p. 135), all rental income acrues to the highest
four income groups who together constitute 15 percent of the formal
sector income recipients. The highest two groups receive the rental
income of large corporations while the next two income classes are
the recipients of rental income from small and medium sized establishments.

The relative share of the highest and next to highest income
classes in the rental income of large firms is assumed to correspond
to the ratio of their wage income. From Table 10, this can be
estimated to be 63:37 for non-agriculture and 65:35 for agriculture.
Similarly the relative share of the next two groups in agricultural
and non-agricultural rental income of small and medium sized establishments
is estimated to be 58:42 and 59:41. Given the rental incomes of each

type of establishment from agricultural and non-agricultural activities, the following table can be constructed.

TABLE 11

Distribution of Rental Income By Income Group,
and by Agriculture and Non-Agriculture, 1974
Experiment I

| Income Group Sh/month | Rental Income Received in £millions | |
	From Agriculture	Non-Agriculture
1000 - 1499	.14	5.75
1500 - 1999	.21	7.95
2000 - 2999	.69	20.06
3000 & over	1.29	34.15
	2.33	67.91

Source: Table 10 and text.

Combining the rental (Table 10) and wage (Table 4) incomes of each income group in the urban and large-farm sectors, the respective distributions within the two sectors can be derived. They are shown in Tables 14 and 15.

Experiment II: An alternative assumption used is that £35 million go to the top two income groups. The remainder is distributed across all income groups above the mean income according to each group's share in wage income. The mean income for formal non-agricultural employment is £411.

Justification:

1. The residual of 70 million includes the imputed value of the services of unpaid managers and directors which is not included in employment income. Rental surplus as shown in the National Accounts amount to £35 [Stat. Abst., 1976, p.47]. If this is the same as "rental" income and imputed labor income of unpaid directors" as defined above, then at least $35 million must go to the top two income groups where managers and directors are located.

2. Income groups receiving wage rates below the average for the formal sector are comprised of unskilled manual workers. It is unlikely that these groups would own rent-generating assets in the formal sector.

There is inevitably an element of arbitrariness in allocating operating surplus to the various income groups because of the lack of information on household asset ownership. The assumption used under experiments I and II, however, conform to the limited evidence that is available (e.g., ILO estimates). Also the economy-wide operating surplus of £500 million has first been broken down into its various components and the amount that acrues to property owners has been estimated as a residual. Any error introduced by the apparent arbitrariness of the assumptions has thus been reduced, at least in absolute terms. A small error in allocating £70 million (rental income) is far less serious for aggregative analysis than an equivalent error in allocating £500 million.

Experiment III: It is assumed that rental income is shared by all income groups above the mean formal-sector wage income for non-agriculture. In agriculture all rental income accrues to the top two income groups. The share of each recipient group in non-agricultural rental income is assumed to equal its share of wage income within the recipient-groups.

TABLE 13

The Distribution of Rental Income
Experiment III

Income Class	Share in Rental Income (£000)
1	----[a]
2	----
3	13,611
4	9,410
5	7,982
6	10,250
7	7,561
8	8,402
9	13,023
	70,240

[a] Income groups receiving less than £411/year do not share in rental income by assumption.

Source: Table 8 and text on next page.

I.5. INCOME DISTRIBUTION WITHIN URBAN AND LARGE-FARM SECTORS

I.5.1. Urban

The distribution of wage (Table 4) and self-employment income
(Table 9) in the formal-urban sector and the informal-urban sector
(Table 3) are combined with that of rental income obtained under the
three different set of assumptions (Tables 11, 12, and 13). The result is Table 14 which shows the distribution of urban income on a
recipient basis.

I.5.2. Large-Farm

The same process is followed for the large-farm sector. The
only differences are that income from casual employment in the formal
sector is included. The distribution of income within the large-farm
sector is shown in Table 15.

I.6. DISTRIBUTION OF INCOME ON A HOUSEHOLD BASIS

The distribution of wage income in urban areas and large farms
is on a personal basis while incomes of small farmers are distributed
on a household basis. To render the different distributions comparable,
personal income can be aggregated to arrive at household distribution
or household incomes can be decomposed to obtain individual distribution. Each has some advantages and disadvantages, the relative weights
of which depend on the intended end-use of data.

If the determination of the pattern of income distribution is the
objective then it is preferable to decompose household distribution to
arrive at individual distribution. The reason is that one must have

TABLE 14

Income Distribution Within Urban Areas Before Taxes and Transfers

	NUMBER OF INCOME RECIPIENTS, 000's				EMPLOYMENT INCOME 000s				% Empl.*	% Inc.	Rental Income 6000			Total Income Received[9]			% Income		
	Hired Labor[1]	Self-Employed		Total	Wage Inc.[4]		Self-Empl. Inc.[5]	Total			Exp.[6]	Exp.II[7]	Exp.III[8]	I	II	III	I	II	III
		Formal[2]	Informal[3]		Formal	Informal													
Under 200	67,940	12,908	123,000	203,848	6,197	1,314	7,488	14,999	27.6	5.6	----	----	----	14,999	14,999	14,999	4.5	4.5	4.5
200-399	159,761	30,449	---	190,210	28,757	6,117	---	34,874	25.7	13.2	----	----	----	34,874	34,874	34,874	10.4	10.4	10.4
400-599	114,798	28,876	---	143,674	34,439	7,341	---	41,780	19.5	15.8	----	6,858	13,611	41,780	48,638	55,391	12.4	14.5	16.5
600-799	56,795	10,839	---	67,634	23,854	5,075	---	28,928	9.2	10.9	----	4,741	9,410	28,928	33,699	38,338	8.6	10.0	11.4
800-999	37,378	7,095	---	44,473	20,184	4,305	---	24,489	6.0	9.2	----	4,022	7,982	24,489	28,511	32,471	7.3	8.5	9.7
1000-1499	34,689	6,602	---	41,291	26,016	5,528	---	31,544	5.6	11.8	5,890	5,165	10,250	37,434	36,709	41,794	11.2	10.9	12.4
1500-1999	18,205	3,449	---	21,654	19,115	4,078	---	23,193	2.9	8.7	8,160	3,810	7,561	31,353	27,003	30,754	9.3	8.0	9.2
2000-2999	14,156	2,661	---	16,817	21,234	4,531	---	25,765	2.2	9.7	20,750	17,823	8,402	46,515	43,588	34,167	13.9	13.0	10.2
Over 3000	13,534	2,562	---	16,096	32,888	7,024	---	39,912	2.2	15.0	35,440	27,822	13,023	75,352	67,734	52,935	22.4	20.2	15.8
	517,256	98,540	123,000	738,796	212,684	45,313	7,488	265,485	100.9	99.9	70,240	70,241	70,240	335,724	335,725	335,723			

Sources and explanations:

[1] All in formal sector (Table 5). This includes all non-agricultural formal-sector jobs, but some, especially government jobs, might be located in rural areas [see pp. for removing this overlap].

[2] Self-employment in formal sector (Table 9). It is assumed that income from formal-sector self-employment has the same distribution as wage income in the sector. Also that all non-agricultural self-employment in the formal sector are in urban areas.

[3] Includes both hired and self-employed individuals in the informal-urban sector. All individuals engaged in this sector earn less than 200 Sh/month and so belong to the first income bracket.

[4] Table 5.

[5] Table 4 and 9.

[6] Table 11.

[7] Table 12.

[8] Table 13.

[9] The relevant experiment column plus total wage income.

TABLE 15

Income Distribution with the Large-Farm Sector

Income Bracket (Sh/month)	Wage Employment		Self-Empl.[3]	Total	Income for Bracket (£000/yr.)				% Workers	% Income
	Regular[1]	Casual[2]			Wage[4]	Casual[5]	Self-Empl.	Total		
Under 100	37,143	76,853	4,414	118,410	1,670	6,603	176	8,449	42.0	25.6
100 - 149	91,254	---	10,816	102,070	6,844	---	721	7,565	36.0	22.9
150 - 199	20,104	---	2,382	22,486	2,111	---	221	2,332	8.0	7.1
200 - 399	20,029	---	2,382	22,391	3,605	---	379	3,984	7.9	12.1
400 - 599	7,131	---	852	8,083	2,140	---	226	2,366	2.9	7.2
600 - 799	3,074	---	371	3,445	1,291	---	136	1,427	1.2	4.3
800 - 999	1,353	---	153	1,506	731	---	78	809	.5	2.5
1000 - 1499	1,478	---	175	1,653	1,109	---	115	1,224	.6	3.7
1500 - 1999	945	---	109	1,054	923	---	105	1,096	.37	3.33
2000 - 2999	1,021	---	131	1,152	1,532	---	161	1,693	.41	5.13
3000 and over	763	---	87	850	1,854	---	196	2,050	.30	6.21
	184,295	76,853	21,850	282,998	23,880	6,603	2,512	32,995	100.2	100.1

Sources and explanations:

[1] Table 5.

[2] Statistical Abstract, 1976

[3] Table 9.

[4] Table 9.

[5] Statistical Abstract, 1976. The average wage rate for casual workers is about 686/year. Most are concentrated in the lowest income group.

fairly detailed knowledge of family size and the number of secondary wage earners in each household to be able to aggregate personal to household distribution while the same is not required for the reverse operation [Szal (82), p. 8)]. But if one needs to estimate, as I do, changes in the private demand resulting from income redistribution, then it is preferable to aggregate personal to household distribution. The main reason for this is that many goods and services are consumed by households as a unit and some items (e.g., housing) cannot be apportioned to different members of the household. Also, most productive assets are jointly owned by household members. This is especially true of rural households who constitute more than 87% of the population. Household members work on the family farm as a unit and jointly consume the product. The relevance of personal distribution in this sector is therefore limited. However, household size would have to be taken into consideration both for cross-sectional welfare comparison and because the consumption of certain items varies directly with household size. Another important reason why household rather than personal distribution should be used is that the latter includes only income recipients and therefore might not give a satisfactory picture of the overall pattern of income distribution. For these reasons, I will convert the urban and estate subdistributions from personal to household basis. To perform this conversion, information on the number of workers for each household is needed. Such information is not available, but can be estimated in a round-about way.

Household income and household size are highly correlated. This could result from either of two factors:

a) Non-family members tend to stay with the relatively affluent relatives. This would increase the relative size of households in the upper income brackets. This line of reasoning is consistent with the concept of extended family.[11] A corollary of (a) is that higher income families have higher fertility. However, evidence from fertility studies suggests an inverse relationship between fertility and income. At any rate, the difference between unitary and extended family members makes little difference for our purposes here.

b) Higher income households contain a relatively higher number of secondary income earners.

It would seem that both factors are operative but not in the manner envisioned. First, secondary income earners need not be workers in the formal sector. They could be property owners or self-employed. Thus, a household could have wage-employed, self-employed, and property-owning members. Second, many of the relatives staying with relatively well-off urban residents need not be of working age. In Kenya, like many other LDCs, some of the children of rural families come to urban centers to go to school and stay with relatively better off relatives. Most urban residents still have close familial ties with some rural areas because of the recency of urbanization.

For these reasons, and also because of lack of data, I assume that secondary workers are equally distributed across households. Moreover, it is assumed that these secondary workers are located in

---

[11]Because of the relative recency of urbanization in Kenya, most urban households still have familial ties with rural areas.

the same production sectors and have similar skill characteristics as the primary wage earners. To estimate the average number of secondary wage earners, the total number of urban jobs are subtracted from the number of urban households and the balance is divided by the latter. The reasoning rests on the implicit, and plausible, assumption that each household has one primary income earner.

There are 517,000 formal-sector jobs (see Table 5) and 123,000 informal-sector jobs (Table 3a) in urban areas. There are also approximately 320,000 urban households. With the above assumptions, the average number of wage earners per household is estimated to be 2.0.[12] Since the number of secondary workers is by assumption evenly distributed across households, the percent distribution of income as shown in Tables 13 and 14 is not affected. However, the number of workers in each bracket is divided by 2.0 to convert it to households and the total income earned by that bracket is multiplied by 2.0. The income brackets are likewise raised by a factor of 2.0. It is assumed that the same holds for large-farms; i.e., that there are two income earners in each household. The urban and large-farm household distribution of income is shown in Tables 16 and 17. The household distribution of income in the small-farm sector has been shown in Table 2.

---

[12] $\dfrac{(517 + 123)}{320}$

TABLE 16

Urban Household Income Distribution
Before Taxes and Transfers, 1974

Income * Bracket	No. of HH's ** (000's)	% of HH's[2]	% Income[3]		
			I	II	III
< 400	102	27.6	4.4	4.4	4.4
400 - 799	95	25.7	10.4	10.4	10.4
800 - 1199	72	19.5	12.4	14.5	16.5
1200 - 1599	34	9.2	8.6	10.0	11.4
1600 - 1999	22	6.0	7.3	8.5	9.7
2000 - 2999	21	5.6	11.2	10.9	12.4
3000 - 3999	11	2.9	9.3	3.0	9.2
4000 - 5,999	8	2.2	13.9	13.0	10.2
over 6,000	8	2.2	22.4	20.2	15.8

* Income brackets in Table 14 multiplied by two.

** Divide number of income recipients in Table 14 by 2. It is assumed that each
household has two income earners.

TABLE 17

Household Income Distribution
in the Large-Farm Sector, 1974

Income Bracket Sh/month	#hhs[1]	Income ($£$ 000/yr.)[2]	%hhs[3]	% Income[4]
Under 200	59,205	8,449	41.8	25.6
200 - 399	51,035	7,565	36.1	22.9
400 - 599	11,243	2,332	7.9	7.1
600 - 799	11,195	3,984	7.9	12.1
800 - 1199	4,041	2,366	2.9	7.2
1200 - 1599	1,722	1,427	1.2	4.3
1600 - 1999	753	809	0.5	2.5
2000 - 2999	827	1,224	0.6	3.7
3000 - 3999	527	1,098	.37	3.33
4000 - 5999	576	1,698	.41	5.13
over 6000	425	2,050	.30	6.21

Sources and explanations:

[1]Table 15. Divide number of workers by 2 to obtain #hhs.

[2]Table 15.

[3]$\dfrac{N_k^H}{N^H}$, where N_k^H = number of hhs in income group k;

$\qquad\qquad N^H$ = total number of households.

[4]Table 15.

I.7. THE DISTRIBUTION OF HOUSEHOLD INCOME AFTER TAXES AND TRANSFERS

The distribution of earned income (Tables 16, 17) is affected by urban-rural remittances and direct taxes. These are discussed below.

I.7.1. Taxes

The major tax that directly affects household income is income tax. The tax rates as well as the average amount paid by households in each income group is shown in Table 18.

Indirect business taxes have already been deducted from sectoral value added before the latter is distributed across households (see p. 130). Import and sales taxes (the latter is mostly limited to beer and cigarettes) go into the cost of purchased products. It should be noted that income taxes are limited to the formal sector.

I.7.2. Remittances

Information on urban-rural remittances can be obtained from the Integrated Rural Survey (IRS) on the recipient-end and from Whitelaw-Johnson and Ankar-Knowles from the remitters (i.e., urban end). According to the IRS, remittances account for a significant proportion of rural income (30% for the poorest groups and 10% overall). The total amount of remittances received amounted to £26 million in 1974 (see Table 3, Chapter 6).

Estimates on urban remittances by Ankar-Knowles are based on a 1974 ILO-University of Nairobi study and a 1968/69 urban household budget study. Remittance ratios estimated from the former are a monotonically decreasing function of income while that obtained under the latter first declines, then rises, then declines again with rise in income (Ankar-Knowles, pp. 8-9). The overall average remittance is 5.3% under the ILO-University of Nairobi study and 7.4% using data based on the 1968/69 household budget survey.

Results from the Whitelaw-Johnson study also differ from that obtained by Ankar-Knowles even though the same data were used. It cannot be ascertained what the basis of this discrepancy is but the Whitelaw-Johnson overall remittance ratio results in a much higher income remitted by urban residents than received by rural households. The different remittance ratios are shown in Table 19.

From Table 19 it could be observed that the total remittances received by rural residents is the equivalent of 7.4% of urban income (column 2 of urban). For this reason, I will use the remittance ratios shown in column 2 but is combined with that of column 1 for the uppermost income groups (see footnote, Table 19).

The distribution of urban household income after taxes and intergroup transfers is shown in Table 20. Assuming that the same rates apply to households in the estate sector, the same could be done for the latter. But because there is no data on this sector and the assumption of similarity might entail more problems than it solves, the latter operation will not be performed. At any rate, the estate sector is small (11% of rural and 8% of urban income) compared to the other two sectors. The distribution of rural income is already inclusive of remittances and there are no direct taxes.

The effects of the direct taxes and voluntary transfers are the following:

a) The distribution of total income in rural areas becomes more equal than it would have been if only earned income was considered.

b) Urban-rural differentials in income are slightly reduced.

c) The distribution of income within urban areas becomes slightly more unequal as a result of the remittances since the ratio of remittance to income falls as income rises for most groups. This is partly compensated for by direct income taxes. Income taxes, however, are progressive only for groups earning more than £1200 per year (i.e., income class 8 and above in Table 20 or only 13% of hhs) and this tends to mitigate its ameliorating effect.

TABLE 18

Income Tax Rates Effective January 1974

Income		Marginal Tax Rate (%)	Average Amount of Tax Paid (£)	Tax Rate for Bracket (%)
First	1200	10	120	10.00
Next	600	15	210	11.66
Next	600	20	330	13.75
"	600	25	480	16.00
"	600	30	680	18.89
"	600	35	890	21.19
"	600	40	1130	23.54
"	600	45	1400	25.92
"	600	50	1700	28.33
"	600	55	2030	30.76
"	600	60	2390	33.19
"	600	65	2780	35.55
Over	9000	70	3200	35.64

Source: Income Tax Regulations, Ministry of Finance, Nairobi, 1974.

TABLE 19

Remittances (±) as a Percent of Earned Income, 1974*

RURAL

Income Group	Remittances as % of Income
1	+28.85
2	+17.57
3	+15.53
4	+11.28
5	+ 9.20
6	+ 5.81
7	+ 2.61
Total	+10.00

Total Rural Income 260 mil.

URBAN

	Remittances(%)		
	Ankar-Knowles		Whitelaw-Johnson
Income Group	ILO/U. of Nair.	HH Survey	
1	-24.1	-12.5	-32.2
2	-10.5	- 8.4	-29.3
3	-12.1	- 7.6	-27.7
4	- 6.0	- 5.9	-24.2
5	- 4.2	-11.0	-21.5
6	- 2.8	- 8.2	-18.6
7	- 2.8	- 7.7	-17.1
8	- 2.8	- 6.8	-16.4
9	- 2.8	- 6.1**	-17.7
10	- 2.8	- 6.1	- 9.9
11	- 2.8	- 6.1	- 9.0

Sources: Ankar-Knowles [ ], Whitelaw-Johnson [90] and
The Integrated Rural Survey [54].

*Some interpolation made.
**Information is given only on classes below.

TABLE 20

Urban Household Income Distribution
After Taxes and Transfers, 1974

Income Bracket (Shs/month)	No. of HHs (000's)	% of HHs	% Income		
			I	II	III
less than 400	102	27.6	4.5	4.5	4.5
400 - 799	95	25.7	10.8	10.8	10.8
800 - 1199	72	19.5	12.9	15.0	17.0
1200 - 1599	34	9.2	8.6	10.0	11.3
1600 - 1999	22	6.0	7.5	8.7	9.9
2000 - 2999	21	5.6	11.5	11.2	12.7
3000 - 3999	11	2.9	9.4	8.0	9.1
4000 - 5999	8	2.2	13.6	12.7	9.9
6000 & over	8	2.2	21.4	19.2	14.9

Source: Tables 14, 18 and 19.

The overall (national) distribution of income has not been calculated partly because data for the three sectors were grouped differently
and their reconciliation and consolidation would require heroic assumptions about the within-group distributions of each of the three sectors.
This, however, does not detract from the completeness of the study.
The objective of this study is to simulate the effect of an exogenous
redistribution scheme on economic growth constraints. Since there is
a great deal of difference between the three sectors (linkages with
other sectors, location of the various income groups, production techniques, consumption characteristics, etc.) it is preferable to disaggregate the data set into these three sectors than to treat them as one.
For example, the effect of income transfer to the urban poor will have a
much different effect on the level and composition of consumption, production and employment than an equivalent transfer to the rural-poor
or to a group of households composed of both rural and urban-poor.

For these reasons it is not necessary to combine three subdistributions into an overall distribution. To obtain meaningful results
from simulating the effect of income redistribution, they would have
to be decomposed later anyway.

I.8   <u>Reconciling National Accounts and Income Distribution Data</u>:

To make National Accounts and Income distribution data comparable and also for consistency check, GDP at factor cost and total income estimated from the distribution data are compared.

Total GDP at factor cost as shown in the National Accounts amounted to £ 900 million in 1974, while Income received by households in the same year amounted to £712 million. The balance of accrues to non-individuals. These are further broken down into monetary and non-monetary sector and by urban and rural and estate sectors from the recipient end and by labor and non-labor from the source end. The results are shown in Tables 21 and 22.

TABLE 24

Factor Income in δ Million

	Income Received (in million) by Households in				Institutions			Total
	U	SF	E	Unsp.	B	G	ROW	
Non-monetary:								
Labor	---	6	---					6
Oper. Surp.	---	146[a]	6	9[b]				169
Monetary:								
Labor	265[c]	60[d]	30[e]	36[f]	---	---	---	394
Oper. Surp.	71[g]	80[h]	3	--	49,14[j]	48[k]	16[l]	330

KEY:

U = urban; SF = small-farm; E = estate; Unsp. = unspecified; B = business/companies; G = government; ROW = rest of world.

Sources and explanations:

Row sums are obtained from the national accounts, e.g., Statistical Abstract, 1976, Table 4C. The value of matrix elements are obtained from sources indicated below.

[a] £96 million of own-consumed food [IRS, Table 13.8] or 25% of the agricultural production of small-farms [I-0 tables, p. 8]. £21 million from non-farm activities [Table 3 & 6] and £29 million as remittances from urban areas [see text for explanations].

[b] Incomes of pastoralists and other rural households outside agriculture. 350,000 households with an average income of £25.

[c] Table 14.

[d] IRS, Table 8.5.

[e] Table 15 of this chapter.

[f] The amount of labor income not directly received by individuals like pensions, employees contributions to the National Security Fund, provident funds [Statistical Abstract, 1976, p. 262].

[g] Table 14.

[h] £70.83 million in farm operating surplus, and £9.42 in non-farm operating surplus. Total farm and non-farm operating surplus are £167 and £31 million respectively [IRS Table 8.5]. The non-monetary portion has been subtracted.

[j] Depreciation and undistributed profits respectively. Tables [see pp. 130,131 of this chapter].

[k] Profits of government enterprises [p. 130].

[l] Profits repatriated by foreign companies [p. 132].

TABLE 22

Monetary Sector GDP: Sources and Receipts by the Different Economic Entities

£ 000

	RECEIVING ENTITIES							
	Households				Institutions			
					G π^d,δ	B π^g	ROW π^r	
	SF	U	E	Unsp.				Total
1. Enterprises*								
Wages	30	152	30					212
Profits	80	71	3	----	14,49	48	16	330
2. Government								
Wages	30	106						136
Profits	--	---						---
3. Households								
Wages	--	7	--					7
Profits	--	---	--					

KEY:

δ = depreciation; π^d = undistributed profits; π^g = profits of government enterprises; π^r = repatriated profits.

*Includes government enterprises.

Source: Statistical Abstract, 1976, Tables 48, 256(c).

I.9. CONCLUSIONS

In this chapter, the size distribution of income within the small-farm (rural) informal-urban and formal sector has been estimated. The latter was then broken down into agriculture and non-agriculture and the latter in turn combined with the informal-urban sector to obtain urban income distribution. Thus the size distribution of income in the urban, rural, and estate (large-scale agriculture) sector has been estimated.

Data on the small-farm sector are obtained from the Integrated Rural Survey [1977] which contains a wealth of information on the economic activities of small-farm households. The size distribution of income within this sector can easily be estimated from the given data. In the formal sector, data on the distribution of wage income have been obtained from official data [e.g., Statistical Abstracts (Annual)]. No data, even an aggregate figure, are available for non-wage income in this sector. The latter was obtained by piecing together information from various sources and distributed across income groups with the help of simplifying assumptions.

Sectoral non-wage income in the formal sector is obtained by subtracting from the total (economy-wide) gross operating surplus the portion that accrues to households in the small-farm and informal-urban sectors. From the balance is subtracted the portion that accrues to non-persons in the form of depreciation, retained earnings, surplus of government enterprises, and expatriated profits. The imputed wage income of those self-employed in the formal sector is then subtracted and the "residual" which is property income is distributed across the top income groups. Income from self-employment and property income are then combined with total wage income for each income group in the formal sector and the size distribution of income thus obtained.

Information on the informal-urban sector is obtained from the ILO [40] and World Bank [91] reports. But estimates on this sector are expectedly only tentative since no official data exist. Nevertheless, there is some agreement between the two reports on the number of workers in this sector and their average earnings. Therefore, employment and earnings as shown in these two studies are used as starting point. Distribution data by income group are not available. However, since everybody in this sector is poor variances in income would tend to be relatively small. In combining the distributions in the informal-urban and non-agricultural formal sectors to obtain the urban distribution, it is assumed that all informal-urban sector households are concentrated in the lowest income group in urban areas. It has been shown that the minimum wage in the formal sector is several times higher than the average earnings in the informal-urban sector.

The overall (economy-wide) distribution has not been calculated partly because data in the three sectors were grouped differently and their reconciliation and subsequent consolidation would have required heroic assumptions. Also, consolidation, even if it could be performed, would have concealed sectoral differences and probably presented a distorted picture of the degree of intersectoral linkages. An important objective of estimating the size distribution of income is to help delimit appropriate policies. But unless the sectoral location of the target groups and the linkages of that sector with the rest of the economy are known the final impact of the policy cannot be determined (one must known where the poor are located and their sources of income to help the poor). For these reasons, it has not been necessary to combine the three subdistributions into an overall distribution. For purposes of subsequent analysis it would have to be decomposed anyway.

To cross-check the accuracy of the income distribution data and to ensure its consistency, the total income received by households in the three sectors and the amount of income received by institutions (government, business and the rest of the world) are combined and the results compared with national accounts data. Thus, the source of income by sector (national accounts) and its receipt by economic units are reconciled.

In the next chapter the source of income by sector and its receipts by urban, rural and estate households are combined. The changes in household income resulting from changes in sectoral output can be determined. This would help estimate not only changes in the size distribution of income as output and employment change, but also identify the source of income, and thus the alternative ways of changing the incomes for the target groups. Moreover, by identifying the recipients of sectoral incomes and combining with this information the consumption patterns, by sector, of these recipients the production, distribution, and consumption patterns can be combined. Such information has important implications for planning.

CHAPTER 6

SECTORAL LOCATION AND SOURCE OF INCOME
FOR EACH INCOME GROUP

I. INTRODUCTION

The main objective of this chapter is to formulate a method by
which changes in sectoral value added can be mapped to personal or
household income. Put differently, a method by which the production
and income matrices can be linked.

As mentioned in Chapter 3, changes in sectoral output can be
mapped into personal income either via the factors of production or
directly with the help of certain simplifying assumptions. The
first method can be used if the occupational and skill characteristics
and asset ownership of the households in each income group are known.
Changes in sectoral output lead to changes in factor income. The
distribution of factoral income across households depends on which
households own which factors. Such information is not available. The
collection of data usually reflects the intended end-use of that data
and since distributional issues have only recently become of major
interest to development economists, there is a dearth of such data.
This is especially true of the distribution of asset ownership (except
land) across households. But even if such information was available

the specification of the appropriate production function and the efficiency of factor markets would have to be considered. To estimate the distribution of factor income, one must know what the appropriate production function is. Problems inherent in this have been extensively discussed in the literature [see Denison and Abramovitz (cited in Chapter 2), among others]. The dualistic nature of the economy, the heterogeneity of assets and the prevalence of institutional rigidities and monopolistic elements mitigate the proper functioning of factor markets. Therefore, the "mapping" of sectoral into personal income via the factor market might not be the most appropriate method even if information of household factor ownership was available. However, the lack of such information is still the main problem in using such a method.

An alternative method directly mapping sectoral to personal income instead of via factoral income can be formulated. Given the prevailing relative share of each income class in the wage and non-wage income of each sector and assuming that this relative share is maintained, at least in the short run, changes in sectoral value added can be mapped directly to personal income. This is accomplished by assigning households to urban, small-farm and estate sectors, thereby homogenizing within-sector composition of households. The assumption that each income group maintains its within-sector share of value added is more realistic than if the whole economy is considered. Thus, if the demand for a certain crop increases, it is likely that small-farm households who were already engaged in the production of that crop will increase their output and thereby incomes. The relative responsiveness of the different households would of course depend on factor availability and its degree of utilization.

But this would have already been taken into consideration when calculating the relative share of each income class in sectoral income.

This direct method, though it by-passes factoral income in mapping sectoral to personal income, does recognize the importance of factor markets. Underlying the assumption that each income maintains its relative share of sectoral income is the fact that household income depends on factor ownership. As factor usage changes so does household income.

In this chapter, the source of income by industry, for each income class in the formal, small-farm and informal-urban sectors are estimated. The formal sector is broken down into agriculture and non-agriculture. The latter is then combined with the informal-urban sector to obtain the source of income for urban households. The percent share of each income class in the wage and non-wage income of each industry ($s_{k_j}^{w}$, $S_{k_j}\Pi$) in the urban, estate and small-farm sectors is then estimated.

II. THE SMALL-FARM SECTOR

II.1. Source of Income for Small-Farm Households

About 80 percent of the household heads covered in the Integrated Rural Survey are self-employed. The rest are employed on other small farms, in non-agricultural rural activities, government employment, or in urban areas. The major source of income is farm operating surplus, accounting for over half of the income by small-holder households. The other sources of income, in descending order of magnitude are: employment, non-farm operating surplus and remittances from relatives in urban areas. Household by type of employment, and major sources of income are shown in Tables 1 and 2.

In Table 1 only heads of households are included. No information is available on secondary workers. But this table is merely intended to give a picture of rural employment and is not used for subsequent analysis. The exclusion of secondary workers therefore poses no problem. It should be observed, however, that the self-employed and workers on other small farms are relatively more concentrated in the lower income groups while "other rural employment," including "teaching/government" are dominated by the higher income households. For poor families casual non-farm employment and remittances from relatives in urban areas are important sources of income. Thus, while over 80% of these households are self-employed, less than 50% of their incomes come from farm and non-farm operating surplus. The reverse holds for the highest income group. Only 60% of these households are self-employed, yet 75% of the incomes come from operating surplus. For middle income groups, the percentage of self-employment and the percent of income from such activities are approximately equal.

These figures indicate several underlying factors. The richest households hire labor to work on their farms and engage in other lucrative employment. Many of them are employed in the formal-rural jobs such as teaching and other public services. This may also imply that there are a higher number of secondary workers in higher income households. This may be supported by the fact that household income and household size are highly correlated (IRS Table 6.10). However, it is not known what proportion of household members are dependents staying with relatively well-off parents and what proportion are workers contributing to household income.

The total income for each income bracket by source of income can be calculated from Table 2. It is merely the product of average income from a particular source, say farm operating surplus, for each bracket and the number of households in that bracket. This is reproduced in Table 3.

Employment income and non-farm operating surplus are further broken down by industry and monetary and non-monetary sectors.

TABLE 1

Percentage Distribution of Heads of Household
By Type of Employment and Household Income Group

	1 Below 0KShs.	2 0000-999 KShs.	3 1000-1999 KShs.	4 2000-2999 KShs.	5 3000-3999 KShs.	6 4000-5999 KShs.	7 6000-7999 KShs.	8 8000 KShs. & over	Percent Total
None	84.01	89.74	86.74	83.75	78.06	76.30	75.02	61.40	80.08
Operate another Holding	0.00	0.00	1.53	1.30	2.03	1.07	0.02	0.42	0.96
Labour on another Holding	0.00	3.28	1.63	2.88	3.15	0.81	1.13	1.05	1.84
Other Rural Work	9.43	3.56	3.88	8.18	6.59	12.00	9.14	15.04	7.99
Teaching/Gov. Employment	1.81	0.94	2.87	0.86	1.30	5.65	11.38	13.30	4.42
Urban Employment	4.75	2.48	3.36	3.02	8.71	4.17	2.19	8.80	4.60
Other	0.00	0.00	0.00	0.00	0.17	0.00	1.13	0.00	0.11
Total	100.00	100.00	100.00	100.00	100.00	100.00	100.00	100.00	100.00

Source: Integrated Rural Survey, Table 6.5.

TABLE 2

Average Value Per Holding of Income and Outlays by Household Income Group

	1 Less than 0KShs.	2 0-999 KShs.	3 1000-1999 KShs.	4 2000-2999 KShs.	5 3000-3999 KShs.	6 4000-5999 KShs.	7 6000-7999 KShs.	8 8000 KShs. & over	Shs/month Total
Farm Operating Surplus	-2,621	128	649	1,327	1,933	2,944	4,239	7,865	2,081
Non-Farm Operating Surplus	-832	87	170	250	409	572	421	1,390	354
Regular Employment	183	46	142	128	457	449	1,290	2,331	566
Casual Employment	159	116	217	350	222	266	439	281	252
Remittances from Relatives	241	159	261	389	390	443	404	322	324
Other Gifts	38	14	46	61	45	141	160	128	75
Total Household Income	-2,840	551	1,485	2,505	3,456	4,815	6,953	12,317	3,652
Total Outlays	-3,690	1,611	2,165	2,721	3,364	3,892	5,618	6,505	3,450
Current Savings	-6,530	-1,060	-681	-216	93	923	1,335	5,812	202
Number of Holdings	98,982	274,000	332,813	204,972	174,002	200,501	117,919	179,176	1,483,422

Source: IRS, Table 8.5.

TABLE 3

Total Income For Each Group by Source of Income

	1* 0-999Sh	2 1000 -	3 2000 -	4 3000 -	5 4000 -	6 6000 -	7 8000 -	£ 000/year Total
Farm Operating Surplus	1,753.6	10,799.4	13,601.8	16,817.1	29,513.6	24,988.9	70,470.4	167,954.8
Non-Farm Operating Surplus	1,191.9	2,828.8	2,562.5	3,558.3	5,734.3	2,481.8	12,454.4	30,812.0
Employment	2,219.3	5,980.4	4,899.5	5,907.3	7,167.9	10,192.5	23,400.4	59,767.4*
Regular	630.3	2,364.3	1,312.0	3,975.9	4,512.5	7,611.0	20,862.5	41,268.5
Casual	1,589.0	3,616.1	3,587.5	1,921.4	2,655.4	2,581.5	2,537.9	18,498.9
Remittances from Relatives	2,178.6	4,343.2	3,986.7	3,393.0	4,441.1	2,382.0	2,884.7	23,609.3
Other Gifts	191.8	765.5	625.2	391.5	1,413.5	943.4	1,146.7	5,477.6

*The poorest group shows a negative income of £142 and a dissaving of £326.5. This is mainly of draught conditions which coincided with the survey. It is assumed that in normal years the income of this group is equal to that of the group above. The two have therefore been added together.

Source: Table 2.

170

II.1.1. Operating Surplus

The distribution of farm and non-farm operating surplus is shown in Table 4.

Table 4

K £ OOO's

Income Group	Farm Oper. Surplus	% of Total	Non-farm Operating Surplus	K£ 000's % of total
1	1,754	1.04	1,192	3.87
2	10,798	6.43	2,829	9.18
3	13,602	8.10	2,563	8.32
4	16,817	10.01	3,558	11.55
5	29,514	17.57	5,734	18.62
6	24,989	14.88	2,484	8.06
7	70,470	41.96	12,441	40.39
	167,945	99.99	30,801	99.99

Source: Table 3.

II.1.1.1. Farm Operating Surplus: Monetary and Non-Monetary

About £96 million worth of agricultural products are self-consumed (IRS Table 8.13) and so would be included in the non-monetary sector. The rest is in the monetary sector.

The share of each income group in each of the monetary and non-monetary sectors is shown in Table 5.

Table 5

The Distribution of Farm Operating Surplus
by Income Group and Monetary and Non-Monetary Sectors

K �£000

Income Group	Total Oper.[a] Surplus	Non-Monetary[b]	Monetary[c]	% Non-Monetary[d]
1	1,754	6,275	-4,521	6.7
2	10,799	12,504	-1,705	13.3
3	13,602	9,922	3,680	10.6
4	16,817	10,379	6,438	11.1
5	29,514	14,907	14,607	15.9
6	24,989	13,346	11,643	14.2
7	70,470	26,367	44,103	28.1
	165,360	93,700	77,340	99.9

Sources:

[a]Table 4

[b]IRS, Table 8.13.

[c]a - b

[d]Elements in b divided by sum of its column.

II.1.1.2. Non-farm Operating Surplus

1. <u>Monetary</u>: Most non-farm operating surplus consists of traditional processing and service activities and is more concentrated
in relatively remote areas with limited access to urban services and
formal-sector goods.[1] No data on the proportion of own-consumed to
marketed non-farm goods and services is available. But most of them
are produced for own-consumption.

It is assumed that of the total non-farm operating surplus of
31.4 million (Table 3) only 25 percent or £7.85 million is traded
and   is included in monetary sector. To cross-check the degree of
accuracy of this estimate, it is compared with figures obtained from
other sources [e.g., ILO, p. 37). According to the ILO, 106,000
individuals were self-employed in small-scale non-agricultural rural
activities in 1969. This figure is projected to 1974 assuming that
self-employment in such activities increases at a rate equal to that
of the population growth (i.e., 3 percent). Total employment of
126,564 is obtained. If the assumption that only 25 percent of non-
farm operating surplus is in the monetary sector holds, then per capita
earning is £72. According to the ILO the average earnings in 1969 were
£56. When projected at 4 percent -- the rate of growth in per capita
earnings -- this comes to about £72. The assumption that only 25 percent of the small-scale non-agricultural rural activities is included
in the monetary sector therefore seems realistic. The subdivision of
non-farm operating surplus into monetary and non-monetary sectors was
also made with the consistency-check of national accounts and income

---

[1]Social Perspectives [55], p. 4.

distribution data in mind. The monetary sector is further disaggregated by industry according to information which was obtained from Social Perspectives [55], published by the Bureau of Central Statistics. This is shown in Table 6. It should be remembered that small-scale non-agricultural rural activities do not include formal-sector rural activities, which produce relatively more sophisticated products.

Table 6

The Distribution of Monetary Sector,
Non-farm Operating Surplus by Industry

Item	%**	£ 000
Manufacturing and Repairing		
Food, beverages & tobacco	22.3	1,233
Wood products	14.0	744
Fibre products & wearing apparel	12.4	686
Other manufacturing	10.0	553
Resource Extraction*	12.1	1,140
Wholesale & retail trade	9.3	876
Services	17.8	1,677
	97.9	6,909

Source: Social Perspectives, Central Bureau of Statistics, Ministry of Finance and Planning, Nairobi, 14 June 1977, p. 2.

*Assume 50 percent of it is for construction and dwellings and 50 percent is in mining and quarrying.

**About 2% could not be allocated to any sector.

The figures in Table 6 are further disaggregated by income group according to each group's share in total non-farm operating surplus (Table 4).

Table 7

Distribution of Non-Farm Operating Surplus
by Industry and Income Class: Monetary Portion   K £ OOO's

| Industry | INCOME GROUP | | | | | | | Total |
	1	2	3	4	5	6	7	
Mining & Quarrying	22.06	52.33	47.42	65.84	106.13	45.94	230.22	570
Manufacturing of:								
Food	47.72	113.19	102.59	142.41	229.58	99.38	498.00	1,233
Wood Products	28.79	68.30	61.90	85.93	138.53	59.97	300.50	744
Apparel & fiber prod.	26.55	62.97	57.08	79.23	127.73	55.29	277.08	686
Other	21.40	50.77	46.01	63.87	102.97	44.57	223.36	553
Building & Construction	22.06	52.33	47.42	65.84	106.13	45.94	230.22	570
Transp. & Comm.	0	0	0	0	0	0	0	0
Trade	33.90	80.41	72.88	101.18	163.11	70.61	353.82	875
Services	64.90	153.95	139.53	193.69	312.26	135.17	677.34	1,677
Total	267.38	634.25	574.83	726.66	1286.44	515.47	2790.54	6,909

Source: Tables 4 and 6.

2. <u>Non-monetary Sector</u>: About £ 22 million of non-farm operating surplus is in the non-monetary sector (£30.4 million - £7.9 million).[2] It consists primarily of building and construction, water supply and ownership of dwellings. Together they account for 22 percent of the total non-monetary sector. Agriculture accounts for the rest.

TABLE 8

Distribution of Non-farm, Non-monetary
Operating Surplus by Sector of Origin

Sector	Share in Output	
	%	£ 000
Building and Construction	38.2	8,404
Water Supply	13.6	3,000
Ownership of Dwellings	48.2	10,604
		22,008

Source: Statistical Abstract, 1976, Table 45(c).

Distribution by income group can be obtained as a residual. Given the total non-farm operating surplus (Table 4) and the monetary portion (Table 7) of each group, the amount of non-farm, non-monetary operating surplus accounted for by each income group can be easily obtained (Table 9).

---

[2]See page 10 for explanations.

TABLE 9

Distribution of Non-Farm, Non-Monetary
Operating Surplus by Sector of Origin (£000)

Income Group	Amount Received*
1	925
2	2,295
3	1,988
4	2,831
5	4,348
6	1,969
7	9,650
	23,306

Sources:

*Column 4, Table 4 minus corresponding column of Table 7.

II.1.2. Wage Income

Income from employment is approximately £60 million. Distribution by income group is shown in Table 3. Income from employment is further subdivided into farm and non-farm components.

II.1.2.1. Farm Employment

Earnings and employment figures on small farms and settlement schemes are obtained from the Statistical Abstract and are reproduced below:

TABLE 10

Employment and Earning on
Small Farms and Settlement Schemes

	Employment 000s	Earnings £ 000s
Regular	237.5	10,332
Casual	238.7	5,374
Total	476.2	15,706

Source: Statistical Abstract, 1975; Table 238(c) and Table 239(c)

Earnings from farm employment as shown above are inconsistent with those obtained from Table 1. The latter is only £4.8 million or less than 30% of that shown in Table 10.[3] However, this inconsistency is more apparent than real. Table 1 refers only to heads of households and does not take into consideration secondary household income earners.

It is assumed that the share of each income group in incomes from employment in small-farms and settlement schemes corresponds to its share in overall casual employment income.[4] The results are shown in Table 11.

---

[3]Table 1 shows that 1.84% of the heads of rural households are employed on farms other than their own. Assuming that the earning-employment ratios for different sources of income are equal for each income class, income from farm employment can be obtained by multiplying 1.84% with total income of households in the small-farm community.

[4]Reason why only casual employment is considered is that most regular employment is in the formal sector (mostly government services) which is concentrated in the highest income brackets.

TABLE 11

Distribution of Small-Farm Employment
Income by Income Group

Income Group	% Share in Casual Income	Share in Wage Income of Small-Farm and Settlement Schemes £000
1	8.6	1,351
2	19.5	3,063
3	19.4	3,047
4	10.4	1,633
5	14.4	2,262
6	14.0	2,199
7	13.7	2,152

Source: IRS Table 8.5 and Table 1.

II.1.2.2. Non-Farm Employment

Most of the employment income for rural areas outside agriculture is in small-scale, non-agricultural activities. There are also some formal sector jobs. The latter is concentrated in government services like teaching and police protection. Small-scale, non-agricultural rural enterprises are mostly owner-operated and have already been included in the non-farm operating surplus.[5]

---

[5] For a full discussion of these activities, see Social Perspectives [55].

II.1.2.2.1. Formal-Rural Sector

Employment in formal-rural activities is estimated in the following way. From total employment in the formal sector, figures for both formal-urban and large-scale agriculture are subtracted. These respectively are 826,000, 386,000, and 261,000 (see Statistical Abstracts). The balance of 179,000 gives formal sector employment in rural areas. The accuracy of these figures is checked with those from other sources in the following way. In 1969 employment in this sector was 138,000 (ILO, p. 40]. During the period 1969-1974 formal employment has been increasing at 5.6 percent a year. Projecting the 1969 figures at this rate, gives 177,000 which is remarkably close to the figure obtained above. To disaggregate total rural-formal employment by industry the 1969 ILO breakdown is used. Earnings are estimated by assuming that sectoral/industry wage rates are half the formal sector sectoral wage rate.[6] The results are shown in Table 12.

To distribute the income in Table 12 by income group, it is assumed that the share of each group is proportional to its share in income from wage employment which is given in Table 3. The results are shown in Table 13.

---

[6]Since high-level manpower is concentrated in urban areas, the average wage rate in formal-rural would be substantially below the overall sectoral wage rate. It is assumed that rural wages are 50% of the overall sectoral wage rate.

Table 12

Distribution of Formal-Rural Employment by Sector

	Percent[a]	# in 000's[b]	Average Wage Rate[c]	Total Earnings (£000's)
Mining & Quarrying	.72	1,290	182	235
Manufacturing	8.70	15,570	218	3,394
Construction	.72	1,290	175	226
Electricity & Water	.72	1,290	245	316
Transportation	5.07	9,080	299	2,715
Commerce	3.62	6,480	252	1,633
Services	81.16	145,280	183	26,586
Sectoral				35,105

[a]Employment divided by total employment in formal-rural in ILO, p. 40.

[b]Col. a X 179,000.

[c]50% of formal sector wage rate.

[d]b X c

Source: Statistical Abstract, 1975, tables 221 and 233, and ILO Report, p. 40.

Table 13

Distribution of Income from Formal Employment by Income Group

	Class	Income from wage[1] Employment in 000's	Percent of[2] Total	Amount Received by each Group[3] in £ 000's
Lowest	1	2,219	3.7	1,299
	2	5,980	10.0	3,511
	3	4,900	8.2	2,879
	4	5,709	9.6	3,370
	5	7,168	12.0	4,213
	6	10,192	17.1	6,003
Highest	7	23,400	39.2	13,762
		59,767		35,106

[1]Table 3, row 3

[2]Each element in column 1 is divided by column sum.

[3]Column 2 X £ 35.105 million. Latter is shown in Table 12.

Source: Tables 3 and 12.

Most of these jobs are in the public sector especially in services like teaching, police and administration, agricultural extension services, etc. Employment in such services is not expected to change as a result of income redistribution.

II.1.2.2.2. Small-scale Non-agricultural Rural Activities

There is very little data available on wage employment in such activities and the limited available information is highly contradictory. For example, the ILO estimates that 82,000 persons were employed in these activities in 1969 [ILO Report, p. 39]. On the other hand, estimates by the World Bank for the same year amount to 150,000 [IBRD, p. 146].

The most plausible explanation for this huge disparity is that the World Bank estimates include self-employed persons while ILO's refer only to wage employment. If self-employment is included in the latter, the two sets of figures are exactly the same. Since income from self-employment has already been included in non-farm operating surplus (Table 6), only wage employment will be considered here.

Assuming that employment in these activities increased at the rate indicated by the World Bank for the period 1969-1971,[8] and average earnings rise at half the rate of increase in the average wage rate of large-scale farming,[9] total employment in 1974 is 98,000 and average earnings would amount to £70 (£ 80 for regular, £ 62.5 for casual).

----

[8] Total employment (including self-employment) rose from 96,000 in 1969 to 102,000 in 1971 or an average of 3% a year.

[9] Average wage rate of large farm employment rose from £73.85 in 1969 to £116.56 in 1974 [Statistical Abstracts, 1974, Tables 225 and 241, and 1976 tables 237 and 250]. This comes to an average of 8.5%. Such an assumption is arbitrary but not unrealistic. The rate of increase in the wage rate of the small farm sector where population pressure is most acute would have to be considerably less than that in the relatively "protected" large-farm sector. But whether the former increases at 30% or 5C% of the latter cannot be ascertained.

These aggregate figures are broken down by industry using World Bank estimates (p. 146) and by regular and casual employment, using ILO figures (p. 39). The results are shown in Table 14 and 15.

The sectoral earnings are subsequently distributed by income class according to the share of each group in income from regular and casual employment which is obtained from the Integrated Rural Survey (IRS) and reproduced as Table 16. The lowest class is excluded because its average income is only £27 per household [see Table 8.5], while the average earnings for casual employment in non-farm activities is £62.5. Households in this class are concentrated in farm employment where earnings are considerably less. The shareof the rest of the income classes is shown in Table 15. The information in Tables 14 and 15 is combined to obtain distribution of earnings by industry and income group. The results are shown in Table 16. This is then combined with information on the distribution of all wage income and farm and non-farm operations.

TABLE 14

Percent Share of Each Income Class in the
Small-Farm Sector in Non-Farm Wage Income

Income Class	% Share	
	Regular	Casual
2	7	20
3	4	20
4	10	13
5	11	16
6	18	16
7	50	15
	100	100

Source: IRS, Table 8.5

But whatever error is introduced by the relative arbitrariness of this assumption, it would be small because all wage incomes from non-agricultural rural activities account for less than 2% of rural income. It is considered only for the sake of completeness.

Table 15

The Distribution by Industry of Employment & Earnings
in Small-Scale Non-Agricultural Rural Activities, 1974

INDUSTRY	% of Total[a]	Employment			Earnings (£000)		
		Regular[b]	Casual[b]	Total	Regular[c]	Casual[d]	Total
Mining & Quarrying	0.6	311	276	587	25	17	42
Manufacturing of:*							
Food	7.6	3,944	3,497	7,441	316	218.6	534
Wood products	4.8	2,480	2,200	4,680	198	138	336
Apparel	4.2	2,179	1,933	4,112	174	121	295
Other	3.4	1,972	1,748	3,721	158	109	267
Building & Const.	0.6	311	276	587	25	17	42
Transport. & Comm.	2.0	1,037	920	1,958	80	58	138
Wholesale & retail trade	64.0	33,210	29,450	62,661	2,657	1,841	4,498
Services	12.7	6,575	5,830	12,405	526	364	890

Sources:

[a] IBRD, Table

[b] The ratio of regular to casual employment is 53:47.

[c] Col. 2 X 80 (see p. 21).

[d] Col. 3 X 62.5 (see p. 21).

*The manufacturing sector is disaggregated into its component industries using Table 6.

Table 16

Amount Received by Each Income Group From Employment
in Small-Scale Non-Agricultural Rural Activities (£000)

INDUSTRY	2			3			4			5			6			7		
	R	C	T	R	C	T	R	C	T	R	C	T	R	C	T	R	C	T
Mining & quarrying	1.7	3.5	5.2	.1	3.5	3.6	2.5	2.5	5.0	2.7	2.8	5.5	4.5	2.8	7.3	12.5	2.6	15.1
Manufacturing of: food	22.1	43.7	65.8	8.7	43.7	52.4	31.6	28.4	60.0	34.7	35.0	69.7	56.8	35.0	91.8	157.8	32.8	190.6
Wood products	13.9	27.5	41.4	5.5	27.5	33.0	19.8	17.9	37.7	21.8	22.0	43.8	35.7	22.0	57.7	99.2	20.6	119.8
Apparel & Fiber	12.2	24.2	36.4	4.8	24.2	29.0	17.4	15.7	33.1	19.2	19.3	38.5	31.4	19.3	50.7	87.2	18.1	105.3
Other	11.0	21.8	32.8	4.4	21.8	26.2	15.8	14.1	29.9	17.4	17.5	34.9	28.4	17.5	45.9	78.9	16.4	95.3
Building & Construction	1.7	3.5	5.2	.1	3.5	3.6	2.5	2.5	5.0	2.7	2.8	5.5	4.5	2.8	7.3	12.5	2.6	15.1
Transp. and Commerce	5.6	11.5	17.1	2.3	11.5	13.8	8.0	7.5	15.5	8.8	9.2	18.0	14.3	9.2	23.5	39.8	8.6	48.8
Wholesale & retail trade	186.0	368.1	554.1	73.6	368.1	441.7	265.7	239.3	505.0	292.2	294.5	586.7	478.2	294.3	772.5	1328.4	276.1	1605.5
Services	36.8	72.9	109.7	14.6	72.9	87.5	52.6	47.4	100.0	57.9	58.3	116.2	94.7	58.3	153.0	263.0	54.7	317.7
			867.7			690.8			791.2			918.8			1209.7			2312.2

Symbols:
R = Income from regular employment
C = Income from casual employment
T = Income from overall employment (R + C)

Source: Tables 14 and 15.

II.2. <u>Summary of the Sources by Sector and Income Group in the Small-Farm Sector</u>

The information contained in Tables 5, 7, 9, 11, 13, and 16 is summarized by income group in Table 17 and by income group and sector of origin in Table 18. The percent of each group, derived from Table 18, is shown in Table 19.

Table 17

Income Distribution in the Small-Farm Sector
by Factor and Income Group (£ 000's)

Income Class	WAGE INCOME				OPERATING SURPLUS					
	Agriculture[a]	Non-Agriculture		Total	Agriculture			Non-Agriculture		
		Formal[b]	non-farm rur. activities[c]		Total[d]	Monetary[e]	Non-Monetary[f]	Total[g]	Monetary[h]	Non-Monetary[i]
1	1,351	1,299	-	2,650	1,754	-4,521	6,275	1,192	267	814
2	3,063	3,511	868	7,442	10,806	-1,705	12,504	3,415	634	2,377
3	3,047	2,879	691	6,617	13,602	3,680	9,922	2,563	575	1,783
4	1,633	3,370	791	5,794	16,817	6,438	10,379	3,558	727	2,487
5	2,262	4,213	919	7,394	29,588	14,607	14,907	5,734	1,286	4,181
6	2,199	6,003	1,210	9,412	25,010	11,643	13,346	2,484	515	1,717
7	2,152	13,762	2,312	18,226	70,392	44,643	26,367	12,441	2,791	8,627
		35,106	6,791		165,360	74,245	93,700*	31,387	6,795	21,986

Source:

aTable 11.
bTable 13.
cTable 14 and 15.
dTable 5.
eTable 5.
fTable 5.
gTables 7 and 9.
h = Table 7.
i = Table 9.

*The amount of self-consumed food is £96 million [IRS 8.13]. The low figure in this table (lower by £3 million) results from the exclusion of the lowest income group which received negative income for the year [see footnote to Table 3 for explanations.]

TABLE 18

Income Distribution in the Small-Farm Sector
By Factor, Income Group and Industry (£000)

Industry	1 W	1 Π M	1 Π NM	2 W	2 Π M	2 Π NM	3 W	3 Π M	3 Π NM	4 W	4 Π M	4 Π NM	5 W	5 Π M	5 Π NM	6 W	6 Π M	6 Π NM	7 W	7 Π M	7 Π NM	Total W	Total Π M	Total Π NM
Agriculture, forestry & fishing	1,351	-4,521	6,275	3,063	-1,705	12,504	3,047	3,680	9,922	1,633	6,438	10,379	2,262	14,607	14,907	2,199	11,643	13,346	2,152	44,103	26,367	15,706	86,697	93,700
Mining & quarrying		23		5	63		4	46		5	63		6	103		7	46		15	228		42	572	
Manufacturing of:																								
food		49		66	136		52	99		60	136		70	222		92	99		191	493		531	1,233	
wood products		30		41	82		33	60		38	82		44	134		58	60		120	298		336	744	
apparel & fiber products		27		36	76		29	55		33	76		39	124		51	55		105	274		295	686	
other		22		33	61		26	44		30	61		35	100		46	44		95	221		267	553	
Building & construction		23	311	5	63	908	4	46	681	5	63	950	6	103	1,597	-7	46	656	15	228	3,294	42	570	8,404
Water supply			111			324			243			339			570			234			1,176			3,000
Transportation & comm.				17			14			16			18			24			49			138		
Trade	35		---	554	96	---	442	70	---	505	96	---	587	158		773	70		1,605	350		4,498	876	
Ownership of dwelling			392			1,145			859			1,198			2,014			827			4,157			10,604
Service		67		110	185		88	135		100	185		116	302		153	134		318	617		890	1,667	

Symbols:
W = wage income
M = monetary
Π = operating surplus
NM = non-monetary
SF = small-farm

Sources: W - agriculture, Table 17
    non-agriculture, Table 11

Π - Agriculture: monetary, Table 17
    non-monetary, Table 17

Non-agriculture: monetary, Table 7
    non-monetary, Table 9

Table 19

Percent Distribution of Sectoral Wage Income and Operating Surplus by Income Class (S^w_{kj}, S^{Π}_{kj}) in the Small-Farm Monetary Sector

	INCOME CLASS													
SECTOR	1		2		3		4		5		6		7	
	W	Π	W	Π	W	Π	W	Π	W	Π	W	Π	W	Π
Economy	8.6	3.7		10.8		8.1		11.3		19.0		7.8		39.2
Agriculture, Forestry, & Fishing		0	19.5	0	19.4	4.2	10.4	7.2	14.4	16.8	14.0	13.4	13.7	51.0
Mining and Quarrying		4.0	11.9	11.1	9.5	8.1	11.9	11.1	14.3	18.1	16.7	8.1	35.7	40.0
Manufacturing:														
Food preparations		4.0	18.1	5.5	14.8	8.0	17.1	11.0	19.9	18.0	26.2	8.0	54.4	40.0
Wood products		4.0	12.2	11.0	9.8	8.1	11.3	11.0	13.1	18.0	17.3	8.1	35.7	40.0
Apparel & fiber		4.0	13.5	11.0	10.9	8.1	12.4	11.0	14.6	18.0	19.1		39.3	40.0
Leather		4.0	12.4	11.0	9.7	8.0	11.2	11.0	13.1	18.0	17.2	8.1	35.5	40.0
Building and Construction		4.0	11.9	11.0	9.5	8.0	11.9	11.0	14.3	18.1	16.7	8.1	35.7	40.0
Transport and Comm.		---	12.3	---	10.1	---	11.6	---	13.0	---	17.4	---	35.5	---
Trade		4.0	12.3	11.0	9.8	8.0	11.2	11.0	13.1	18.0	17.2	8.1	35.7	40.0
Services		4.0	12.3	11.0	9.9	8.0	11.2	11.0	11.6	18.0	17.2	8.1	35	40.0

Source: Table 18.

III. INFORMAL-URBAN SECTOR

The distribution of income in this sector has been discussed in Chapter 5 (See table 5.3). Since everybody in this sector is poor, there is little variance in income and therefore no distinct income classes. But in general, the self-employed fare better than hired labor in this sector. The former are included in operating surplus while the latter are in wage income.

About 60 percent of those engaged in informal-sector activities are self-employed with a total income of about £4.7 million. The other 40 percent are hired labor and with a total wage income of £2.7 million (Table 5.3).

These figures are disaggregated by industries with the help of World Bank estimates of the sectoral breakdown of informal sector employment (p. 54).

Table 20

Distribution of Income in The Informal-Urban Sector by
Industry and Employment Status (Self-Employed or Wage Employed 60:40)

SECTOR	Lowest 40%	Highest 60%
Manufacturing:food	423.6	752.0
Construction	313.4	565.2
Transportation & Comm.	26.4	46.9
Trade	847.2	1,504.0
Services	1,084.6	1,925.6

*I assume that the ratio of self-employment to wage employment is the same across sectors.

IV. FORMAL SECTOR

IV.1. Wage Income by Industry and Income Group

The average wage rate and the number of workers from each of 11 income groups in each of 9 main productive sectors is shown in the appendix 8. Table 21 shows the distribution of wage income by industry and income group. This is merely the product of the average wage rate and the number of workers of each income group in each sector ($\bar{w}_{k_j}$, L_{k_j}). Income from the informal-urban sector (Table 20) can then be added to the income from non-agricultural employment to obtain the distribution of wage income in urban areas. This is shown in the last column of Table 21.

The share of each class in the wage income of each industry ($s_{k_j} w$) in the formal and urban sectors (including informal-urban) is shown in Tables 22 and 23.

Table 21

Distribution of Wage Income By Industry and Income Group, 1974

	1	2	3	4	5	6	7	8	9	10	11	TOTAL	Total-urban (Incl. informal)
1. Agriculture, forestry & fishing	8,449.0	7,656.0	2,332.0	3,984.0	2,366.0	1,427.0	809.0	1,224.0	1,104.0	1,685.0	2,053.0	32,995.0	
2. Mining & Quarrying	.5	10.6	21.3	194.0	150.3	88.6	53.5	113.3	54.6	85.5	277.0	1,049.2	Unchanged (same as Col. 12)
3. Manufacturing:													
.1 Food, bev. & tobacco	8.3	93.7	171.8	953.1	1,654.4	1,016.8	743.0	1,210.5	694.1	904.4	1,606.2	9,056.3	10,231.9
.2 Textile, apparel & leather	2.3	14.6	146.9	2,216.9	1,022.7	297.5	105.3	245.3	203.7	324.0	286.4	4,865.6	Unchanged
.3 Wood, paper products and publishing	6.2	81.8	187.6	809.8	779.5	458.6	329.4	668.3	935.6	634.5	1,326.8	6,218.1	"
.4 Chemicals, petroleum and rubber products	---	---	74.0	320.0	594.6	282.2	204.1	375.8	346.5	579.0	1,509.0	4,225.1	"
.5 Non-metallic mineral products excl. petrol.	4.9	6.2	6.2	185.8	255.0	142.4	54.5	86.3	57.8	160.5	442.3	1,401.9	"
.6 Basic metal and metal products, machinery, equipment	2.9	13.8	47.6	2,037.6	1,841.4	1,075.6	871.5	1,005.0	839.0	1,093.5	2,009.6	10,837.5	"
4. Electricity and Water	.6	.2	.5	62.1	343.2	178.9	186.3	324.0	192.2	366.0	483.5	2,155.5	"
5. Construction	11.7	20.2	194.9	2,200.0	2,117.4	1,144.9	867.2	1,235.2	895.6	1,129.5	2,087.4	11,904.0	12,787.6
6. Trade, rest. & hotels	52.8	127.7	339.9	3,789.0	2,539.2	1,925.7	1,335.4	2,381.2	1,903.6	3,265.5	6,842.9	24,502.9	26,854.2
7. Transp. and Comm.	3.5	7.4	358.0	1,729.8	2,319.0	2,604.8	4,690.4	3,123.7	1,921.5	2,200.0	3,010.8	21,958.9	22,042.2
8. Finan'l & Bus. Services	1.6	9.7	46.1	984.6	753.0	524.6	1,360.8	2,143.5	1,572.9	2,467.5	5,960.8	15,825.1	Unchanged
9. Community, Social & Personal Services													
.1 Public (Administ. defence & social)	263.4	167.0	225.6	10,582.5	19,928.1	13440.0	8,914.3	12,271.5	9,302.0	7,185.0	5,486.9	87,766.3	"
.2 Personal & Household	87.7	298.6	292.0	268.8	906.3	738.4	469.8	815.2	557.5	741.0	1,154.2	6,329.5	9,339.7

Source: Statistical Abstract, 1976, Table 256(c), p. 298. For informal-urban, see Table 20, for estate (agriculture, forestry, and fishing) Table 15, ... Chapter 5.

Table 22

Share of Each Income Class in Formal Sector Wage Income*
by Industry (S_{kj}^{w})

(Sector/class)	1	2	3	4	5	6	7	8	9	10	11	
1	.26	.23	.07	.12	.07	.04	.02	.04	.03	.05	.06	1.00
2	.00	.01	.02	.18	.14	.08	.05	.11	.05	.08	.26	1.00
3.1	.00	.01	.02	.11	.18	.11	.08	.13	.08	.10	.18	1.00
3.2	.000	.003	.03	.46	.21	.06	.02	.05	.04	.07	.06	1.00
3.3	.001	.013	.03	.13	.13	.07	.05	.11	.15	.10	.21	1.00
3.4	.00	.00	.003	.08	.14	.06	.05	.09	.08	.14	.36	1.00
3.5	.003	.004	.004	.13	.16	.10	.04	.06	.04	.11	.32	1.00
3.6	0	.001	.004	.19	.17	.10	.08	.09	.08	.10	.19	1.00
4	0	0	0	.03	.16	.08	.09	.16	.09	.17	.22	1.00
5	0	.002	.01	.18	.18	.10	.07	.10	.08	.09	.18	1.00
6	.002	.005	.01	.15	.10	.08	.05	.10	.08	.13	.28	1.00
7	0	0	.02	.08	.10	.12	.21	.14	.09	.10	.14	1.00
8	0	0	.003	.062	.048	.033	.086	.14	.10	.16	.38	1.00
9.2	.014	.047	.046	.042	.14	.12	.07	.13	.09	.12	.18	1.00

Source: Table 21.

*Excludes government service.

Table 23

Share of Each Income Class in Sectoral Wage Income in 000*
(Urban Sector Including Informal-Urban)

	1	2	3	4	5	6	7	8	9	10	11
3	.00	.01	.02	.18	.14	.03	.05	.11	.05	.08	.26
4	.04	.08	.02	.09	.16	.10	.07	.12	.07	.09	.16
5	.00	.00	.03	.46	.21	.06	.02	.05	.04	.07	.06
6	.00	.01	.03	.13	.13	.07	.05	.11	.15	.10	.21
7	.00	.00	.0	.08	.14	.06	.05	.09	.08	.14	.36
8	.00	.00	.00	.14	.16	.10	.04	.06	.04	.11	.32
9	.00	.00	.00	.19	.17	.10	.08	.09	.08	.10	.19
10	.00	.00	.00	.3	.16	.08	.09	.16	.09	.17	.22
11	.03	.05	.02	.17	.16	.09	.07	.10	.07	.09	.16
12	.03	.06	.01	.14	.10	.07	.05	.09	.07	.12	.25
13	.00	.00	.02	.08	.11	.12	.21	.14	.09	.10	.14
14	.00	.00	.00	.07	.05	.03	.09	.14	.10	.16	.38
15	0	0	0	0	0	0	0	0	0	0	0
16	.13	.24	.03	.03	.10	.08	.05	.09	.06	.08	.12

*Excludes government services (item #9.1)

Source: Tables 20 and 21

IV.2. Non-Wage Income by Industry and Income Group

The distribution of non-wage income in the formal sector has been discussed in Chapter 5. It is further disaggregated by industry in the following way:

1. Since formal sector operating surplus is obtained as a residual, each of the items to be deducted from the economy-wide operating surplus (i.e., informal-urban and small-farm sector operating, depreciation, profit expatriation, undistributed profits and profits of government enterprises) is disaggregated by industry.

2. These are then subtracted from sectoral operating surplus to obtain formal sector operating surplus.

3. The imputed wage incomes of the self-employed, broken down by industry, are subtracted to obtain sectoral rental income.

4. The latter is then distributed by income group according to the assumptions discussed in Chapter 5.

A major thrust of this section is the disaggregation by industry of that portion of non-wage income that does not accrue to individuals.

1. <u>Depreciation</u>:

The ratio of depreciation to sectoral value added is obtained
from the input-output tables for Kenya, 1971 [9]. Since this differs
slightly from that obtained from the 1967 input-output table, the average
of the two is applied to current-year (1974) sectoral value added to
obtain total value of depreciation. This is shown in Table 24.

2. <u>Profit of Government Enterprises</u>

This is estimated by multiplying the share of the public sector
in sectoral value added with total sectoral profit and is shown in Table 25.

3. <u>Undistributed Profits</u>

The total undistributed profits were estimated to be   14 million
(see Table 7 in Chapter 5). No data are available on its sectoral
distribution. To disaggregate the total figure by sector of origin,
I will assume that the ratio of undistributed to total profits is equal
across sectors. Given sectoral profits, the percent share of each sector
in undistributed profits can be estimated. This is shown in Table 26.

4. <u>Indirect taxes</u>

The amount of indirect taxes paid by each sector is obtained as
the product of the ratio of indirect taxes to gross value added obtained
from the input-output tables and the 1974 sectoral gross value added.
This is shown in Table 27.

Table 24

Ratio of Depreciation to Gross Value-Added,
and Total Depreciation by Sector, 1974

SECTOR	Ratio	Total ($ million)[d]
Non-Monetary		0
Agriculture and Forestry	.0853	11.059
Mining and Quarrying	.1770	.453
Manufacturing and Repairing	.0998	12.540
Building and Construction	.1296	3.940
Electricity and Water	.1695	1.235
Transportation and Comm.	.1389	8.158
Wholesale and Retail Trade	.0615	7.219
Banking, Insurance & Real Estate	.0224	2.448
Ownership of Dwellings	0	0
Other Services (excl. government)	.0479	1.196
Central Government	.0064	.870
Total		49.118

Source: Input-Output Table for Kenya [53].

Table 25

Profits of Government Enterprises, 1974

INDUSTRY	% V.A.[a]	Profits of Public[b] Enterprises* (£mil.)
Agriculture, forestry & fishing	3.71	3,506
Mining and quarrying	0	0
Manufacturing**		
Food, beverages & tobacco	22.54	3,531
Textile, apparel & leather prod.	"	2,865
Wood products and furniture	"	2,677
Chemical, petroleum, rubber & plastic	"	941
Mineral products	"	622
Basic metal, equip., machinery and other mfc	"	3,835
Subtotal	22.54	14,471
Electricity and Water	13.17	1,029
Construction	16.47	1,441
Trade, restaurants & hotels	0	0
Transportation & Communication	38.01	8,203
Financial & Bus. Services	14.19	3,705
Ownership of Dwellings	3.72	1,316
Other Services	.92	.065

*Includes depreciation.

**Percent share of each manufacturing subsector is assumed to equal its percent share of manufacturing output. This in turn is based on two implicit assumptions: 1) profit-making government corporations are as efficient as privately-owned ones, and 2) the same profit-output ratios hold for all government enterprises in the manufacturing sector. Both of these assumptions seem realistic but have also been necessitated by unavailability of information on the distribution of the profits of government-owned enterprises between the subsectors in manufacturing.

Source: [a]Economic Survey, 1977, Table 2.5.

[b]Statistical Abstracts, 1976, Table 48.

Table 26

Estimates of Undistributed Profits by Sector*

	(£million)
Non-monetary sector	0
Monetary sector:	
Agriculture, forestry & fishing	3.971
Mining and quarrying	.063
Manufacturing	2.812
Electricity and water	.328
Building & construction	.368
Wholesale, retail trade, restaurants and hotels	2.667
Transport, storage and comm.	.907
Finance, insurance, real estate	1.097
Ownership of dwellings	1.487
Other services (excl. government)	.299
Government	0

*Sectoral profits divided by total monetary profits multiplied by 14 million.

Source: Economic Survey, 1976, Table 2.3 and preceding text of this section.

Table 27

SECTOR	Ratio of indirect taxes to gross value added in base year	Amount of tax in K£000
Agriculture, forestry & fishing	-.0037	-481
Mining and quarrying	.0327	102
Manufacturing	.2347	29,548
Electricity & water	.0049	51
Building & construction	.0104	451
Trade, hotels & restaurants	.0344	3,986
Transp. and comm.	.0199	1,107
Finance, insurance & Bus. services	.0300	1,404
Ownership of dwellings	.1183	4,187
Other services (excl. gov't)	.0302	669

Source: Input-Output Table for Kenya, 1977.

5. Profit Repatriation

The total amount of repatriated profits amounts to £36 million and has been discussed in Chapter 5. Disaggregating profit repatriation by sector is very difficult because of the unavailability of information on the sectoral location of foreign-owned businesses. If the latter were available then foreign share in sectoral profit could have been estimated given their share in output, taking into consideration the differential capital intensity between domestic and foreign-owned firms. Assuming that the ratio of remitted to earned profits is the same across sectors, the total repatriated profits could then have been disaggregated by sector. Such data, however, do not exist and have to be estimated indirectly.

I will assume that Asian and European expatriates employed in the private sector are concentrated in foreign-owned firms so that the relative concentration of expatriates is an indication of the extent of foreign investment in a particular sector.[10] But differences in the capital intensity of sectors would have to be taken into consideration. The ratio of sectoral non-wage bill to sectoral value added is taken as a surrogate of the capital intensity. The amount of profits repatriated from each sector is then calculated using the following equation:

$$\pi_j^r = \alpha_j \left[\frac{W_j^x}{W^x} \cdot \frac{\pi_j}{V_j} \right] \pi^r$$

_____

[10]This is a reasonable assumption. For a country like Kenya where local entrepreneurship has not yet been well developed, most of the highly paid expatriates (usually non-African) are employed either by the government or foreign-owned corporations.

where:

W_j^x = Expatriate wage earnings in sector j

W^x = Total expatriate (Asians and Europeans only) wage earnings

Π_j = Profits of sector j

V_j = Value added in sector j

Π^r = Total profits remitted by foreign corporations

Π_j^r = Profits remitted by sector/industry j

The constant α_j is chosen such that

$$\sum_j \alpha_j \frac{W_j^x}{W^x} \frac{\Pi_j}{V_j} = 1$$

Table 28 can then be constructed.

According to Table 28, 35 percent and 29 percent of profit repatriation are respectively accounted for by manufacturing, and trade restaurants and hotels. Assuming that profit-remittance ratios are equal across sectors, these two sectors account for 75 percent of the profits of foreign corporations.[11] Assuming that the rate of return to foreign investment is equal across sectors, this would in turn mean that 75 percent of all foreign investment is located in these two sectors. This is generally in accord with outside estimates.

According to the ILO [pp. 437-457] most of the foreign investment is in the highly protected and lucrative sectors of manufacturing and tourism.[12] But exactly what proportion of it is in these two sectors

---

[11] It is assumed that profit remittance is dependent on as-yet-undetermined set of economic and political factors that are common to all sectors.

[12] Most of the tourism is in the sector labeled "trade, restaurants, and hotels."

Table 28

SECTOR	Ratio of expatriate earnings in each sector to total expatriate earnings (W^x_j/W^x)	Ratio of gross profits to sectoral value added (Π_j/V_j)	$\alpha_j \dfrac{W^x_j}{W^x} \dfrac{\Pi_j}{V_j}$ [a]	Repatriated profits (Π^R_j) (K£million)
Agriculture & forestry	.01	.73	.1437	2.256
Mining and quarrying	--	--	--	--
Manufacturing	.34	.53	.3546	5.567
Electricity and water	--	--	--	--
Construction	.13	.20	.0517	.811
Trade, rest. and hotels	.27	.55	.2922	4.588
Transp. and comm.	.04	.39	.1102	.577
Financial and bus. services	.10	.56	.1102	1.730
Other services (incl. government)	.02	.32	.0124	.193
				15.722

a. $\alpha_j = .82$.

Table 29

Employment and Earning in the Private Sector
by Industry and Race for Non-Citizens

	Employment in 000's[a]		Earnings in £mil[b]		
	Asian	European	Asian	European	Total
Agriculture & forestry	.10	.5	.140	.950	.090
Mining and quarrying	--	--	---	---	
Manufacturing	1.48	.75	2.133	1.425	3.558
Electricity and water	--	--	---	---	---
Construction	.51	.30	.735	.570	1.305
Trade, restaurants & hotels	1.06	.67	1.527	1.273	2.800
Transp. and comm.	.08	.13	.115	.247	.362
Finance, insurance, real estate & business services	.31	.61	.447	.598	1.045
Community, social and personal services	.04	.06	.058	.114	.162
TOTAL	3.58	2.57	5.155	5.177	10.332

[a] Economic Survey 1975, Table 5.9, p. 39 and Table 29 above. The number of expatriates in the private sector is calculated by multiplying sectoral expatriate employment and the percent of private to total sectoral value added.

[b] Average earnings for Asians are £1441 and for Europeans £1,890.

Source: Economic Survey, 1975, Table 5.9.

was not mentioned. This, however, can be estimated with relevant scattered information. An UNCTAD [9] study estimated that 35 percent of capital formation in modern manufacturing was accounted for by private foreign investment over the period 1966-1969. Assuming this ratio still holds and that profit share corresponds to the share in capital formation, foreign firms would then get 35 percent of manufacturing profits. This corresponds to the figure for manufacturing in column 4 of Table 28. Modern sector manufacturing profits amount to £43.5 million. Foreign firms would then receive £15.225 million or 35 percent of the total. The amount of profits repatriated from manufacturing is about £5.5 million or 43 percent [ILO, p. 36] of £15.225 million. This is only 16 percent more than that shown in column 5 for manufacturing. Considering that this difference reflects the cumulative errors of all the items that are deducted from economy-wide operating surplus for manufacturing (Table 30), this difference is relatively small especially when taken in light of the indirectness of the method necessitated by the paucity of the data and the fact that the 6.5 million is itself a rough estimate.

While similar figures are not available for non-manufacturing sectors, there is limited evidence that tourism, large-scale farming and finance, insurance and business services account for most of the foreign investment in non-manufacturing. After manufacturing, tourism is the most important sector for foreign investment [ILO, p.438]. Many estates, especially tea and coffee plantations are owned by foreign firms [ILO (40)].

Many banks and other financial institutions are also foreign-owned. Unlike many other African countries Kenya did not nationalize foreign

Table 30

Distribution of Formal Operating Surplus by Destination and Productive Sector

SECTOR	2 Monetary sector operating surplus	3 O.S. of small farmers SF	4 O.S. of informal-urban IU	5 O.S. of gov't enterp.* π^g	6 Depreciation**	7 Undistributed profits π^d	8 Repatriate profits π^f	9 Total of columns 3 - 8	10 Net balance column 2 minus Col. 9 π^h	11 Operating surplus of self-employed SE	12 Non-wage Income column 10 minus column 11 RI
Agriculture, forest. & fishing	106.51***	70.83	--	3.51	11.06	3.97	2.26	91.63	12.88	2.51	12.33
Mining & quarrying	1.49	.50	--	0	.40	--	--	.90	.59	.47	.22
Manufacturing	59.47	5.53	.75	14.47	12.54	2.81	5.57	41.67	22.53	5.58	12.22
Electricity & water	7.81	---	--	1.03	3.94	---	---	4.97	2.84	----	2.84
Building & const.	8.75	---	.57	1.44	1.24	.37	.811	4.43	4.32	.35	3.97
Trade	63.48	.88	1.46	0	8.16	2.67	4.59	17.76	45.72	29.75	15.97
Transp. & Comm.	21.58	---	.05	8.20	7.22	.91	.58	16.96	4.62	1.84	2.78
Financial & bus. services	26.11	---	--	3.71	2.44	1.10	1.73	8.98	17.13	2.25	14.88
Ownership of dwelling	35.39	.57	--	1.32	---	1.49	----	3.38	32.01	4.77	27.24
Other services: personal & household	7.12	1.68	1.88	.07	2.07	.30	.19	6.19	.93	.72	.21
Total	330.44	80.25	4.71	33.75	49.12	14.00	15.72				

*. Includes depreciation.

**. Includes depreciation of the capital of government-owned enterprises. Government share is assumed to be proportionate to its share in sectoral gross value added.

***. National Accounts show an operating surplus of only 94 million. This would result in a rental income of only 2 million. The problem is that the operating surplus of the small-farm sector was understated in the National Accounts by about 10 million [compare table 5 above which is obtained from ... IRS, and Tables 82(c) and 260(c) of the Statistical Abstracts 1976].

Sources by column: 2) Statistical Abstract and Economic Survey; 3) Table 19; 4) Table 20; 5) Table 25; 6) Table 24; 7) Table 26; 8) Table 28; 11) Table 22 this chapter and Table 9, Chapter 5.

banks after independence although it acquired an increasingly larger share in these banks.[13]

These three sectors account for most of the foreign investment (almost 100 percent according to Table 18).

IV.3. Formal-Sector Operating Surplus Accruing to Individuals

The amount of operating surplus which accrues to individuals can then be estimated by subtracting from the economy-wide gross operating surplus the following items:

a) The monetary portion of farm and non-farm operating surplus of small farms (Table 17).

b) Operating surplus of those self-employed in informal-urban activities.

c) The portion of sectoral value added that does not acrue to individuals: depreciation (Table 24), profits of government enterprises (Table 25), undistributed profits (Table 26), and profits repatriated by foreign corporations (Table 28).

The balance is shown in column 10 of Table 30.

Column 10 of Table 30 shows the portion of sectoral operating surplus that accrues directly to individuals. The low figure for "transportation and communication" and "building and construction" and for "electricity and water" indicates the preponderance or absolute domination of the public sector in these industries. The figures for agriculture reflect the relative importance of small-scale agriculture. About 80 percent of rural households are self-employed on small family holdings and their earnings are included in agricultural operating surplus. The remainder, after appropriate deductions, accrues to the owners of large farms and plantations. The high figure for

---

[13] Ali I. Abdi, Commercial Banks and Economic Development: The Experience of Eastern Africa. Praeger, 1977, p. 58.

"wholesale and retail trade and restaurants" relative to its share in either gross value added or total operating surplus reflects the fact that trade is dominated by neither the government nor foreign corporations.

For both rental and self-employment income, the manufacturing sector is further disaggregated into the component industries to make it comparable to the sectoral/industrial classification of wage employment (Table 14) as well as the input-output and expenditure tables. The latter two will be discussed in Chapter 7.

IV.3.1. Disaggregating the Manufacturing Sector by Industry

In disaggregating the manufacturing sector by industry, it is assumed that the share of each industry in manufacturing operating surplus is proportional to its share in manufacturing output. But since owner-operated and large firms employing more than 50 workers would probably differ in technology and thereby in their respective share of profits in total value added, each industry is first divided by firm-size using information in Stat. Abst. The items deducted from operating surplus (π^g, π^d, π^f, α in Table 30) are also disaggregated by industry. The methods used and the assumptions made are in the footnotes to Table 32.

IV.3.2. The Distribution of Operating Surplus

The recipients of sectoral operating surplus can, as mentioned in Chapter 5 (p. 27) be classified into the self-employed and recipients of "rental" income.

Table 31

Distribution of Output and Employment By
Industry In the Manufacturing Sector

| INDUSTRY | EMPLOYMENT | | | OUTPUT[c] | |
| | Wage-employment[a] | | Self-empl.[b] | | |
	# in 000's	%	%	000's	%
Manufacturing of:					
food, bev. & tobacco	24,426	24.4	13.9	61,543	41.4
textile, apparel & leather	19,804	19.8	33.2	14,519	9.8
wood & furniture	18,493	18.5	28.4	13,900	9.4
chemical, petrol., rubber	6,557	6.5	3.2	25,366	17.0
non-metallic mineral	4,341	4.3	2.0	5,903	4.0
basic metal	26,550	26.5	19.0	27,412	18.4
	100,170			148,651	

[a]Table

[b]The total manufacturing self-employment is disaggregated by industry according to the number of establishments with zero employees [see Statistical Appendix].

[c]Statistical Abstracts, 1976, Table 106.

Table 32

The Distribution of Operating Surplus of Formal-Sector Manufacturing
by Industry and Non-Household Recipient Entities (in million)

Sector/Industry	DEDUCTED ITEMS				OPERATING SURPLUS OF:*			
	Π^g	Π^d	Π^f	α	SF	IU	SE	RI
Manufacturing of:								
food, beverages & tobacco	3.53	1.16	2.05	1.25	2.10	.60	1.70	2.98
textile, apparel & leather	2.86	.28	1.37	.74	1.17	---	4.06	2.42
wood products & furniture	2.68	.26	.68	.44	1.32	.15	3.47	2.26
chemical, petroleum, rubber, plastic	.94	.48	.89	.58	.94	---	.39	.79
mineral products (non-metalic)	.62	.11	1.25	.33	---	---	.24	.53
basic metal, mach., equip. & other mfc	3.84	.52	1.42	9.14	---	---	2.32	3.24
Subtotal**	14.47	2.81	11.35	12.54	5.53	.75	5.58	12.22

*Symbols are defined in Chapter 3, page 7, and in Table 30 of this chapter.
**Summation errors due to rounding.

Sources:

Column
1. Π^g: obtained from Table 25.
2. Π^d: assumed that percent share in profits is proportional to percent share in manufacturing output. Statistical Abstracts, 1976, Table 106.
3. Π^f: ILO Report, Table 73, p. 443 for percent share of each industry. Total figures from Table 28.

Column
4. α: I-O table for Kenya, 1977 for % share of each industry. Total figure from Table 25.
5. SF: Table 18.
6. IU: Sundry sources incl. author's knowledge. Also Table 20.
7. SE: According to % share of self-employment in the manufacturing sector.
8. RI: According to % share of wage-employment in the manufacturing sector.

IV.3.2.1. <u>The Self-Employed</u>

The sectoral income of self-employed individuals has been shown in Table 30. Subtracting the portion of sectoral operating surplus that accrues to individuals (Table 30, column 10) from self-employment income yields "rental" income which accrues to property owners in the formal sector.

IV.3.2.2. <u>Rental Income</u>

In distributing sectoral rental income across households, the same assumptions as in Chapter 5 (pp. 135-141) are used. But unlike Chapter 5, rental income is distributed across sectors as well as income groups. To recapitulate, rental income is apportioned under three different sets of assumptions. These are:

1. All rental income goes to the top four income groups with the highest two receiving the rental incomes of large firms (more than 50 workers) and the next two groups receiving rental income of small to medium-sized firms.

2. To reconcile rental income as estimated (£70 million) with rental surplus from the national accounts (£35 million) it is assumed that the former includes the imputed labor value of unpaid managers and directors. It is assumed that the latter goes to the top two income groups and that the rest is shared by all income groups above the mean wage rate according to their share in wage income.

3. Rental income is shared by all groups receiving wage rates greater than the mean according to their share in sectoral wage income.

For both rental and self-employment income the manufacturing sector is further disaggregated into the component industries to make it comparable to the sectoral/industrial classification of the distribution of wage income (Table 14), as well as the input-output and expenditure tables. The latter two will be discussed in Chapter 7.

The absolute distribution of rental income ($\Pi_{k_j}^h$) under experiments I, II, and III embodying the first three sets of assumptions mentioned above, is shown in Tables 33, 34, and 35. The share of each income group in sectoral rental income ($S_{k_j}^{\Pi}$) is shown in Tables 36, 37, and 38. The latter are obtained by dividing each element in Tables 33, 34, and 35 ($\Pi_{k_j}^h$) by the sum of the elements in its row (Π_j^h).

Table 33

Distribution of Rental Income by Size
of Establishment and Income Group, 1974   (£Million)
EXPERIMENT I

	FIRMS						HOUSEHOLDS							TOTAL
	1 - 49		50 and over		Total		Group 2 (£000/month)				Group 1 (£000/month)			
							1 - 1.5		1.5 - 2		2 - 3		3+		
Sector/Industry	%¹ £million²		%¹ £million²		% £ mil.		%³ £ mil.⁴		%³ £ mil.⁴		%⁵ £ mil.⁶		%⁵ £ mil.⁶		%
1 Agriculture, forestry and fishing	15	1.85	85	10.48	100	12.33	6.3	.78	8.7	1.07	32	3.95	53	6.53	100
2 Mining & quarrying	18	---	82	----	100	0	7.6	---	10.4	---	30	---	52	----	100
3 Manufacturing	17	2.07	83	10.13	100	12.20	7.1	.87	9.9	1.21	31	3.79	52	8.35	100
3.1 food, bev. & tob.	9	.27	91	2.71	100	2.98	3.8	.11	5.2	.15	34	1.01	57	1.70	100
3.2 textile, app.,lea.	15	.37	85	2.05	100	2.42	6.3	.15	8.7	.21	32	.77	53	1.28	100
3.3 wood & paper prod.	27	.61	73	1.65	100	2.26	11.3	.25	15.7	.35	27	.61	46	1.11	100
3.4 chem.,petro.,rubber & plastic	15	.12	85	.67	100	.79	7.1	.056	9.9	.078	31	.24	52	4.1	100
3.5 non-metalic mineral products	11	.06	89	.47	100	.53	4.6	.024	6.4	.034	33	.17	56	.30	100
3.6 basic metal, mach., equip.	20	.65	80	2.60	100	3.24	8.4	.27	11.6	.38	30	.97	50	1.62	100
4 Electricity & water	7	.20	93	2.63	100	2.83	2.9	.08	4.1	.12	34	.96	59	1.67	100
5 Construction	17	.67	83	3.30	100	3.97	7.1	.28	9.9	.39	31	1.23	52	2.06	100
6 Trade, rest., & hotels	57	9.10	43	6.87	100	15.97	21.9	3.50	33.1	5.29	16	2.56	27	4.31	100
7 Transp. & Comm.	14	.39	86	2.39	100	2.78	5.9	.16	8.1	.23	32	.92	54	1.50	100
8 Fin. & bus. services	38	5.66	62	9.22	100	14.88	16.0	2.38	22.0	3.27	23	3.42	39	5.80	100
9 Ownership of dwellings	44	12.00	56	15.24	100	27.24	18.5	5.04	25.5	6.94	21	5.72	35	9.53	100
10 Other services	100	.93	0	---	100	.93	100	.93	---	---	---	---	---	---	100

Sources: 1. Sectoral employment for each firm-size divided by total employment
for that firm size. Obtained from appendix.
2. Col. 1 x total sectoral rental income. Latter is obtained from
Tables 20 and 5, and reproduced under the "total" for firms.
3. Share of wage income for each class of income group 2 (Table)
multiplied by the percent share in sectoral profit of the
"1-49" firms (column 1 of this table).

4. Col. 3 x total sectoral rental income. The latter is reproduced in column 6 of this table.
5. Share in wage income of each income class of group 1
(Table) multiplied by percent share in sectoral
profits of the "50+" firms (column 3 of this table).
6. Col. 5 x sectoral rental income.

TABLE 34

Distribution of Sectoral Rental Income

by Group (Π^h_{kj}) in £000

EXPERIMENT II

SECTOR	5	6	7	8	9	10 a	10 b	10 c	11 a	11 b	11 c	Total
1	1,356.3	739.8	370.0	739.8	616.5	896.7	+ 2,802.3	= 3,699.0	952.8	+ 3,362.7	= 4,315.5	12,330.0
2	17.6	11.0	6.6	13.2	6.6	19.1	+ 25.9	= 44.0	26.9	+ 84.1	= 110.0	220.0
3.1	274.5	169.9	117.6	196.1	104.6	156.8	+ 615.9	= 772.7	274.5	+ 1,053.1	= 1,327.6	2,963
3.2	436.7	127.8	42.6	106.5	85.2	138.5	+ 719.5	= 858.0	127.8	+ 635.5	= 763.3	2,420
3.3	149.1	89.5	59.6	129.2	178.9	119.2	+ 410.2	= 529.4	258.4	+ 855.8	= 1,114.2	2,249.9
3.4	52.1	24.3	17.4	34.7	31.3	52.1	+ 122.7	= 174.8	135.3	+ 320.3	= 455.6	790
3.5	48.9	28.0	11.7	16.3	11.7	30.3	+ 79.0	= 109.3	86.2	+ 218.0	= 304.2	530
3.6	299.3	171.0	142.5	171.0	142.5	185.3	+ 638.9	= 824.2	327.8	+ 1,176.1	= 1,503.9	3,254
4	199.2	112.1	112.1	199.2	124.5	211.7	+ 683.1	= 894.8	286.4	+ 901.9	= 1,188.3	2,830
5	384.3	209.6	157.2	227.1	157.2	209.6	+ 870.3	= 1,079.9	384.3	+ 1,442.9	= 1,827.2	4,042
6	913.4	702.6	419.8	843.1	632.3	1,124.2	+ 2,888.6	= 4,012.6	2,388.8	+ 6,054.4	= 8,443.2	16,039
7	146.8	159.0	281.3	195.7	122.3	134.5	+ 657.1	= 791.6	183.5	+ 899.9	= 1,083.4	2,780
8	327.4	261.8	589.2	916.6	720.2	1,113.0	+ 2,441.6	= 3,554.6	2,618.8	+ 5,891.4	= 8,510.2	12,261.2
9	2,277.2	1,588.0	1,318.3	1,797.8	1,318.3	1,438.2	+ 6,102.0	= 7,540.2	2,277.2	+ 9,153.0	= 11,430.2	27,270.0
10												

Source: Tables 21 and 30.

a = Share in rental income.

b = Imputed value of the salaries of managers and directors.

c = a + b.

TABLE 35

Distribution of Sectoral Rental Income
By Income Group (£ 000)
EXPERIMENT III

	Income Group						
Sector	5	6	7	8	9	10	11
1	0	0	0	1,233	2,466	3,699	4,932
2	37	22	13	31	13	22	66
3.1	626	387	268	447	238	358	626
3.2	992	290	97	242	194	315	290
3.3	339	203	136	294	407	271	588
3.4	119	55	40	79	71	119	308
3.5	111	64	27	37	27	69	196
3.6	680	389	324	389	324	421	745
4	454	256	256	454	284	488	653
5	873	476	357	516	357	476	874
6	2,076	1,597	1,118	1,916	1,437	2,555	5,430
7	334	361	639	445	278	305	417
8	744	595	1,339	2,083	1,637	2,530	5,952
9	5,176	3,541	2,996	4,086	2,996	3,269	5,176
10	0	0	0	0	0	84	126

Source: Tables 21, 32, 34 and assumptions in text (p. 241).

Table 36

The Proportion of Sectoral Rental Income
Received by Each Income Class (S^{II}_{kj})

EXPERIMENT I

	8	9	10	11
1	.06	.09	.32	.53
2	.08	.10	.30	.52
3	.07	.10	.31	.52
3.1	.04	.05	.34	.58
3.2	.06	.09	.32	.53
3.3	.11	.15	.27	.49
3.4	.08	.10	.30	.51
3.5	.04	.06	.30	.54
3.6	.08	.12	.30	.50
4	.03	.04	.21	.59
5	.07	.10	.31	.52
6	.22	.33	.16	.27
7	.06	.08	.33	.54
8	.16	.22	.23	.39
9	.19	.25	.21	.35
10	.19	.25	.21	.35

Source: Table 33.

Table 37

Share of Each Income Class in Rental Income (S_{kj}^{II})
EXPERIMENT II

Sector/Class	5	6	7	8	9	10	11
1	.11	.06	.03	.06	.05	.30	.35
2	.08	.05	.03	.06	.03	.20	.50
3.1	.09	.06	.04	.07	.04	.26	.45
3.2	.18	.05	.02	.04	.04	.35	.32
3	.07	.04	.03	.06	.08	.24	.49
4	.06	.03	.02	.04	.04	.22	.58
5	.09	.05	.02	.03	.02	.21	.57
6	.09	.05	.04	.05	.04	.25	.46
4	.07	.04	.04	.07	.04	.32	.42
5	.10	.05	.04	.06	.04	.27	.45
6	.06	.04	.03	.05	.04	.25	.53
7	.05	.06	.10	.07	.04	.28	.39
8	.03	.02	.05	.07	.06	.29	.69
9	.10	.06	.05	.07	.05	.28	.42
10	---	---	---	---	---	.40	.60

Source: Table 34.

Table 38

Share of Sectoral Rental Income Received by Top 5 Income Groups
EXPERIMENT III

Sector/Income Group	5	6	7	8	9	10	11
1				.10	.20	.30	.40
2	.17	.10	.06	.14	.06	.10	.30
3							
3.1	.21	.13	.09	.15	.08	.12	.21
3.2	.41	.12	.04	.10	.08	.13	.12
3.3	.15	.09	.06	.13	.18	.12	.26
3.4	.15	.07	.05	.10	.09	.15	.39
3.5	.21	.12	.05	.07	.05	.13	.37
3.6	.21	.12	.10	.12	.10	.13	.23
4	.16	.09	.09	.16	.10	.17	.23
5	.22	.12	.09	.13	.09	.12	.22
6	.13	.10	.07	.12	.09	.16	.34
7	.12	.13	.23	.16	.10	.11	.15
8	.05	.04	.09	.14	.11	.17	.40
9	.19	.13	.11	.15	.11	.12	.19
10	---	---	---	---	---	.40	.60

Source: Table 21.

V. Summary of the Distribution of Sectoral Wage and Non-Wage Income and Operating Surplus

So far, in this chapter the distribution of sectoral wage income and operating surplus by urban, rural, and estate has been discussed. But this information has been scattered throughout the chapter. Moreover, the exposition mostly concentrated on the share of each income group in urban, rural, and estate incomes. Without first determining the distribution of sectoral income between the urban, rural and estate sectors, also, the information so far compiled would be of little use. For example, the 7th group in the rural sector receives about 40% of sectoral income in rural areas. However, outside of agriculture, rural production is almost insignificant compared to the economy-wide income and output. The distribution of income and output between the three main sectors would have to therefore be determined if the within-sector distribution data which have so far been compiled are to be of use for subsequent analysis.

This has been done and is summarized in Tables 39 and 40. Table 39 shows the total amount of sectoral income received by households in the urban, rural, and estate sectors as well as the income received by institutions (government, business, and the rest of the world). Sectoral income is further broken down into wage income and operating surplus to conform to the data contained in previous tables of this chapter. Table 40 shows the percent distribution of the corresponding elements in Table 39.

TABLE 39

Amount Received in Wage Income and Operating Surplus by Urban, Rural, and Estate in Wage and Non-Wage Income

SECTOR	Operating Surplus (Π_j)		Households			Wage Income (W_j)				
	Total*	Inst.	U	R	E	Total**	I	U	R	E
1. Non-Monetary	175.69									
2. Agriculture, forest.&fish.	104.03	20.48	--	70.83	12.88	83.71	39.20	--	5.70	33.50
3. Mining & quarrying	1.49	.42	.49	.57	--	1.06	1.09	1.05	.04	--
4. Manuf. of food	12.11	7.90	2.98	1.23	--	4.21	10.76	10.23	.53	--
5. Manuf. of textiles	8.42	5.25	2.42	.75	--	3.17	5.21	4.87	.34	--
6. Manuf. of wood products	7.01	4.06	2.26	.69	--	2.95	6.52	6.22	.30	--
7. Manuf. of chemical, rubber & petroleum	3.60	2.81	.79	--	--	.79	4.50	4.23	.27	--
8. Manuf. of non-metallic prod.	3.43	2.31	.53	.59	--	1.12	1.40	1.40	--	--
9. Manuf. of basic metal	18.16	14.92	3.24	--	--	3.24	10.84	10.84	--	--
SUBTOTAL	63.79	37.25	23.28	3.26			44.25	40.86	3.39	--
10. Electricity & water	7.82	4.97	2.84	--	--	2.84	2.48	2.16	.32	--
11. Construction	9.41	3.86	4.89	.57	--	5.46	13.02	12.79	.23	--
12. Trade	63.76	15.50	47.38	.88	--	48.26	28.48	26.85	1.63	--
13. Transport. & Communication	21.61	16.90	4.71	--	--	4.71	24.76	22.04	2.72	--
14. Financial Services	26.11	8.98	17.13	--	--	17.13	15.83	15.83	--	--
15. Ownership of dwellings	35.39	2.81	32.01	.57	--	32.58	--	--	--	--
16. a)Government services	--	--	--	--	--	--	110.77	87.77	23.00	--
b)Private services	7.82	2.63	2.81	1.68	--	4.49	13.93	9.34	3.59	--

*The total might slightly differ from those shown in the official accounts due to rounding and small errors in estimation.
**Does not include self-employment and employee compensation that does not go to individual, e.g., pension fund.

U = Urban   R = Rural   E = Estate

SOURCES BY COLUMN: 1. Stat. Abstracts; 2. Tables 30, 32; 3. Table 33; 4. Tables 4&7 and 30; 5. Table 30; 6. Stat. Abstract
7. Table 21; 8. Table 16; 9. Stat. Abstracts.

TABLE 40

The Percent Share of the Urban, Rural and Estate Sectors
in the Wage and Non-Wage Income by Industry

Sector	Inst. (D_j)	NON-WAGE Households U	R	E	WAGE U	R	E
1							
2	19.68	---	68.09	12.38	---	14.54	85.46
3	28.19	32.88	39.60	---	96.33	3.67	---
4	65.23	24.61	10.16	---	95.07	4.93	---
5	62.35	28.74	8.91	---	93.47	6.52	---
6	57.92	32.24	9.84	---	95.40	4.60	---
7	78.05	21.19	---	---	94.00	6.00	---
8	67.35	15.45	17.20	---	100.00	---	---
9	82.16	17.84	---	---	100.00	---	---
10	63.55	36.32	---	---	87.10	12.90	---
11	41.02	51.97	6.06	---	98.23	1.77	---
12	24.31	74.31	1.38	---	94.28	5.72	---
13	78.20	21.80	---	---	89.01	10.99	---
14	34.39	65.61	---	---	100.00	---	---
15	7.94	90.45	1.61	---	---	---	---
16	33.63	35.93	21.48	---	67.05	25.77	---

Source: Table 39.

CONCLUSIONS:

In this chapter the amount of income, by source, received by each income group in the urban, rural, and estate sectors has been estimated. This information is used to calculate the percent share of each income group in sectoral wage and non-wage income. Given changes in sectoral income resulting from income redistribution, via changes in consumption and production, and assuming that group share in sectoral income does not change during the period of analysis, changes in personal income and thus its distribution can be calculated. The consumption, production and income formation processes can thus be integrated. But first, the consumption and production data will have to be analyzed and arranged in a form conformable to the income formation block. This is the objective of Chapter 7.

CHAPTER 7

CONSUMPTION AND PRODUCTION ANALYSIS

I. Introduction

Changes in private consumption resulting from income redistribution are central to this study. Therefore, the estimation of consumption coefficients is of particular importance. Unfortunately, there is a paucity of data on household expenditure patterns. A number of budget surveys are available but they are either limited only to one area (e.g., Nairobi) or pertain to different years. Reconciling data of different calendar years, and piecing together information from different sources and on different sectors or areas is a major thrust of this section.

Once the data are appropriately arranged, they are then fitted into regression equations to obtain the MPC of each consumption item across income groups. This is done for both rural (small-farm) and urban areas. The estate sector is very similar to the urban sector with most of the food and non-food items purchased. Unlike the small-farm sectors, few items are produced for own-consumption. A large number of estate workers also live in urban areas [see the Statistical Abstracts; e.g., 1976, Table 11]. But unlike urban residents, these workers spend little on rent (housing is usually provided by the estate) or transportation (most live on or near the estates). Consumption patterns are likely to be similar to urban residents in the same income brackets on other items.

Once the MPC for each good is estimated, changes in the amount consumed by the average household of each income group can be obtained by multiplying the MPC of that good with the average income change of that class. However, with the MPC of a good constant across income classes, changes in income resulting from intergroup income transfer may not lead to a net change in the consumption of that good except as each good shares in the changes in overall expenditures resulting from differences in class MPCs. For this reason, it may be more appropriate to calculate the MPC of each good for each income class. This is not, however, possible with the limited available data. So instead, the average propensity to consume will be used. However, the MPCs were estimated for comparison purposes.

II. Data

There are three major sources of data on consumption patterns of different income classes in Kenya:

1. The Integrated Rural Survey [54]
2. The Consumer Price Index for Nairobi [48]
3. The Income and Expenditure Patterns of Middle Income African Workers in Nairobi [58]

The Integrated Rural Survey (IRS) contains data on consumption patterns of small-farm households and applies to 1974. The IRS is a major source of information on all facets of the small-farm community. The Consumer Price Index for Nairobi (CPI) is based on a 1974 household survey and covers over 100 expenditure items grouped under nine main headings. These are recombined into twenty-two main groups to make

them comparable to rural expenditure items (which covers only fifteen

items) and the I-O sectors.

It is assumed that the consumption pattern in other urban cen-

ter is similar to that of Nairobi. This is a big assumption, partly

necessitated by lack of data, but is not unrealistic. Nairobi accounts

for over 65% of the urban population and has a strong demonstration

effect on the consumption pattern in other urban centers. Actually,

Mombassa is the only other major city. Together they account for over

80% of the urban population. Mombassa is a major part and the center

of large commercial and governmental activities. It should be kept

in mind, however, that the income in Nairobi is much higher than those

in other urban centers (including Mombassa).[1]

A major problem with the CPI is that it covers only three broad

income classes:

> Lower income group: Ksh 0 - 699/- a month
>
> Middle income group: Ksh 700 - 2499 a month
>
> Upper income group: Ksh 25,000 and above a month.

The lower and upper income groups each cover 25% of the households

while the middle income group covers 50% of the households in Nairobi.

The range of these classes is very wide concealing the differences

within each group. For example, the consumption pattern of the middle

income group is the weighted average of that of 50% of the households.

Interpolation would not be appropriate unless one knows what the weights

for the various subgroups are. Also meaningful results cannot be

obtained from a mere three observations. The problem is solved in the

---

[1] By urban is meant population centers with 2,000 or more inhabitants
(see p. 112).

following way.

The middle income group is broken into seven income groups using data from the Income and Expenditure Patterns of Middle Income African Workers (EPMAW) which applies only to the middle income group. But there are two additional problems. First, EPMAW applies to 1963 while CPI covers 1974. Second, the definition of middle income group is somewhat arbitrary and there is no a priori way of knowing whether it is defined the same in the two studies.

The first problem is solved by inflating the 1963 consumption figures to the 1974 price level. This is done by multiplying the overall consumer price index in 1974, using 1963 as a base, with the expenditure of each item and average income of each income group in 1963. The price index in 1974 was estimated to be 1.96 of the 1963 level.[2]

To find out whether the definitions of middle income group in the 1974 and 1963 surveys are the same, the combined average expenditure and income of the seven income groups is multiplied by the price index and the result compared to the income and expenditure patterns of the single class contained in the 1974 CPI. The results are remark- ably close even though the composition of non-food consumption has changed somewhat during the 1963-74 period (Table 1). For example, there has been a move away from household servants (HH operations) for the

---

[2] Increases in the price level is obtained by subtracting the private expenditure in 1974 in current year prices, from expenditures for the same year in constant 1963 prices. The difference is then divided by the latter. This information is obtained from National Accounts.

TABLE 1

The Consumption Pattern of Middle Income Group,
Nairobi 1963 (adjusted and unadjusted) and 1974

| | EPMAW (1963) | | CPI (1974) |
	Unadjusted	Adjusted*	(Shs/mth)
Income:			
Income bracket covered	350 - 1399	686 - 2744	699 - 2499
Average income	641	1257	(est.)**
Consumption:			
Cereals & bread	48.10	94	88
Meat & fish	39.00	76	83
Eggs & milk	29.65	58	54
Oils & fats	13.60	27	37
Fruits & vegetables	24.15	47	51
Sugar & sweets	12.45	24	29
Drinks, bev. & tobacco	55.40	108	58
Salt & flavorings	3.85	8	9
Eating out	28.30	55	36
	207.40	406	404
Clothing	56.25	110	136
Rent	44.90	88	183
Furniture & utensils	23.45	48	66
Fuel & power	24.25	46	49
Household operations	20.80	41	26
Health & personal	17.50	34	26
Education & recreation	18.85	37	51
Transportation & Comm.	38.80	75	90
Financial & legal services	36.90	72	53
Remittances to relatives	66.30	130	42

*1.96 x Column 1.

**Midpt of class.

Source: EPMAW 1a, 2a, 3a, 4a
CPI Appendix C

middle income group probably brought about by wage increases. The

amount paid for rent has also more than doubled. This probably resulted

from the housing shortage in Nairobi which was brought about by the

post-independence (1963) boom. Remittances also declined, probably

reflecting the loosening of ties with rural residents. But in general

the adjusted 1963 figures roughly correspond to 1974 ones. The assump-

tion that the same definition of "Middle Income Class" was used in the

two surveys is therefore realistic.

The one middle income group is disaggregated into seven using

EPMAW. But since the pattern of consumption has changed for some

items, the 1974 figures are used for those items. The average for each

class is assumed to correspond to its proportion of total consumption of

that item in 1963. Implicit here is the assumption that the consumption

patterns of the middle class are affected by the same extraneous factors

and that though this pattern might change for this group as a whole,

within-group changes in consumption follow a similar trend.

The lower and upper income groups from the CPI are then appended

to the disaggregated-middle-income group. Thus the consumption

patterns of nine income groups are obtained (Table 2). The upper and lower

groups account for 25% of the households each while the seven sub-

groups of the middle income class together account for 50%. This,

however, does not pose any problem since the variable of interest

is average household consumption rather than total income-group con-

sumption.

From this data the consumption coefficients by good and income

are estimated. But before this is done, the average income for the

TABLE 2

The Consumption Patterns of Urban Hhs

ITEM	INCOME GROUP								
	1	2	3	4	5	6	7	8	9
Income Bracket	< 700	700						2499	2500 +
1. Cereals	36	64	70	58	84	71	75	70	48
2. Breads, biscuits &cakes	16	19	21	20	23	34	28	31	38
3. Meat & fish	35	52	72	75	83	91	86	94	145
4. Milk and eggs	23	44	49	58	60	63	74	71	113
5. Oils & fats	15	23	22	27	34	28	27	30	223
6. Fruits & vegetables	33	36	40	53	55	43	56	57	127
7. Sugars & sweets	14	21	23	25	24	28	29	23	32
8. Drinks, bev.& tobacco	25	39	53	52	74	78	90	125	90
9. Salt & flavorings	1	3	2	4	6	11	3	4	3
10. Eating out	14	24	21	44	49	47	37	44	72
	212	325	373	416	493	494	505	549	691
23. Processed	120	181	214	247	293	326	300	351	562
24. Unprocessed	92	144	159	169	200	168	205	198	129
11. Clothing & footwear	47	95	99	130	133	188	159	213	226
12. Rent	110	101	124	130	135	207	203	335	912
13. Fuel,water & light	17	33	57	34	42	54	58	68	159
14. Furniture & furnish.	14	34	30	31	40	38	42	71	74
15. Appliances & utensils	9	18	16	15	16	18	30	18	55
16. Cleaning,wash.,misc. hh	4	11	12	13	18	15	17	23	24
17. Domestic services	1	4	6	13	13	10	18	21	130
18. Health&per.(cosmetics)	7	16	19	24	20	48	29	41	97
19. Transp. & Comm.	17	57	59	102	92	104	112	138	480
20. Financial & legal ser.	1	7	23	50	38	74	83	152	166
21. Remittances	32	23	29	39	51	72	49	58	98
22. Recreation	6	14	14	21	24	33	31	33	128
	265	413	488	602	622	861	831	1171	2556
25. Total consumption	477	738	861	1018	1115	1336	1355	1720	3247
Average income	415	729	874	1080	1289	1464	1721	2242	4007

Sources:
1. Consumer Price Index, Nairobi, 1974. Central Statistical Bureau, Ministry of Planning and Finance, Nairobi, 1977.

2. Income and Expenditure Patterns for Middle Income African Workers, 1963. Directorate of Planning, Nairobi, 1964.

upper and lower income groups which are open-ended need to be estimated. There are accepted procedures for estimating this [see Cline (22), Chp. 2, Mazumdar (17a), and Szaal (19), for example]. The mean income for grouped data is usually assumed to be its midpoint. So for the lowest income group, the minimum income received by any household is first estimated. The midpoint between ceiling and minimum income of this group is then taken as its average income. Alternatively, the mean income is taken as .65 of the upper bound of the lowest income group [Szaal]. The latter will be adopted.

For the upper income group, the mean income is estimated by using the following formula relating the number of income recipients to the per-recipient income level.

(1) $N = AY^{-\alpha}$

where: Y = household or individual income
        N = number of recipient units receiving Y or more
        A = a constant.

The value of α is an indicator of the pattern of income distribution. The higher its value the more equal the distribution. Thus, with a high α, the value of N quickly approaches zero as Y increases because there is little difference between the upper and lower income groups. The value of α is estimated by fitting the above equation to the the highest and next to highest income groups. With two equations, σ and A can be estimated. Given α and A, the mean for the upper income group can be estimated by the following formula [Cline (22), p. 60]:

(2) $\bar{Y}_u = \dfrac{\alpha A}{1 - \alpha} Y_{fu}^{1-\alpha}$

where $\bar{y}_u$ = mean income of the upper income class

y_{fu} = income flow of the upper bracket

Applying the data from the CPI to equations (1) and (2), $\bar{y}_u$ is estimated to be 4007 shillings.[3]

An average monthly income of ksh.4007 for the upper 25% of the households would seem too high when compared to data from other sources [see Table 16, p. 43 of Chapter 5]. However, the figures in Chapter 5 refer to all urban areas while the above figures applies only to Nairobi. Most high-paying jobs and recipients of property income from the formal sector are concentrated in Nairobi. So the mean income in Nairobi is considerably higher than that for the urban sector as a whole.

II.1. Rural

There are seven income groups and 15 consumption items. Ten of these are food items. A large proportion of food consumption by small-farm households is own-produced and thus outside the monetary sector. Since the purpose of this study is to estimate the effect of income transfer on several growth constraints via changes in private consumption, it would seem that the non-monetary consumption is not relevant. But while the latter is not directly affected by exogenous income changes, it could be affected indirectly. A farmer may increase the consumption of his own produce because he does not have to sell as much in order to buy the same amount of goods as before the income transfer. In other words, he could buy his own products. On the

---

3) α = 1.157

   A = 13.86

other hand, he may spend the full amount of the transfer on purchased
items or divide them between the two sets of goods. In sum, he could
sell less (consume more) of his products, buy more purchased items or
a combination of the two. The first option is not very probable, though
certainly possible. He would spend at least some of the new-found
income on purchases. It is most likely that his production of subsistence crops are constrained by factors other than money income.
The consumption coefficients are therefore estimated only for the last
two options.

II.2. Urban

Consumption coefficients are estimated for 16 (aggregated from 22
as in Table 2) different items. There are items like rent, financial
and legal services, and electricity and water that do not enter the
expenditure of rural households.

III. Estimation

1. The Marginal Propensity to Consume (MPC)

The MPC and APC are estimated separately. Given consumption by
good and income group and the average income of each group, the MPC
for each good is estimated cross-sectionally by regressing consumption
on income using appropriate functional relationship.[4] To discern what
this function is, consumption-income pairs have been plotted on a
graph. Linear and log linear equations were chosen as reflecting the
appropriate relationships. The consumption coefficients are then
estimated for both urban and rural.

---

[4]Family size is an important determinant of the quantity consumed of certain
items like food and housing. But because of data limitations, family size
is not included in the equations. At any rate, such an omission would
affect only the MPCs and not the APCs since the later is not obtained by
regression but by simply dividing average consumption per item of each
group by its income.

2. The Average Propensity to Consume

The MPCs as estimated above give a vector of coefficients for
different expenditure items but are constant across income groups as
mentioned in the introduction to this chapter. However, the model (see
Chapter 3) calls for an n X k matrix (n goods and k income classes) of
consumption coefficients so that it could be linked with the production
and value added matrices (see below). Changes in either can then be
directly translated to the others.

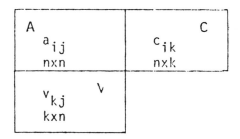

Estimating an n x k matrix of MPCs is not possible because of data
limitations. Moreover, the consumption function is not smooth and estimated
MRCs are very erratic. For this reason, the APC for each income class by
type of good is more appropriate than MPC for each good across income groups.

An alternative to estimating MPCs $(\frac{\partial C_i}{\partial Y})$ is to directly estimate
the APC of each good by income group (C_{ik}/Y_k). The average household
expenditure on each item is divided by the average income for a particular class. The result is an n x k matrix that is comformable to both
the production and income matrices as shown above. This is what several
authors [see Paukert-Skolka-Maton (74), for example] using models
similar to mine have done.

Also,

$$\sum_i C_{ik} - 1 \quad \text{budget constraint}$$

$$\sum_k C_{ik} - 1 \quad \text{reverse Simon-Hawkins condition}$$

where C_{ik} is the APC of class k for good i. The APC for urban house-holds is shown in Table 16. For rural areas the APC is calculated including and excluding the non-monetary consumption and income.

1. Rural

Tables 4-8 shows the consumption characteristics of rural households.

Tables 4 and 5 show the weight of each commodity item in the consumption basket of rural households (C_{ik}/C_k). Surprisingly, the weight of the own-produced items increases with income while those of purchased items behaves in the opposite manner. This would tend to contradict the oft-held notion that subsistence consumption falls with increases of income. But while the inverse relationship between the size of the subsistence sector and the level of income holds when the economy as a whole is considered, the opposite might be true when only the rural sector is taken.

Tables 6 and 7 show the average propensity to consume (C_{ik}/Y_k) by item and income group. These are obtained by merely dividing the average consumption of each item by the average income of households in that group. Table 6 shown the APCs when the non-monetary sector is included and Table 7 when it is excluded.

There is considerable dissaving by the lowest three income classes and so the sum of their APCs would be greater than unity thus violating the budget constraint. This is corrected for by using total consumption rather than total income as the denominator. Implicit here is the assumption that the share of each item in the consumption of the lowest three groups would remain unchanged at least during the period of analysis.

2. Urban

The APCs obtained from Table 10 fall with income for all food items. Non-food items do not display as consistent a pattern. The APCs rise with income for such items as rent, transportation (especially private transportation), financial and domestic services. It should be noted that the latter are luxury goods while food is a necessity. Similar demarcation is not observed when regression equations are used, probably indicating that the latter is not appropriate. This probably results from the fact that consumption functions are not smooth and the number of cases are too small to warrant the use of regression techniques (only three in the original data set, page 1 of this chapter).

An alternative set of consumption data for the urban sector is obtained from the CPI [2]. The average consumption per item of the three income groups in the CPI is plotted against the group income. The consumption of each of the eleven income groups in the urban sector is then obtained by interpolation. The circuitous route of first estimating the consumption patterns of nine income groups and then interpolating for eleven (Table 1 to Table 2) is bypassed. The results are shown in Table 11.

Conclusion

In subsequent analysis the APC rather than MPCs would be used. As mentioned above, this is done for several reasons. The consumption characteristics of different income groups vary with factors other than income. Thus there tends to be a clustering around group means. This would tend to favor the use of APC over MPC. Also, the MPCs are constant across income classes and so changes in composition of consumption would not result from income group income transfer except insofar as the overall MPCs of the various groups differ. Thus, one possible impact of the changes in the composition of private demand has been eliminated by applying a constant MPC. The APC on the other hand allows for the impact of income transfer on consumption through group-differences in both aggregate and per item expenditures.

The data on urban consumption apply only to Nairobi. It is assumed that households in other urban centers have the similar consumption patterns. Nairobi accounts for about 60% of the urban population and up to 70% of urban income. It also has a powerful demonstration effect on consumption in other urban centers. Consumption for the urban sector as a whole is obtained by interpolation since the income brackets for Nairobi (see Table 2) differ from that for the urban sector as a whole (see Table 16, Chapter 5).

TABLE 3

Expenditure Survey Items

I. <u>Rural (1974)</u>

Consumption of own-produced items:

1. { Maize
Finger Millet
Sorghum
Beans
English potatoes
Other crops } Cereals and crops

2. { Beef
Other meat and poultry
Milk } Meat and fish

Consumption of purchased items:

3. Grains, flours and root crops
4. Dairy products and eggs
5. Meat and fish
6. Fats and oils
7. Sugar and sweets
8. Fruits and vegetables
9. Drinks and beverages
10. Salt and other flavorings

11. Clothing
12. Appliances and utensils
13. Furnishings
14. Miscellaneous purchases

15. Miscellaneous expenses

Source: Integrated Rural Survey, Central Bureau of Statistics, Ministry of Finance and Planning. Nairobi, 1977.

TABLE 4

THE AVERAGE WEIGHT OF EACH GOOD IN THE TOTAL
CONSUMPTION OF EACH INCOME GROUP (C_{1k}/C_k).
RURAL HOUSEHOLDS, 1974

Kshs/Year

Good	Class						
	1 0- 999	2 1,000- 1,999	3 2,000- 2,999	4 3,000- 3,999	5 4,000- 5,999	6 6,000- 7,999	7 8,000 & Over
Own-produced Items							
1. Cereals and crops	.270	.295	.328	.302	.343	.376	.405
2. Meat	.052	.062	.045	.037	.046	.044	.043
3. Milk	.047	.083	.084	.107	.129	.130	.167
Purchased Items							
4. Grains, flours & root crops	.269	.225	.213	.228	.171	.184	.121
5. Dairy products & eggs	.029	.018	.022	.023	.017	.011	.014
6. Meat & fish	.127	.104	.095	.090	.093	.076	.079
7. Fats & oils	.023	.031	.028	.031	.033	.033	.032
8. Sugar & sweets	.067	.067	.073	.069	.071	.056	.058
9. Fruits & vegetables	.039	.042	.037	.046	.038	.032	.021
10. Drinks & beverages	.069	.056	.058	.052	.049	.048	.053
11. Salt & other flavorings	.018	.017	.017	.015	.012	.011	.009
12. Clothing	.088	.088	.092	.063	.090	.086	.110
13. Appliances & utensils	.005	.007	.005	.005	.010	.006	.009
14. Furnishings	.016	.006	.013	.006	.012	.010	.014
15. Miscellaneous purchases	.050	.052	.051	.047	.046	.038	.044
16. Miscellaneous expenses	.068	.058	.061	.084	.104	.123	.086

SOURCE: Same as Table 2.

TABLE 5

THE AVERAGE WEIGHT OF EACH PURCHASED ITEM
IN THE TOTAL CASH CONSUMPTION OF EACH
INCOME GROUP

Rural Households, 1974

	Income Group						
Good	1	2	3	4	5	6	7
4	.291	.271	.258	.281	.204	.225	.163
5	.022	.023	.026	.028	.020	.014	.018
6	.137	.125	.115	.110	.111	.093	.106
7	.024	.036	.034	.039	.039	.040	.043
8	.055	.081	.088	.085	.084	.068	.077
9	.042	.050	.044	.056	.045	.039	.027
10	.075	.067	.070	.064	.059	.059	.071
11	.019	.020	.021	.019	.014	.013	.012
12	.123	.135	.142	.098	.145	.144	.201
13	.007	.011	.008	.008	.016	.010	.016
14	.022	.001	.020	.010	.019	.017	.026
15	.070	.080	.079	.072	.074	.063	.080
16	.095	.088	.094	.130	.169	.214	.157

SOURCE: Same as 2.

TABLE 6

THE AVERAGE PROPENSITY TO CONSUME BY TYPE
OF GOOD AND INCOME GROUP (C_{ik}/Y_k)*
RURAL HOUSEHOLDS, 1974**

Class

Good	1	2	3	4	5	6	7
1	.208	.233	.256	.176	.204	.179	.157
2	.040	.048	.035	.029	.028	.024	.017
3	.036	.065	.065	.082	.077	.077	.065
4	.208	.178	.166	.176	.102	.109	.047
5	.016	.015	.017	.017	.010	.007	.005
6	.098	.082	.074	.069	.055	.045	.031
7	.017	.024	.022	.024	.020	.019	.012
8	.039	.053	.057	.053	.042	.033	.022
9	.030	.032	.029	.035	.022	.019	.008
10	.053	.044	.045	.040	.029	.029	.020
11	.014	.013	.013	.012	.068	.006	.003
12	.088	.088	.089	.062	.073	.070	.058
13	.005	.007	.005	.005	.008	.005	.005
14	.016	.006	.013	.006	.010	.008	.007
15	.050	.052	.051	.045	.037	.030	.023
16	.068	.058	.061	.082	.084	.103	.045

SOURCE: Same as Table 2.

    *The first three income groups dissave. The commodity weight
(as in Tables 8 and 9) rather than APC is used, i.e., C_k rather than
Y_k is denominator.

    **Total consumption including own-produced good and total income.

TABLE 7

THE AVERAGE PROPENSITY TO CONSUME PURCHASED GOODS
OUT OF MONETARY INCOME BY EACH INCOME GROUP.
RURAL HOUSEHOLDS, 1974

	Income Group*						
Good	1	2	3	4	5	6	7
4	.291	.271	.258	.270	.147	.161	.062
5	.022	.023	.026	.026	.015	.010	.007
6	.177	.125	.115	.106	.080	.066	.040
7	.024	.036	.034	.037	.028	.029	.016
8	.055	.081	.088	.081	.061	.049	.029
9	.042	.050	.044	.054	.032	.028	.010
10	.075	.067	.070	.061	.042	.042	.027
11	.019	.020	.021	.018	.010	.009	.004
12	.123	.135	.142	.094	.105	.103	.076
13	.007	.011	.008	.007	.011	.007	.006
14	.022	.001	.020	.097	.014	.012	.010
15	.070	.080	.079	.069	.053	.045	.030
16	.095	.008	.094	.125	.122	.153	.060

SOURCE: Same as Table 2.

* First three classes from Table 12.

TABLE 8

**AVERAGE INCOME OF RURAL HOUSEHOLDS
BY MONETARY AND NON-MONETARY AND
BY INCOME GROUP, 1974**
(Kf000)

Income Group

	1	2	3	4	5	6	7
Average Income	551	1,485	2,505	3,456	4,815	6,953	12,317
Non-monetary Income	458	751	968	1,193	1,487	2,262	2,946
Monetary Income	93	737	1,537	2,263	3,328	4,691	9,371
Average Consumption	1,611	2,165	2,721	3,364	3,892	5,618	6,505
Monetary	1,153	1,414	1,753	2,171	2,405	3,356	3,559
Non-monetary	458	751	968	1,193	1,487	2,262	2,946
Total AV. Savings	-1,060	-681	-216	93	923	1,335	5,812

SOURCE: IRS Tables 8.5 and 8.13.

TABLE 9

II. A.   Urban (1974)

Purchased items:

1.   Cereals
2.   Breads and biscuits
3.   Dairy products and eggs
4.   Meat and fish
5.   Oils and fats
6.   Sugar and sweets
7.   Fruits and vegetables
8.   Drinks, beverages and tobacco
9.   Miscellaneous (salt and falvourings)
10.   Purchased food (i.e. eating out)
11.   Clothing and footwear

Housing:

12.   Rent
13.   Fuel, power and water
14.   Furniture and furnishings
15.   Household equipment (i.e. appliances and utensils)

Household operations:

16.   Washing and cleaning
17.   Domestic services
18.   Health and personal care
19.   Transport and commerce
20.   Insurance premiums and legal fees
21.   Remittance to relatives
22.   Recreation. entertainment, education & cultural servcies.

Source: Consumer Price Indices, Nairobi, Central Bureau of
         Statistics,
         Ministry of Finance and Planning, Nairobi (1972)

TABLE 10

Urban Consumptions (1)

Expenditure Item	Income Class									Sh/month	
	1	2	3	4	5	6	7	8	9	10	11
1	0	0	0	0	0	0	0	0	0	0	0
2	72	96	108	145	192	235	264	315	375	453	564
3	0	0	0	0	0	0	0	0	0	0	0
4	42	50	62	76	114	145	176	234	318	442	678
5	3	18	34	62	98	126	147	172	212	225	246
6	0	0	5	15	28	36	42	54	65	75	60
7	3	5	7	12	32	40	48	56	60	60	60
8	0	0	0	0	0	0	0	0	0	0	0
9	2	3	6	12	18	24	28	36	45	58	85
10	0	0	5	13	33	48	60	84	120	174	282
11	0	0	0	0	0	0	0	0	0	0	0
12	6	10	12	16	24	32	38	48	60	75	93
13	3	8	15	27	45	68	85	128	193	245	645
14	3	6	12	20	33	48	62	86	122	174	273
15	60	90	105	120	132	165	204	305	504	1,140	1,750
16	0	0	0	5	10	15	24	50	108	246	536
Average Income	130	250	350	600	1,000	1,400	1,800	2,500	3,500	5,000	7,800

SOURCE: Expenditure Patterns of Middle Income African Workers in Nairobi, Nairobi, 1964.

TABLE 11

Urban Consumptions (2)

Expenditure Item	1	2	3	4	5	6	7	8	9	10	11
						Class				Sha/month	
1	0	0	0	0	0	0	0	0	0	0	0
2	72	96	108	127	235	280	255	314	370	447	602
3	0	0	0	0	0	0	0	0	0	0	0
4	42	50	62	84	127	185	192	235	305	405	600
5	3	18	34	55	125	178	160	230	288	400	505
6	0	0	5	30	38	42	68	68	60	72	80
7	3	5	7	4	10	15	18	23	24	24	27
8	0	0	0	0	0	0	0	0	0	0	0
9	2	3	6	10	16	18	28	24	38	60	84
10	0	0	6	22	40	52	55	82	118	190	270
11	0	0	0	0	0	0	0	0	3	0	0
12	6	10	12	15	36	45	38	60	102	175	305
13	3	8	15	42	84	105	114	190	330	532	908
14	3	6	12	15	32	72	92	150	160	168	302
15	60	90	105	106	128	162	220	400	636	990	1,650
16	0	0	0	15	30	36	48	78	150	245	450
Average Income	130	250	350	600	1,000	1,400	1,800	2,500	3,500	5,000	7,800

SOURCE: Consumer Price Index in Nairobi, 1977.

TABLE 12

RECONCLING THE EXP. ITEMS IN URBAN ('74, '63)
AND RURAL (1974)

	Item No.	
Product	Rural	Urban (1974)
a. Own-consumed products	1,2	NA
b. (i) Cereal and (ii) cereal products	3	1,2
c. Milk and eggs	4	3
d. Meat and fish	5	4
e. Oils and fats	6	5
f. Sugar and sweets	7	6
g. Fruits and vegetables	8	7
h. Drinks, bev. and tobacco	9	8
i. Salt and other flavorings	10	9
j. Eating out	NA	10
k. Clothing and footwear	11	11
l. Furniture, furnishing	13	14
m. Appliances and utensils	12	15
n. Fuel and power	NA	13
o. Washing and cleaning	15,16*	16
p. Domestic services	NA	17
q. Rent	NA	12
r. (i) Health and (ii) personal care	15,16**	18
s. Transportation	15,16***	19
t. Financial and legal services	NA	20

* .30; ** .30; *** .40

SOURCES: Tables 1, 6

KEY: NA = Not applicable.

TABLE 13

Reconciling the Expenditure Items and I-O Sectors

I-O Sectors

Exp. Items (from Table 4)

Non-monetary Sector:

1. Agriculture, fishing and forestry
2. Water Supply, building and ownership of huts

Non-monetary (1) → a

Monetary Sector:

3. Agriculture, forestry & fishing* — (2) → b(i), c, d (rural), g
   (3) → None (all into construction)
4. Prospecting, mining and quarrying
5. Mfc. of food preparations
6. Mfc. of bakery products, chocolate & sweets — manufacture of food,* (4) beverage and tobacco → b(ii), e, f, h, i, d (urban)
7. Mfc. of beverages and tobacco
8. Mfc. of textile, raw-materials, rope & twine
9. Mfc. of finished textiles
10. Mfc. of garments, knitwear, & made-up textiles — Mfc. of textile and leather products (5) → k
11. Mfc. of footwear, leather & fur products
12. Mfc. of saw-mill products — Mfc. of wood and wood products (6) → l
13. Mfc. of wood products; printing & publishing
14. Mfc. of rubber products
15. Mfc. of paint, detergent & soap — Mfc. of rubber, chemical & petrol. products (7) → o, s (80%)
16. Mfc. of petroleum products & other chemicals
17. Mfc. of misc. non-metallic mineral products — (8) → none
18. Mfc. of metal products, machinery & misc. — (9) → m
19. Mfc. of building & repair of transport equip. — (9) → s
20. Electricity and water — (12) → n
21. Building & construction — (10)
22. Trade and distribution — (11) → none (reflected in ownership of dwellings)
23. Transport & communication — (13) → none (reflected in value purchased merch.)
24. Restaurant & hotel services — (12) → s (80%)
25. Ownership of dwellings — (13) → j
26. Financial services — (15) → q
27. Misc. services (excluding gov't.) — (14) → t
28. Gov't services — (15) → p, r(ii)
29. Ownership of business premises — (15) → q
30. Unspecified (incl. hunting)** — ** → none

---

* Food is divided into processed and unprocessed.
** The unspecified item cannot be matched with any expenditure item. At any rate, it is relatively insignificant in terms of magnitude.
SOURCE: Tables 16 and I-O; Tables from Kenya, 1977.

B.   DATA ON PRODUCTION

I.   Inter-Industry Matrices (a_{ij})

Inter-industry matrices are shown in the I-O tables for Kenya which have been published in 1977. The absolute figures in these tables refer to the calendar year 1971 and these would have changed by 1974--the year my study is concerned with. However, it is safe to assume that the coefficients have not changed during this period.

The level of disaggregation in the I-O tables is different from that of the tables shown in previous chapters. For example, the manufacturing sector is broken down into fourteen subsectors in the I-O tables while a single aggregate figure is given in the tables of Chapter 5 and 6. The coefficients in the I-O subsectors can be combined into an aggregate figure for manufacturing using subsectoral output as weights. The converse could be done disaggregating the tables in other chapters to conform to the I-O level of aggregation. A middle road is adopted and the manufacturing sector is broken down into six main subsectors. Both sets of tables are then appropriately changed.

The Input-Output tables also contain information on sectoral output (X_j) and value added (V_j). The latter is broken into wages (W_j) and non-wage (π_j) incomes, depreciation (δ_j) and indirect taxes (T_j^i). Intermediate imports (M_j^r) with or without duties are also shown. Import coefficients for final (M_j^c) and capital (M^k) goods can be obtained from the same tables with almost straightforward computations.

II. Capital and Labor-Output Ratios

The method used to estimate these ratios depends on the available data and intended end-use of the ratios. In this study, these ratios are needed to estimate changes in factor usage resulting from change in sectoral output. So changes in employment and investment requirements hinge on the estimated values of capital and labor-output ratios.

Ideally, these ratios should be estimated from specified production functions which include technological change. But in addition to the problems inherent in completely specifying such functions, the date base is very scant and is available only for a short period. Moreover, the structural changes of a developing economy continually alters the production coefficients. The latter, however, is not important here since the present study is limited to a single period (1974).

1. Capital-Output Ratios

Several methods were tested in estimating the lucramental capital-output ratios (ICORS). These were:

1. Dividing net sectoral capital formation in 1974 by lagged changes in sectoral output.

2. A longer period was used since ICOR values might change with the rate of capital utilization in any one year.

3. Using constant rather than current prices for both investment and output.

4. The investment-output lags were changed. The ICOR values were very erratic. A major shortcoming of these methods is that the effect of existing capital stock is not considered.

An alternate method adopted by Professor James Tobin [83] is used in this Study. In a paper written while in Kenya, Tobin used formal regression techniques to estimate capital-output ratios.

He regresses sectoral GDP on capital formation and its survival rate (defined as one minus depreciation rate). A number of alternative depreciation rates are assumed and an estimate of capital-output ratios for each is obtained using the following equation:

$$Y_t = \sigma K_o s^t + \sigma V_t$$

$$= a s^t + b V_t$$

where $s^t = (1-\delta)^t$, $\quad V_t = \sum_{j=0}^{t-1} I_j s^{t-j-1}$,

σ = reciprocal of ICOR,

δ = depreciation rate.

The above equation is obtained in the following way. The initial capital stock is assumed gain so that $K_o = \overline{K}_o$. The capital stock in year one is the sum undepreciated stock and investment in the base year.

$$K_1 = K_o S + I_o$$

$$|||^1 \gamma \ ,$$

$$K_2 = K_o S^2 + I S_o + I_1$$

.

.

.

$$K_t = K_o s^t + I_o s^{t-1} + I_1 s^{t-2} + \ldots\ldots + I_j s^{t-j-1} + I_{t-1}$$

Let $\quad \sum_j I_j s^{t-j-1} = V_t, \quad K_t = K_o s^t + V_t, \quad$ or $\quad Y_t = \sigma k_o s^t + \sigma V_t$.

Tobin's estimates using alternative depreciation ratio are shown in Table 2 of his paper. It seems the ICOR values thus obtained lie within the expected range and therefore will be used in subsequent analysis. However, since the relevant sectoral depreciation ratios can be obtained from the I-O tables, only one estimate (that corresponds to the relevant depreciation ratio) will be chosen for each sector.

III. Labor-Output Ratios

Labor-Output Ratios are estimated by dividing sectoral employment by the corresponding sectoral GDP. This is done for a number of years and the results averaged. The estimates so derived are generally comparable to outside estimates (see the IBRD (91), p. 54, for example). The results are shown in Table 22.

Sectoral employment is then broken down by skill level. This information is essential for ascertaining changes in skill mix as overall employment changes. Data on the distribution of skill level across sectors is obtained from the "Manpower Survey" conducted by the Central Bureau of Statistics (see Appendix 5). The employment coefficients by skill level is shown in Table 23.

TABLE 14

ESTIMATED ICORS

Sector	Method				
	1	2	3	4	Tobin's
Non-Monetary	.40	-	.76	.54	0
Monetary:					
Agriculture	.14	6.64	1.70	.56	1.02
Mining & quarrying	-	32.00	10.63	8.0	1.65
Manufacturing	.12	1.43	2.41	1.62	1.98
Electricity & Water	.94	6.21	11.97	6.86	3.14
Bldg. & Const.	.08	2.32	3.61	2.13	2.48
Transport & comm.	.12	128.64	5.97	5.24	2.67
Trade & hotels	.19	3.2	.85	.70	.64
Bus. & Fin. Serv.	.03	1.03	.56	.41	.26
Ownership of dwellings	.004	34.75	6.02	4.86	3.11
Private services	.11	2.72	2.04	1.50	1.77
Gov't services	.03	3.06	3.79	2.07	1.43

SOURCE: Statistical Abstracts, Various Issues. Tobin's estimates from his "Estimates of Capital-Output Ratios for Kenya," Institute of Development Studies Discussion Paper #171, Nairobi, Kenya, 1972.

TABLE 15

LABOR-OUTPUT RATIOS BY YEAR,
NUMBER OF EMPLOYEES PER f1000 PRODUCT

	Year				
Sector	1972	1973	1974	1975	Total[1]
Non-Monetary	-	-	-	-	-
Agriculture	2.489	2.605	2.581	2.363	2.506
Mining & quarrying	1.420	.965	1.334	1.189	1.227
Manufacturing	1.088	1.069	1.083	1.035	1.069
Electricity & Water	1.052	1.163	1.388	1.347	1.237
Building & Const.	.576	.582	.564	.692	.604
Commerce (Trade)	.718	.610	.732	.746	.702
Transport & Comm.	1.144	1.007	1.071	1.119	1.085
Financial Services	.556	.623	.569	.599	.587
Private Services	4.284	4.403	4.553	4.870	4.527

SOURCE: Statistical Abstract, Various Issues.

[1] Assumed L/O ratios.

TABLE 16

SKILL LEVEL AS A PERCENT OF
SECTORAL EMPLOYMENT, 1972

Skill Type

Sector	Total Empl. (000's)	Managerial & Professional	Technical & Clerical	Skilled Manual	Unskilled Manual
Agriculture	246.85	2.08	.69	.29	96.95
Mining & Quarrying	3.17	4.32	1.23	3.85	90.60
Manuf. & repair	84.80	4.19	5.60	13.85	76.36
Electricity & water	5.15	2.00	18.27	4.72	75.00
Bldg. & const.	37.60	1.97	2.10	8.91	87.02
Commerce	65.12	9.69	13.65	3.49	74.30
Transport & Comm.	45.31	1.93	12.76	2.64	82.67
Services	231.78	1.99	14.69	.79	82.53

SOURCE: Statistical Abstract, 1976, Table 24.

PART IV

CHAPTER 8: RESULTS

CHAPTER 9: SUMMARY AND CONCLUSIONS

CHAPTER 8

RESULTS OF SIMULATION EXPERIMENTS
INVOLVING INCOME REDISTRIBUTION

I.1. Introduction

The purpose of this chapter is to simulate the potential effects
of various income redistribution policies on selected growth-related
variables and the size distribution of income. These policies involve
direct and indirect (through other policy changes) transfers. The
specific choice of some policies (to the exclusion of others) does not
reflect any prior determination of their relative effectiveness in
terms of changing the size distribution of income or even their feasibility. Several policies were arbitrarily chosen and their potential
effects, both absolutely and in relation to each other, investigated.
This was partly necessitated by the difficulty inherent in the prior
determination of what the set of "appropriate" policies are and partly
the desire to limit the scope of this study within manageable bounds.[1]

---

[1]There have been numerous studies in recent years about the determination of "appropriate" redistributive policies [see Chapter 1].
Briefly, most of those studies attempted to isolate factors that may
be most responsible for the existing patterns of income distribution.
It has been hoped that once these "determining" factors were isolated
the choice of policy would follow. However, there are a multitude of
social, political, and economic variables that affect the size distribution of income which cannot all be considered in a theoretical model.
Many of these factors are also not amenable to quantification and mere
ranking would entail a great deal of subjectivity. In addition, the
interaction between the various factors may depend on yet another set
of unobserved factors which may reflect localized conditions, thus reducing the generality of any results obtained. For these reasons,
there has been little success.

The policies adopted here are all gradualist in nature and do not aim at disrupting the existing socioeconomic structure. The feasibility of their adoption and subsequent implementation would depend on the commitment of the government and the relative strengths of the parties affected. Assuming that the government is committed to achieving greater equality in the distribution of income, such policies might engender lesser resistance by entrenched interest groups than "radical" policies that aim at changing the whole socioeconomic structure.

I.2.   Income Redistribution Policies

I.2.1.   Direct Transfers:

1.   The income of all households in the urban, rural, and estate sectors earning less than the average sectoral income are raised. The total amount transferred to each group is the difference between the average and actual sectoral income multiplied by the number of households in that income group. Households earning at least three times the average sectoral income pay for the cost of the transfer with the burden progressively distributed. The average sectoral incomes are:

$$
\begin{array}{lll}
\text{Urban:} & \text{£ 420/year} & \text{or} \quad \text{770 shs/month} \\
\text{Rural:} & \text{£ 100/year} & \text{or} \quad \text{167 shs/month} \\
\text{Estate:} & \text{£ 180/year} & \text{or} \quad \text{300 shs/month}
\end{array}
$$

Under this plan transfer is limited,by assumption, to within each sector, and thus no net losses or gains to any sector occur. Households making less than the average sectoral income comprise 52.3% 40%, and 70% of total households in the urban, rural, and estate sectors (see Tables 2, 16, & 17, Chapter 5). These households gain as a result of the transfer. The highest 7.3%, 2.0%, and 1.1% of the urban and estate households pay for the transfer.[2] The total amounts transferred are 33.80 million, 28.66 million, and 7.57 million. This represents about 10%, 10%, and 18% of total sectoral income.

2. The second transfer plan and the amount transferred is the same as #1 above for the lower income groups. However, the burden of the transfer in any one sector no longer falls on the more well-off members of that sector, but is distributed according to the level of income regardless of sectoral location. Thus, transfer takes place both within and between sectors although adjustments are made for such factors as cost differentials between sectors so that minimum taxable income (for purposes of the transfer) is higher in urban than in rural areas. It is assumed that an urban household needs twice the income of a similar and similarly placed rural household and about 1.6 times that of estate households to be as well off. It is also assumed that those earning more than 2,000 shs/month, 1,200 shs/month, and 1,000 shs/month bear the burden of the transfer which is progressively distributed between them.

There obviously is an element of arbitrariness in the choice of these figures but the choice is not without some logical basis. The figures for urban and estate sectors correspond to the salary of professional and managerial classes and that of the rural sector to the highest 10% of the rural households. It also closely follows #1, except that burden on high-income urban residents is greater than in #1.

─────────────

[2]These percentage figures provide a rough picture of the degree of concentration within each sector.

The total amount transferred to lower income households in each sector stays the same as #1 but the amount transferred from upper income groups changes between sectors (56 million, 9.6 million, and 5 million transferred from high income groups in the urban, estate, and rural sectors).

3. The share of the lowest 50% of the population (all rural) is doubled and upper income urban households are taxed to pay for the cost. Under this plan only between-sector transfer takes place (cf. #1). The burden to the urban sector is distributed as in #2 above.

The amount of income transferred from (-) or to (+) each income group under the above three plans is shown in Table 1.

4, 5, & 6. The amount of income transferred under 1-3 is reduced by 50%. This is intended to measure the sensitivity of the simulation experiments to the amount of the transfer. Since most of the parameters are fixed it is expected that the results obtained under this set of transfer plans would be exactly 50% of those obtained under plans 1-3.

1.2.2. Other Redistributive Policies:

The above transfer plans are complemented with the following policies:

1. Changing the factoral distribution of income. The wage share in the formal sector is doubled at the expense of the non-wage. One way in which factoral redistribution could be accomplished is to adopt a more labor-intensive technology. This in turn could be accomplished by:

TABLE 1

Amount of Income Transferred (±)
By Urban, Rural, and Estate (£000)

	PLAN I	PLAN II	PLAN III
URBAN			
Class:			
1	10,431	10,000	0
2	11,799	11,000	0
3	5,817	6,000	0
4	5,700	6,000	0
5	0	0	0
6	0	0	0
7	0	0	0
8	0	-7,000	-7,000
9	-5,300	-8,000	-9,000
10	-10,440	-16,000	-16,000
11	-18,007	-25,000	-25,000
RURAL			
Class:			
1-2	28,660	28,600	49,600
3	0	0	7,400
4	0	0	0
5	0	0	0
6	-8,024	0	0
7	-20,640	-5,000	0
ESTATE			
Class:			
1	6,038	6,000	0
2	1,530	1,500	0
3	0	0	0
4	0	0	0
5	0	0	0
6	0	0	0
7	0	-500	0
8	0	-1,200	0
9	-1,500	-1,800	0
10	-2,568	-2,600	0
11	-3,500	-3,500	0

(a) Changing the relative factor prices by raising the cost of capital relative to labor. The cost of capital is kept artificially low by numerous government policies designed to encourage industrialization and by overvalued exchange rates that lower the effective cost of importing capital. On the other hand, wage rates in the modern sector are kept artificially high by minimum wage legislation and the relative strength of trade unions in the relatively protected modern sector.

The combination of artificially low prices of capital and high wage rates lead to the adoption of a technology more capital-intensive than would be warranted by domestic factor availabilities. Removing these factor price distortions might lead to the adoption of more labor-intensive technology at least within the range where factor substitution is possible.

(b) Adopting a technology more "appropriate" to the LDC factor endowments. Most of the current technology is produced in the developed countries (DCs) and therefore reflects the relative factor scarcities in these countries. But it is argued [see Fei-Ranis (27)] that there is a technological "ladder" containing technologies perfected in the past by the present DCs or may be even currently in use in relatively more developed LDCs. Each country can choose the relevant step in that ladder and subsequently "assimilate" it into the domestic, economic structure. There is no evidence, however, that such a ladder exists. Even if it does, knowing about it and transferring it to the relevant LDC would still pose a problem. But assuming that such a technology exists and that it could be adopted, the effect on factor use would be to increase the demand, and subsequently the income, of labor.

2. The income of the sector is doubled. One way this could be achieved is through increased small-farm productivity. But however it is brought about, the focus is not rural productivity per se, but to investigate the effect of changing the income of one sector without reducing that of another as in the transfer policies and factoral redistribution discussed above.

3. Import substitution: A large portion of the increases in domestic demand resulting from income redistribution goes to imported products. These leakages reduce the size of the multiplier. To investigate the potential effect of these leakages it is assumed that any increases in domestic demand can be satisfied domestically.

Comparative static experiments are performed with the above redistributive policies. The effect of each policy (or policy package) on the level and composition of output, private consumption by sector, employment by skill category, imports (final, intermediate and capital goods), capital requirements, and savings (public, personal and business) are measured. The sensitivity of the results to changes in parametric values are investigated. In all, over 50 computer runs were made.

I.3. Changes in Parametric Values

I.3.1. Consumption Coefficients

1. Rural: The most important items in the consumption basket
of rural households are self-produced products. Such consumption is by
definition outside of the monetary sector and would not therefore be
directly affected by income transfers. But it could be indirectly
affected. A farmer could consume more of his own products because the
income transfer could enable him to sell less of his products and still
maintain a given amount of money income. Thus he could "purchase" his
own products.

It is also possible that all additional income resulting from
income transfer would be spent on purchased items. Since both consumption behaviors are theoretically plausible, two sets of simulation runs
are made under each alternative: one including the non-monetary consumption, the other considering only monetary consumption.

2. Urban: Data on the consumption pattern of urban households
is based on two surveys: The expenditure pattern of Middle Income
African Workers in Nairobi (1964) and the Consumer Price Index in
Nairobi (1977). The former covers only the middle 50% of the households in Nairobi and so cannot be used in isolation. In the latter
all urban households are broken down into three broad income groups
(Chapter 7, p. 222) and this would necessitate interpolation of the consumption pattern of households lying within the three broad groups.

An urban household budget survey was conducted in 1968/69 but
it is not published and a copy could not be obtained. Consumption
coefficients were estimated using two alternative expenditure patterns:

the first obtained by concatenating the two sets of data mentioned above,
(see pp.   , Chapter 7), and the second obtained by interpolation from
the consumer price index. The model is estimated using these two alternative
consumption coefficients of urban households. The sensitivity of results
to changes in expenditure pattern are then investigated.

I.3.2.   The Size Distribution of Non-Wage Income

The lack of information on the distribution of asset ownership
across households necessitated explicit assumptions about the size
distribution of non-wage income (Chapter 5, pp. 135-141, and Chapter 6,
p. 214). Three alternative distributions of non-wage income have been
postulated (assumptions, Chapter 6, pp. 214-215). The model is simulated
for each alternative under each income redistribution policy.

I.3.3.   Investment from Non-Wage Income Received by Institutions

1. It has been discussed above (Chapter 5, pp. 129-132) that some of the
sectoral non-wage income acrues to institutions (business, government
and the rest of the world) in the form of retained earnings, repatriated
profits, or operating surplus of government-owned enterprises. It is
assumed that some of the income which in effect represents a leakage
flows back into the system as investment. The proportion of the inflow and the time between the leakage and the reentry cannot be ascertained. Three alternative assumptions are made about the proportion
that flows back into the system, in the current year, through investment. The model is then estimated for each alternative under each of
the redistribution policies.

TABLE 2

Experiments with Income Transfer Plans

	Experiment No.		
Redist. Policy	I	II	III
1. Single Policies (Transfer only)			
1.1. Monetary sector only	4	5	6
1.2. Non-monetary incl.	1	2	3
2. Policy Packages (transfers & other policies)			
2.1. Changing factor shares	7	8	9
2.2. Raising rural incomes	10	11	12
2.3. Import substitution	13	14	15
2.4. Quasi-nationalization	16	17	18
3. Changing Parametric Values			
3.1. Distribution of Rental income			
3.1.1. Alternative #1	19	20	21
3.1.2. Alternative #2	22	23	24
3.1.3. Alternative #3	25	26	27
3.2. Consumption coeff. (urban)	28	29	30
3.3. Changing Z values*			
3.3.1. Z = .5	31	32	33
3.3.2. Z = .8	34	35	36
3.3.3. Z = .5, $M^{K^1}=\frac{1}{2}M^K$	37	38	39

*See text for explanation; M^K = imports of capital goods

2. Most capital equipment is imported in the case of Kenya and so some of the flow-back in (1) above will leak to capital exporting countries, thereby reducing the size of the multiplier. To investigate the sensitivity of the results to the proportion of capital imported, it is assumed that the additional (induced) capital imports can be reduced by 50%.

II. Empirical Results

II.1. The Effect of Redistribution on Output, Factor Usage, Imports, and Savings

The effect of income redistribution policies on the above variables are shown in Tables 3-9. Most of the variables estimated are very sensitive to the type of policy and amount transferred. The effect of each type of policy is discussed below.

EXPERIMENTS 1-3:

Employment and output increase under all three experiments, but while the increase in output is not substantially different between the three experiments, employment increase in Experiment 1 is twice that of 3 and 40% higher than that obtained under 2. The relatively small value under 3 reflects the fact that the net gainers under this plan are rural households. Increases in the consumption of rural households, especially of own-products, and the resulting increases in output do not always lead to increases in the number of persons employed. Most small farms (and other non-farm activities) use family rather than hired labor and the number of workers depends more on factors like population growth and urban migration than on farm output at least to the extent that underemployment exists.

Capital requirements is the most sensitive variable. It ranges from + 34 million for Experiment 1 to - 40 million for 3. Experiment 3 would imply the development of excess capacity. The wide variation in capital requirements is probably due to the fact that the capital-output ratio is greater than unity and so changes in capital requirements are a multiple of the changes in output. For example, if the capital-output ratio is four, capital requirements would have to increase four times a given increase in output unless there was considerable under-utilization of plant and equipment to start with. The large negative figure for Experiment 3 could be explained in the following way: The gainers under this redistribution experiment are rural households while all the losers are urban residents. Both sectors register gains and losses under the other plans. Sectors catering to rural households are less capital-intensive than those

268

catering to urban households. Since income of the rural sector increases and that of the urban sector decreases more under redistribution Plan III than under other plans, reduction in capital requirements under the former is to be expected. Moreover, the single most important item in the consumption basket of rural residents is subsistence crops which require little or no input of reproducible capital.

The huge increase in capital requirements under Experiment 1 reflects the fact that transfer under this plan is limited to within each sector and that the factor intensity of goods consumed by various income groups does not vary within sectors as much as it does between sectors. Nevertheless, there is still some reduction in the capital-output ratio even under this plan. For each additional unit of output, only 1.25 more units of capital is required as opposed to an overall capital-output ratio of approximately 3.0.

Total imports increase slightly for Experiment 1 but decline for 2 and 3. The imports of capital goods decline and that of final goods increase for all three experiments. But the decline of capital imports in 2 and 3 is strong enough to overcompensate for the increase in final imports thus resulting in an overall reduction of imports. The reduction in capital imports results from the reduction in overall capital requirements -- import coefficients are assumed constant.

Aggregate savings decline substantially under all three experiments. Almost all of the reduction results from declines in personal savings. This confirms the theory that the APCs of the poor are higher than those of upper income groups.[3] It should be noted that no

---

[3] It has been sometimes argued that in the LDCs, the MPC of the rich might be as high as that of the poor because of external demonstration effect and conspicuous consumption (see Chapter 2, p. 34).

a priori savings propensities were postulated for the different income groups. Only data on consumption by good and income group were used.

Government revenues decline due to the fall in personal income taxes as income is transferred from those in higher tax brackets. This, however, is limited to the urban and estate sector as rural households usually do not pay income taxes.

EXPERIMENTS 4-6:

This set of experiments exclude non-monetary consumption by rural households, i.e., rural households spend the additional income on purchased goods.

In comparison to Experiments 1-3, gross output increases slightly for #7, but declines for 5 and 6. Employment, however, increases substantially for all three experiments as compared to corresponding experiments which include non-monetary consumption (i.e., Experiments 1-3). However, the relative strength of the increase in employment is reversed. In Experiments 1-3, increase in employment for #1 is twice that for #3. But in Experiments 4-6, the situation is reversed with the smallest increase occurring under #4 and the largest under #6. It should be recalled that Experiments 1 and 4 both refer to transfer Plan I except that in Experiment 1, the self-consumed agricultural products (i.e., non-monetary consumption) are included while in #4 they are not. The increase in employment for #6 is three times that obtained under Experiment 3.

There are two reasons for the huge employment increases in Experiments 4-6 over 1-3, and the reversal of the direction of increase within each set of experiments. First, it is assumed that employment would not increase if output of the subsistence or non-monetary sector rises partly because of the existence of high amounts of underemployment. The family unit shares whatever work is available. Approximately 30% of the increase in output is in the non-monetary sector. This explains the difference in the employment increases between Experiments 1-3 on the one hand (which includes the non-monetary sector) and 4-5 on the other (which considers only the monetary sector).

The reversal of the direction of increase in employment in the two sets of experiments (i.e., decreasing from 1 to 3 in the first set and increasing from 4 to 6 in the second set) can be explained in the following way.[4] Under income transfer I, redistribution is limited to within each sector and so the post-redistribution aggregate rural income stays the same as the pre-redistribution level. Under transfer III, however, redistribution is from urban to rural and so the latter is a net gainer. The non-monetary consumption is limited to the rural sector and

---

[4]Corresponding experiments in the two sets of experiments refer to the same income transfer plans. Any difference is therefore due to factors other than the type and magnitude of income transfer.

non-monetary output would expand more under III than under I. But by assumption (see p. 280 above) increases in the non-monetary sector would not lead to employment increases. Therefore, Experiment 3 results in less employment increases than Experiment 1. However, when only the monetary sector is considered (Experiments 4-6) transfer Plan III results in greater increase in employment than I or II because III favors the rural sector which has a more labor-intensive consumption pattern.

Capital requirements rise both in absolute terms and over Experiments 1-3. The reasons for the absolute rise are the same as those explained for Experiments 1-3. The relative increase over the latter is due to the fact that only the monetary sector, which as a whole is more capital-intensive than the non-monetary sector, is considered in Experiments 4-6.

Imports rise slightly for Experiments 7 and 9 but decline for 8. The import of final and intermediate goods rise while that of capital goods decline for all three experiments. The latter is mainly brought about by the decline in the sectors that use relatively more imported capital compared to the expanding sectors. But total capital requirements still rise because of the increase in sectoral output even though overall capital-intensity of production falls. The increase in final and intermediate imports merely reflects the fact that Kenya is still at an early stage of import substitute industrialization and that a large proportion of consumer goods, including food, and intermediate inputs are imported.

Total Savings decline but by a much smaller amount than under Experiments 1-3. Most of the decline is in personal savings followed closely by government savings. The decline in the former is largest in Experiment 4 and smallest in Experiment 6. The reverse is true for government savings.

The decline in personal savings for all three experiments is due to the fact that the MPS rises with income. As income is transferred from higher to lower income groups, total personal savings decline. The largest decline is in Experiment 4 implying that the rural MPS is higher than that of urban households in the same income bracket. In Experiment 4 income is transferred from the rich to the poor within each sector while in 6 it is transferred from high income groups in the urban sector to low income groups in the rural sector. The small decline in 6 (less than 50% of 7) implies that the MPS of households in the rural households is much higher than that of urban households in comparable income brackets. A possible explanation is the availability of credit in urban areas and possible demonstration effect which might increase dis-savings by more than would otherwise obtain.

The component of government savings most responsible for the latter's decline are direct taxes resulting from the transfer of income. Implicit here is the assumption that recurrent government expenditures do not fall as revenue falls. If this assumption is dropped then savings would fall by less than indicated.

Corporate savings (depreciation and undistributed profits) are positive but very small. It is assumed that corporate savings are a constant function of sectoral output. But with total capital requirements rising and aggregate savings declining, it is likely that retained earnings and thus corporate savings will rise at the expense of the amount paid to owners.

EXPERIMENTS 7-9:

Transfer Plans I-III are coupled with redistribution of factoral income. Wage shares are doubled at the expense of non-wage income outside the rural sector. The latter is excluded because most of the rural farmers are self-employed and therefore the recipients of non-wage income. Reduction in the non-wage share in this sector would hurt the poorest segments of the population. It is assumed that the objective of redistributing income is to alleviate poverty and so the rural sector is excluded.

Gross output, capital requirements, imports and savings remain almost unchanged from Experiments 4-6. Total employment rises but by slightly less than under 4-6. The smaller increase in employment results from two factors. First, the lowest income group in the urban sector is found in the informal sector where most are self-employed and therefore the recipients of operating surplus.[5] Such groups consume labor-intensive products. Second, the highest income groups in the formal sector receive "rental" income (operating surplus minus imputed wage income of the self-employed minus the amount received by institutions). Such groups are the largest consumers of personal and domestic services. A decline in their income would lead to a reduction in the consumption of such services. At any rate, the decline of employment from Experiments 4-6 is very small.

The constancy of the variables estimated and the very small value of the change in employment would imply that there is little congruence between the factoral and personal distribution of income even when the

---

[5]In the National Accounts and the distribution derived therefrom (see Chapter 5) the income of the self-employed is labelled as "imputed wage income" rather than operating surplus.

rural sector is excluded. This would tend to refute the argument that the redistribution of factor income in favor of labor would lead to greater equality in the personal distribution of income. This argument rests on the assumption that wage income is less concentrated than non-wage income. Before this line of reasoning is rejected, however, a distinction must be made between "non-wage" and "rental" incomes. The latter is a subset of the former and is concentrated in the highest 1 or 2% of the population. The former, on the other hand, includes incomes from self-employment in formal and informal-urban sectors and small farms, corporate retained earnings, surplus of government-owned enterprises and expatriated profits. Changes in retained earnings, government profits and expatriated profits need not affect the personal distribution of income except insofar as they change against the portion that is received by individuals. The effect of changing the portion of non-wage income received by individuals or households on the overall personal distribution of income will depend on the relative weights of the imputed wage income of the self-employed and property income. If the latter is greater, then redistribution of factor income against non-wage income recipients would tend to improve the overall size distribution of income. The reverse would be true if income from self-employment predominates.

Another distinction that would need to be made is between overall distribution of income and the percent share of each group. The former is indicated by such summary measures as Gini coefficient which measures inequality over the entire population and may thus be insensitive to the degree of inequality within particular ranges. The percent share, on the

other hand, is sensitive to changes within any particular range. Thus,
if property income is reduced the concentration of income in the top 1 or
2% can be shown if the distribution of income is indicated by percent
share of each group rather than inequality indices like Gini coefficient.

EXPERIMENTS 10-12:

Under this set of experiments, rural income is raised in addition
to the income transfers. The most marked results, as compared to previous
experiments, are obtained. Gross output and employment increase substantially both in absolute terms (see Table 5) and in relation to other experiments (c/w 4-6). Within Experiments 10-12 the biggest increase in employment occurs in Experiment 12 and in Experiment 19 for gross output. The
reasons for this have been explained earlier (see p. 303).

Capital requirements rise a little while the ICORs decline a little.
This is because while the increase in output would raise aggregage capital
requirements, the increase would be at a much lower rate than the overall
capital-output ratio.

Total imports increase slightly over 4-6, but the import of capital
goods stays almost the same. The reason for the increase in final imports
over Experiments 4-6 is mainly due to the increase in rural income over
and above the income transfer and the fact that the marginal propensity
to import by rural households is positive. The constancy in capital
imports implies that most of the capital equipment used by the rural
sector is domestically produced.

Total savings decline both absolutely and relative to Experiments
4-6. The reasons for the decline have been explained earlier under 4-6.

EXPERIMENTS 13-15:

A large amount of the increase in consumption leaks out in the form of imports thus reducing the size of the production-consumption multiplier. The major component of imports is that of consumer products. If the additional consumption occasioned by the income transfer can be met from domestic sources, the size of the multiplier and thus the results observed would be markedly increased. This in fact is what happens. But the changes are greatest under Transfer Plan I, i.e., Experiment 15 where the transfer is limited to within each sector. The urban sector, which has a relatively high propensity to import, does not lose income to the other sectors through this transfer plan. Since imports of final goods would be highest under Plan I, a policy of import substitution would have the most marked effect here (see Table 6).

EXPERIMENTS 16-18:

The objective of this set of experiments is to investigate whether the decline in savings could be averted or at least reduced by the government siphoning-off all the incremental operating surplus. The government does not take over establishments nor do all the profits of these establishments accrue to it. But it just siphons off the incremental non-wage income. Employment and output are slightly reduced over Experiments 4-6, but savings are increased. This is especially so for Experiment 31 (Transfer I). But the changes in aggregate savings are still negative even though the government component has increased.

Changes in Parametric Values

Alternative Assumptions about the Size Distribution of Rental Income

EXPERIMENTS 19-27

In the absence of information of the distribution of household asset ownership, the size distribution of rental income is based on assumptions. The following experiments are intended to investigate the sensitivity of the results to alternative assumptions about the distribution of rental income. Experiments 19-21 apply to alternative #1, Experiments 22-24 to alternative #2, and Experiments 25-27 to alternative #3 (see pp. 29-36, Chapter 5). From Table 7 it could be seen that the first two alternative assumptions make little difference for the results observed. The main reason for this might be that the recipients of rental income are the top income groups in the urban and estate sectors and there is little variation in the consumption patterns of these groups. Since both alternative assumptions about the distribution of rental income change merely the within-group distribution but do not change overall distribution of income, there is no reason to believe the level and composition of private consumption and subsequently sectoral output, employment and the other variables estimated would be affected.

Under alternative 3, however, there are slightly higher changes especially under I (Experiment 25). The reason is that under this experiment, rental income is assumed to be no more concentrated than wage income in the non-agricultural formal sector. But it is still limited to groups above the mean wage rate.

Alternative Urban Consumption Patterns

EXPERIMENTS 28-30

The alternative consumption pattern chosen is obtained by project-ing the Three-Income-Group data contained in the Consumer Price Index (1977). A small increase in output, employment, capital requirements and imports, and a decline in savings in relation to Experiments 16-18 are obtained.

The small increases obtained under Experiments 25-27 could be explained in the following way. In interpolating the consumption patterns of 11 income groups from the broad three groups that are given, it is assumed that the segments of the consumption functions connecting pairs of these three groups are linear. Moreover, such segments are upward sloping. Therefore, the consumption of each good continually rises with income. On the other hand, there are some reversals in the alternative consumption data which have been used in previous experiments. These reversals are especially prevalent in the middle 50% of the urban households. It should be recalled that this group has already been disaggregated into seven sub-groups and the actual consumption for each group has been obtained from survey data (see Page 227).

Changing the Z-values (Experiments 31-39

In previous experiments it has been assumed that $Z = 0$, so that the income received by institutions represents a net leakage from the system uncompensated for by any corresponding inflor--at least in the current year. Alternatively, it is assumed that $Z = .5, .8$.

Gross output, employment and capital requirements increase slightly over the case when $Z = 0$ and higher for $Z = .8$ than when $Z = .5$ (Table 9, columns 1-3, cols. 4-6). Nevertheless, the changes are rather small which probably reflects the fact that the inflows, which are in the form of investment, subsequently leak out through imports of capital goods. To investigate the sensitivity of the result to the amount of capital imports, the latter is reduced by 50%. The only change was in the amount of capital imported. Since most capital is imported, a 50% reduction in capital import would be expected to have an impact on sectoral output and thus employment, capital requirements and savings. The reason behind this apparent anamoly is that the impact of a positive Z value is very small to start with (compare Tables 1 and 7) and so a fractional change of that would have an even less impact.

TABLE 3

Changes in Output, Employment, Imports and Domestic Savings
Results from Various Income Transfer Experiments

Changes in	Actual (1974)	REDISTRIBUTIVE EXPERIMENTS					
		1	2	3	4	5	6
Gross Output (£000)	1,725.11 mtl[a]	27,661	21,814	23,374	28,404	20,000	16,682
Employment: Total	826,300[b]	44,000	31,103	22,961	51,561	51,498	70,512
Skill-Level 1	24,673	1,122	696	393	1,294	1,203	1,602
Skill-level 2	65,475	-339	-1,746	-1,640	-190	-1,106	13
Skill-level 3	24,647	991	425	184	1,054	893	1,452
Skill-level 4	711,505	42,000	31,556	23,865	49,199	50,769	67,107
Capital Requirements (£000)	--[c]	34,178	821	-40,070	33,293	14,668	-6,119
Imports: Total (£000)	105,810	4,628	-6,717	-7,854	3,856	-2,454	2,510
Consumption	22,420[d]	4,416	2,056	3,012	4,611	3,895	7,034
Intermediate	59,345	1,778	580	-79	2,135	1,686	2,985
Capital Goods	17,149	-1,666	-9,353	-10,787	-2,890	-8,034	-7,479
Savings: Total (£000)	--[e]	-31,394	-28,214	-40,979	27,959	-22,172	-24,502
Private Indiv.		-31,394	-20,163	-26,285	28,468	-15,804	-13,912
Business		1,710	741	-197	1,995	1,520	1,630
Government: Total		-1,362	-8,792	-14,497	-1,485	-7,888	-12,239
Direct Taxes		-2,730	-8,655	-12,407	-2,989	-8,252	-11,457
Indirect Taxes		696	-74	-1,389	742	78	-977
Operating Surplus		672	-63	-700	762	286	193

Sources and Explanations:

a) Monetary = £1,524.87
Non-monetary = £190.24
Intermediate Consumption = £817.49
GDP at Factor Cost = £907.63
(Economic Survey, 1976, Table 2.3).

b) Refers only to wage employment
Skill level 1 = Managerial & Professional
Skill level 2 = Technical & Clerical
Skill level 3 = Skilled-manual
Skill level 4 = Unskilled
Figures obtained from Stat. Abst. 1976, Table 245.
They refer to 1972 and have been project to 1974.

c) Not available.

d) Only private consumption is included. Information on imports obtained from Stat. Abst., 1976, Table 77a.

e) No accurate figures available for this.

TABLE 4

Effect of Redistributing Factor Income in Favor of Labor Share

	7	8	9
Gross Output (f000)	27,140	18,915	15,846
Employment (N. of Employees)			
Total	48,924	48,626	67,178
Skill-Level 1	1,234	1,139	1,529
Skill-Level 2	-224	-1,146	-31
Skill-Level 3	1,039	888	1,444
Skill-Level 4	46,684	47,511	63,903
Capital Requirements (f000)	36,717	13,871	-5,801
Imports (f000)			
Total	3,118	-2,798	2,326
Consumption	4,084	3,739	7,002
Intermediate			
Capital	-3,006	-8,130	-7,558
Savings (f000)			
Total	-26,734	-22,704	-26,063
Private Indiv.	-26,566	-16,397	-15,732
Business	1,267	921	827
Government: Total	-1,435	-7,228	-11,158
Direct Taxes	-2,891	-7,581	-10,424
Indirect Taxes	721	81	-926
Operating Surplus	735	271	192

TABLE 5

The Effect of Rural Productivity Increases

	10	11	12
Gross Output (£000)	31,581	23,641	20,923
Employment (N. of Employees)			
Total	58,889	59,902	80,303
Skill-Level 1	1,458	1,391	1,821
Skill-Level 2	70	-970	177
Skill-Level 3	1,110	957	1,527
Skill-Level 4	56,118	58,273	76,428
Capital Requirements (£000)	41,898	18,788	-1,311
Imports (£000)			
Total	6,184	146	5,560
Consumption or final	6,363	5,842	9,288
Intermediate Capital	-2,588	-7,694	-7,080
Savings (£000)			
Total	-34,749	-29,704	-33,361
Private Indiv.	-35,711	-23,853	-23,357
Business	2,261	1,825	1,987
Government: Total	-1,299	-7,675	-11,991
Direct Taxes	-2,881	-8,129	-11,314
Indirect Taxes	751	89	-964
Operating Surplus	831	365	286

TABLE 6

Effect of Import Substitution Policies

	13	14	15
Gross Output (£000)	47,671	15,656	16,261
Employment (N. of Employees)			
Total	81,271	51,170	75,138
Skill-Level 1	2,172	1,187	1,767
Skill-Level 2	1,106	-1,914	-627
Skill-Level 3	2,439	1,007	2,050
Skill-Level 4	75,168	50,598	71,483
Capital Requirements (£000)	69,298	1,990	12,714
Imports (£000)			
Total	5,172	-13,003	-10,298
Final Goods	0	0	0
Inter. Goods			
Capital Goods	169	-14,584	-14,388
Savings (£000)			
Total	-31,727	-20,170	-22,470
Individual or HH	-35,935	-12,151	-10,793
Business	3,281	1,151	1,486
Government: Total	928	-9,170	-13,163
Direct Taxes	-1,978	-8,982	-12,142
Indirect Taxes	1,291	-190	-1,121
Operating Surplus	1,615	1	100

TABLE 7

QUASI NATIONALIZATION

	16	17	18
Gross Output (f000)	25,596	38,173	15,085
Employment: (N. of Employees):			
Total	46,065	69,930	64,134
Skill-Level 1	1,166	1,799	1,463
2	-310	598	-71
3	1,006	1,817	1,435
4	44,006	65,405	60,979
Capital Requirements (f000)	34,495	52,323	-5,517
Imports (f000):			
Total	3,810	10,043	5,959
Final Goods	3,525	7,094	6,988
Interm. Goods			
Capital Goods	-1,627	-681	-3,815
Savings (f000):			
Total	-17,319	-24,360	-34,768
Personal	-24,355	-38,489	-17,311
Business	0	0	0
Government: Total. From:	7,036	14,129	-17,457
Direct Taxes	-2,897	-2,832	-9,496
Indirect Taxes	685	913	-879
Operating Surplus	9,248	16,045	-7,081

TABLE 8

Effect of Alternative Values of Share
In Sectoral Rental Income
By Top Income Groups

	19	20	21	22	23	24	25	26	27
Gross Output (£000)	31,761	23,993	21,286	31,699	24,008	22,889	17,213	24,712	22,889
Employment (N. of Employees)									
Total	59,121	60,338	80,741	59,099	60,327	82,481	70,960	61,770	82,481
Skill-Level 1	1,464	1,401	1,831	1,463	1,401	1,872	1,613	1,433	1,872
Skill-Level 2	-62	-954	192	-63	-954	232	31	-928	232
Skill-Level 3	1,128	993	1,563	1,127	992	1,579	1,489	1,003	1,579
Skill-Level 4	55,377	58,648	76,805	55,358	58,638	78,446	67,490	60,009	78,446
Capital Requirements (£000)	42,385	19,781	-285	42,215	19,827	3,135	-4,599	20,776	3,135
Imports (£000)									
Total	6,722	1,167	6,506	6,727	1,165	7,637	7,157	1,658	7,637
Final	6,854	6,770	10,142	6,865	6,766	11,056	7,833	15,208	11,056
Intermediate Capital	-2,562	7,643	7,029	-2,567	-7,642	-6,888	-3,707	-7,576	-6,888
Savings (£000)									
Total	-37,123	-34,270	-37,623	-37,159	-34,273	-41,793	-28,745	-35,983	-41,793
Private Indiv.	-38,612	-29,483	-28,650	-38,572	-29,539	-34,092	-19,421	-31,625	-34,092
Business	2,266	1,834	1,996	2,263	1,835	2,097	1,648	1,891	2,097
Government: Total	-778	6,621	-10,969	-850	6,569	-9,798	-10,972	-6,249	-9,798
Direct Taxes	-2,373	7,100	-10,319	2,437	7,050	-9,289	-10,240	6,757	-9,289
Indirect Taxes	753	92	958	747	94	-865	-954	105	-865
Operating Surplus	842	386	308	840	387	356	222	403	356

TABLE 9

THE EFFECT OF USING DIFFERENT CONSUMPTION COEFFICIENTS
FOR URBAN HOUSEHOLDS

	28	29	30
Gross Output (f000)	33,843	30,283	27,264
Employment (N. of Employees)			
Total	60,970	66,941	87,043
Skill-Level 1	1,566	1,667	2,071
Skill-Level 2	91	-392	768
Skill-Level 3	1,182	1,241	1,818
Skill-Level 4	57,927	64,175	82,029
Capital Requirements (f000)	44,648	28,813	8,2661
Imports (f000)			
Total	11,131	10,004	15,120
Final Goods	7,840	9,064	12,501
Inter. Goods			
Capital Goods	432	-2,093	-1,714
Savings (f000)			
Total	-40,057	-42,188	-46,055
Private Indiv.	-42,120	-39,195	-38,735
Business	2,541	2,441	2,530
Government: Total	-478	-5,435	-9,851
Direct Taxes	-2,204	-6,361	-9,598
Indirect Taxes	762	203	-877
Operating Surplus	966	723	624

TABLE 10

Institutional Income Flowing Back as Investment

	g = .5			g = .8			g = .5, $M^{kl} = h_h^k$		
	31	32	33	34	35	36	37	38	.39
Gross Output	29,272	21,418	18,401	29,973	22,103	19,272	28,183	21,272	18,268
Employment									
Total	53,632	54,386	74,185	55,119	55,962	76,263	51,322	54,268	74,087
Skill-Level 1	1,341	1,268	1,683	1,377	1,303	1,729	1,286	1,265	1,681
Skill-Level 2	-202	-1,098	69	-190	-1,103	96	-218	-1,121	48
Skill-Level 3	1,083	956	1,531	1,101	973	1,559	1,055	951	1,526
Skill-Level 4	51,203	53,015	70,555	52,622	54,540	72,528	48,996	52,928	70,485
Capital Requirements	39,242	16,855	-3,477	40,046	17,618	-2,446	37,992	16,517	-3,792
Imports									
Total	4,414	-1,201	3,783	4,594	-1,056	3,987	4,138	2,582	7,284
Final Goods	5,112	4,919	7,975	5,175	4,974	8,043	5,029	4,904	7,952
Interm. Goods									
Capital Goods	-2,920	-7,944	-7,362	-2,852	-7,917	-7,312	-3,006	-4,122	-3,823
Savings									
Total	-30,310	-27,043	-29,153	-30,481	-27,206	-29,352	-30,018	-27,007	-29,120
Private Indiv.	-31,353	-21,882	-19,763	-31,623	-22,131	-20,073	-30,935	-21,803	-19,689
Business	2,061	1,615	1,749	2,118	1,671	1,820	2,000	1,599	1,735
Government:									
Total	-1,018	-6,775	-11,139	-976	-6,746	-11,099	-1,083	-6,804	-11,166
Direct Taxes	-2,532	-7,190	-10,421	-2,512	-7,178	-10,405	-2,564	-7,203	-10,433
Indirect Taxes	734	86	-964	739	89	-959	726	83	-966
Operating Surplus	780	329	246	797	243	265	755	516	233

TABLE 11

PERCENT CHANGE IN GROSS OUTPUT, EMPLOYMENT, IMPORTS AND SAVINGS BY EXP. NO.

Exp. #	Gross Output	Employment	Imports	Savings
1	1.60	5.32	4.37	-17.44
2	1.26	3.76	-6.35	-15.67
3	1.35	2.78	-7.42	-22.77
7	1.65	6.24	3.64	-15.53
8	1.16	6.23	-2.32	-15.65
9	.97	8.53	2.37	-13.61
13	1.57	5.92	2.95	-14.85
14	1.10	5.88	-2.64	-12.61
15	.92	8.13	2.20	-14.48
19	1.83	7.13	5.84	-19.31
20	1.37	7.25	.14	-16.50
21	1.21	9.72	5.25	-18.53
25	2.76	9.84	4.89	-17.63
26	.91	6.19	-12.29	-11.20
27	.94	9.09	-9.73	-12.48

SOURCE: Tables 1-6.

Effect on Demand and Output Composition

Aggregate private demand and subsequently output rise for all the above experiments. But the aggregate is merely a summation of sectoral changes and therefore conceals sectoral differences. The consumption and output of some sectors fall while that of others rise. In general, sectors supplying necessities like food register an increase and conversely for sectors producing "non-necessities".

Composition of Sectoral Demand

For analytical purposes, changes in private demand are broken down into "exogenous" and "endogenous" components. The exogenous portion results from the initial income transfer ($\Delta \bar{C}$ in the model, Chapter 3), and the endogenous portion from the subsequent changes in employment and income started by the income transfer. The purpose of this breakdown is to investigate the strength of secondary changes. Many studies on the effect of redistribution of income (see first-genre models) neglect these secondary changes and this might lie behind the small results obtained.

There are 6 sets of changes in the exogenous consumption corresponding to the six income transfer plans described above (three for monetary sector only and three when non-monetary is included). But there are 54 sets of endogenous consumption changes (as many as there are experiments). The reason why there is a higher number of endogenous than exogenous consumption changes is that the latter, by assumption, is dependent only on the exogenously-introduced income transfers and there are only three such transfer schemes. The endogenous component, on the other hand, depends on complementary policies aimed at changing the structure of the economy (import substitution -- Experiments 13-15; improvements in rural productivity and therefore rural incomes -- Experiments 10-12) or on alternative assumptions about parametric values (the size distribution of rental income -- Experiments 19-27; alternative consumption behavior of urban households -- Experiments 28-30) in addition to the secondary changes resulting from the initial income transfer.

Changes in the two components of private demand as well as the initial level of consumption are shown in Tables 11&12. It should be observed that the endogenous changes are small relative to the exogenous ones. This is probably a reflection of low linkages within the Kenyan economy which in turn might reduce the magnitude of the feedback effects. Since the same consumption coefficients are used, differences in magnitude between the two components merely reflects the difference between the amount of the income transferred and the incomes endogenously-generated therefrom. The latter influences the final pattern of income distribution and will be discussed later under that heading.

The item showing the greatest increase in consumption, under transfer schemes, is "unprocessed food" supplied by the agricultural sector. This is followed by "processed food" produced by the sector labeled "manufacture of food" (see Table VII.20). Items for which consumption has declined include personal and business services, housing, electricity and water, and machinery and equipment. Most other items show a modest increase.

When non-monetary consumption (i.e., part of the income transferred is used to "purchase" own-products -- Experiments 1-3) is included the non-monetary sector displays the greatest rise under transfer scheme III. But the consumption of unprocessed food still predominates under the other four transfer schemes. The magnitude of the changes depends on the amount of income transfer and the composition and sectoral location of the groups receiving (paying) the transfer. Demand for unprocessed food is highest under transfer schemes III (urban-rural transfer) and lowest under I (within-sector transfers). Conversely for housing and merchandising.

The above results are generally in line with accepted consumption behavior obtained by other studies [Cline, Adelman-Robinson, etc., cited in bibliography]. An income transfer that benefits the poor would change the composition of demand in favor of "necessities," especially unprocessed food. This is especially true when the transfer is from urban to rural rather than from the relatively well-off to the poorer members of the same sector.

Because of Kenya's early stage in import substitution a high proportion of consumer items are imported. This would tend to reduce the multiplier effect as some of the changes in final demand leak out to the rest of the world. Even for unprocessed food, 15% of total consumption is on imported items (especially rice and cereals). If the additional demand can be met domestically, sectoral output and thus induced demand would increase.

Changes in Sectoral Output

Changes in sectoral output pretty much follow that of consumption, the extent of the change depending on the size of the relevant multiplier. The changes in sectoral output are shown in Table 13. These changes reflect the direct (income transfer) and indirect (through secondary changes) effects of the initial income transfer. The exogenous change in consumption resulting from the transfer leads to changes in output through the production (Leontief) multiplier. This in turn leads to changes in employment, income, consumption, and secondary changes in output. The final output reflects the combined impact of the production and consumption multipliers.[6]

To show the impact of secondary changes (through endogenous consumption), final output is separated into that resulting from the production multiplier and from that reflecting the combined production-consumption multiplier. The results are shown for several experiments in Table VIII.13.

---

[6]"Consumption" here refers only to the endogenous component. The exogenous portion represents the initial shock to the system (see equation, Chapter 3).

TABLE 12   293

First-Round Changes in Sectoral Demand
Resulting From Income Transfer
(£000)

Income Transfer Plan

Sector/

	Actual 1974 Consumption	1	2	3	4	5	6
1 Non-monetary	87332.7	13704.7	8187.08	20868.2	178.077	115.626	-112.799
2 Agriculture & forestry	111193	34722.1	16232.5	13402.2	17766.4	20603.7	23840.3
3 Mining & quarrying	60.6144	39.3018	17.1313	26.9749	20.2129	24.815	41.9473
4 Manufacture of food	66187.6	14356.1	5491.6	3642.33	6534.27	7146.46	8335.68
5 Manufacture of clothing	52963.7	3950.16	-444.399	1206.73	-280.254	537.664	4312.7
6 Manuf. of furniture & wood	11368.9	646.831	-221.39	-184.991	1.70729	-76.4429	176.349
7 Manuf. of chemical, rubber, petro.	6141.28	1586.52	760.96	889.504	814.722	992.637	1556.6
8 Manuf. of non-metallic products	1456.04	432.593	189.041	-34.0767	271.054	220.675	8.20249
9 Manuf. of metal & machinery	6341.36	394.795	-102.609	-253.95	15.01	-41.7743	-43.2679
10 Electricity and water	12704.4	-974.004	-1927.61	-1936.09	-1055.5	-1895.98	-1893.81
11 Construction	1456.04	432.593	189.041	-34.0767	271.054	220.675	8.20249
12 Trade	12052.2	325.718	-979.087	-1889.13	-150.717	-947.453	-1846.85
13 Transportation & communication	35487.8	-2221.49	-5225.71	-5055.47	-2995.6	-5041.89	-4525.28
14 Business & financial services	14925.5	-353.618	-1802.96	-2258.25	-644.367	-1771.33	-2215.
15 Ownership of dwellings	64055.9	6030.97	-1421.63	-11133.2	3292.63	-1390	-11050.5
16 Personal services	17796.9	-891.077	-2525.08	-1580.77	-1654.91	-2280.53	-874.128

TABLE 13
Secondary Change in Sectoral Demand
(£000)

Sector/Transfer Plan

	4	5	6	1	2	3
1	10.7418	-13.0632	-15.3243	2802.92	5318.29	70410.5
2	2926.35	2147.74	2506.81	2526.58	2366.02	4927.35
3	2.31121	2.51834	2.96806	1.71641	3.65028	7.56603
4	1487.86	775.08	833.519	1349.76	738.568	1724.85
5	990.833	308.099	267.139	921.051	236.142	892.415
6	121.374	-44.2596	-61.5346	142.229	-82.8455	-53.1726
7	162.197	116.015	135.226	140.391	134.679	295.45
8	15.5389	-7.83367	-9.17635	22.0901	-16.8405	-26.0281
9	93.9549	-5.87938	-21.5176	97.8702	-29.0116	-10.4832
10	-24.3648	-357.77	-482.641	78.559	-437.762	-668.743
11	15.5389	-7.83367	-9.17635	22.0901	-16.8405	-26.0281
12	47.0403	-250.327	-357.231	121.338	-342.198	-569.278
13	87.9816	-824.941	-1175.57	305.597	-1019.67	-1525.16
14	-32.3075	-449.244	-592.858	109.333	-554.398	-836.709
15	40.7979	-1733.64	-2365.27	507.996	-2236.52	-3550.5
16	137.902	-267.969	-420.228	194.885	-315.371	-384.494

	7	8	9	10	11	12
1	12.9268	-2.16961	-.0546589	14.3439	-8.9391	-10.5135
2	1879.39	1328.97	1710.39	6034.94	5592.66	6551.86
3	1.23154	1.30253	1.58838	5.22616	5.72969	6.74139
4	972.332	503.487	647.466	3105.05	2571.49	2940.56
5	581.753	134.522	181.098	2301.87	1767.11	1977.83
6	75.9164	-36.9266	-30.9882	294.809	148.246	165.105
7	100.777	68.7089	88.7193	347.757	321.476	376.537
8	15.5496	.616001	3.3247	25.1842	2.95037	3.44463
9	62.5573	-1.303	.283431	206.668	119.803	125.702
10	4.75558	-198.061	-245.979	1.33852	-328.654	-448.564
11	15.5496	.616001	3.3247	25.1842	2.95037	3.44463
12	65.4773	-112.753	-146.1	78.8771	-214.161	-314.963
13	102.74	-442.805	-576.968	317.942	-568.099	-874.438
14	12.8028	-238.517	-290.089	.803858	-411.656	-548.89
15	193.293	-867.176	-1073.5	176.359	-1578.92	-2184.31
16	85.381	-157.965	-217.454	391.487	13.8841	-89.5645

	13	14	15	20	23	26
1	34.3006	-26.9734	-27.2316	9.90947	10.688	20.4204
2	4803.43	1678.68	2220.33	6373.11	6393.64	7007.8
3	3.15579	2.61808	3.16928	5.73336	5.73422	5.85143
4	2661.02	371.598	531,119	3227.46	3233.2	3601.93
5	1914.05	-71.9364	-41.4343	2385.13	2390.34	2599.51
6	301.174	-144.852	-145.35	273.198	281.084	312.552
7	267.477	88.9711	117.204	372.052	374.304	405.035
8	40.8482	-21.5287	-20.6568	21.8065	22.5668	32.5611
9	207.185	-61.6826	-68.6086	201.932	201.885	232.907
10	201.465	-537.283	-651.245	-70.452	-74.8526	-23.5047
11	40.8482	-21.5287	-20.6568	21.8065	22.5668	32.5611
12	275.713	-408.887	-503.676	11.8738	2.70003	84.8152
13	758.043	-1300.78	-1620.76	165.894	138.283	310.215
14	248.767	-672.78	-808.667	-65.8858	-61.5946	5.6963
15	1321.2	-2663	-3236.01	-162.062	-209.527	171.357
16	472.624	-476.203	-611.883	350.419	334.837	408.087

TABLE 14

Changes in Sectoral Output (£000) Resulting from Income Transfer

Δ X₁

Sector	Actual Gross Output 1974 (£ million)	1	2	3	7	8	9
1	190.24	1985.7	8462.97	21572.9	184.404	117.843	-119.497
2	169.99	16120.6	15950.2	12950.4	17642.1	20275.9	23537.6
3	10.51	25.0157	1.61981	-11.8834	33.7333	13.7648	10.4019
4	210.40	5880.77	5072.83	3305.7	6141.45	6645.71	7734.29
5	49.81	306.549	74.3027	1015.97	115.648	562.565	2563.39
6	47.77	156.348	-152.949	-243.263	152.907	10.4617	183.01
7	86.40	694.338	539.073	448.277	765.038	777.328	1076.09
8	20.33	166.706	123.024	19.9754	177.102	110.167	-40.7699
9	93.51	131.156	-50.3501	-162.677	116.663	.560745	-6.67565
10	18.57	-958.319	-1938.08	-2028.76	-918.49	-1836.4	-1802.5
11	130.19	102.474	-370.018	-823.541	141.468	-304.304	-705.63
12	197.84	866.893	-382.062	-1684.08	965.903	6.36681	-700.013
13	147.07	-2290.1	-4888.92	-5282.18	-2220.78	-4498.07	-4224.28
14	62.03	-669.78	-2033.6	-2662.31	-635.2	-1949.9	-2480.93
15	39.05	3305.36	-1446.59	-11129.1	3341.33	-1364.62	-10954.8
16	12.10	-1217.56	-2124.04	-1351.53	-1161.64	-1767.09	-365.62

Δ X₂

Sector	1	2	3	7	8	9
1	2843.12	12117	30887.6	184.437	117.672	-119.795
2	17889	17714	14425.5	20551.6	23613.2	27399.9
3	24.7568	.452612	-13.004	33.5117	12.3517	8.46317
4	6008.56	5185.37	3386.64	6307.35	6824.29	7940.22
5	344.485	139.263	1147.4	158.89	615.98	2646.04
6	165.129	-152.954	-249.2	166.597	17.3929	187.969
7	739.75	575.575	477.199	842.501	856.46	1167.75
8	170.514	138.21	61.4008	177.153	108.253	-43.4525
9	138.153	-41.0786	-135.39	124.69	1.80945	-5.98061
10	-1101.94	-2250.93	-2361.48	-1045.31	-2119.09	-2078.46
11	100.826	-389.641	-855.882	141.911	-320.821	-732.782
12	976.121	-321.761	-1663.04	1128.46	136.256	-578.129
13	-2353.95	-5117.86	-5566.98	-2251.34	-4668.59	-4396.7
14	-681.543	-2101.7	-2765.67	-641.184	-2008.8	-2568.0
15	3590.9	-1563.38	-12057	3637.44	-1464.17	-11852.2
16	-1193.03	-2116.66	-1344.42	-1112.29	-1722.55	-292.676

KEY

$\Delta X_1 = (1-A+M)^{-1}(1-m^c)\Delta\bar{C}$: changes in sectoral output using only production (Leontief) multiplier: equation 10.

$\Delta X_2 = [1-A+M - (1-m^c)CY(1-T) - (1-m^k)ZD]^{-1}(1-m^c)\Delta\bar{C}$: changes in sectoral output when production-consumption multiplier is used.

Table 14 (cont)

Transfer Plan

ΔX_1

Sector/	13	14	15	19	20	21
1	184.404	117.843	-119.497	184.404	117.843	-119.497
2	17642.1	20275.9	23257.6	17642.1	20275.9	23527.6
3	33.7333	13.7648	10.4019	33.7333	13.7648	10.4019
4	6141.45	6645.71	7734.29	6141.45	6645.71	7734.29
5	115.648	562.565	2563.39	115.648	562.565	2563.39
6	152.907	10.4617	183.01	152.907	10.4617	183.01
7	765.038	777.328	1076.09	765.038	777.328	1076.09
8	177.102	110.167	-40.7699	177.102	110.167	-40.7699
9	116.663	.560745	-6.78565	116.663	.560745	-6.78565
10	-918.49	-1836.4	-1802.5	918.49	-1836.4	-1802.5
11	141.468	-304.304	-705.63	141.468	-304.304	-705.63
12	965.903	6.36681	-700.013	965.903	6.36681	-700.013
13	-2220.78	-4498.07	-4224.28	-2220.78	-4498.07	-4224.28
14	-635.2	-1949.9	-2480.93	-635.2	-1949.9	-2480.93
15	3341.33	-1364.62	-1094.8	3341.33	-1364.62	-1094.8
16	-1161.64	-1767.09	-365.62	-1161.64	-1767.09	-365.62

ΔX_2

Sector/	13	14	15	19	20	21
1	184.432	117.766	-119.628	184.537	117.786	-119.66
2	19571.9	22489.3	26096.2	23199.2	26654.2	30928.3
3	33.5978	12.8735	9.20678	33.7902	12.6672	8.83729
4	6259.99	6773.1	7881.62	6388.72	6915.66	8046.53
5	144.472	599.01	2623.65	197.393	660.92	2701.46
6	161.833	15.1548	187.881	178.459	30.8474	203.958
7	816	829.311	1137.17	918.058	943.132	1268.5
8	177.19	109.016	-42.3658	177.942	109.148	-42.4037
9	121.968	1.53849	-5.56044	134.898	13.3921	7.56971
10	-977.6	-1971.99	-1933.64	-1020.85	-2091.1	-2045.75
11	140.952	-316.498	-723.998	146.038	-316.144	-727.204
12	1074.71	91.2315	-618.594	1255.36	281.627	-408.853
13	-2281.02	-4688.2	-4404.81	-2181.07	-4591.04	-4304.51
14	-601.719	-1993	-2540.62	-620.327	-1996.51	-2553.32
15	3485.78	-1410.88	11383.2	3655.18	-1443.89	-11828.5
16	-1132.76	-1742.96	-317.446	-1755.82	-1659.55	-212.525

TABLE 15

Percent Changes in Sectoral Output (ΔX_2) By Experiment No.

Sector	1	2	3	7	8	9	13	14	15	19	20	21
1 Non-Monetary	1.49	6.36	16.24	.10	.06	-.06	.09	.06	-.06			
Monetary:												
2 Agriculture, forestry & fishing	10.52	10.42	8.48	10.27	11.93	13.84	11.51	13.23	15.35	13.65	15.68	18.19
3 Mining and quarrying	0.00	0.00	0.00	0.00	0.00	0.00	0.00	0.00	0.00	0.00	0.00	0.00
4 Manufacture of food	2.85	2.46	1.61	3.00	3.24	3.77	2.97	3.22	3.75	3.04	3.29	3.82
5 Manufacture of clothing	.69	.28	2.30	.32	1.24	5.31	.29	1.20	5.27	.40	1.33	5.42
6 Manufacture of furniture & wood prds.	.35	-.32	-.52	.35	.03	.39	.34	.03	.39	.37	.05	.42
7 Mfc. of chemical, rubber & petrol.	.85	.66	.55	.97	.98	1.34	.94	.95	1.31	1.06	1.09	1.46
8 Mfc. of non-metalic mineral prds.	.84	.68	.30	.87	.53	-.21	.87	.54	-.21	.87	.54	-.21
9 Mfc. of mental & machinery	.15	-.04	-.14	-.13	0.00	-.01	.13	0.00	0.00	.14	0.00	0.00
10 Electricity & water	-5.93	-12.11	-12.71	-5.63	-11.41	-11.19	-5.26	-10.62	-10.41	-5.49	-11.26	-11.02
11 Building & construction	.08	-.30	-.66	-.11	-.25	-.56	.11	-.24	-.56	.11	-.24	-.56
12 Trade, hotels & restaurants	.49	-.16	-.85	.57	.07	-.29	.54	.04	-.31	.63	.14	-.21
13 Transportation & communication	1.60	-3.48	-3.78	-1.53	-3.17	-2.99	-1.55	-3.19	-3.00	-1.48	-3.12	-2.93
14 Business & financial services	-1.10	-3.39	-4.46	-1.03	-3.24	-4.14	-1.03	-3.21	-4.10	-1.02	-3.22	-4.12
15 Ownership of dwellings	9.20	-4.00	-30.87	-9.31	-3.75	-30.35	-8.92	-3.61	-29.15	-9.36	-3.70	-30.29
16 Personal services	-9.86	-17.50	-11.10	-9.19	-14.23	-1.72	-9.36	-14.40	-2.62	-8.73	-13.72	-1.75

SOURCE: Table 13.

Final Pattern of Income Distribution

The initial distribution of income is affected by the direct transfers and the subsequent changes in group-income which result from the changes
in sectoral output. The effect of the transfers depend on the amount
transferred and the recipient (paying) groups. It could affect the distribution between sectors, between groups in the same sector or both.
In Plan I, the transfer is limited to within each sector and so inter-
sectoral distributions are not directly affected. In redistributive Plan
III, the transfer affects the distribution between the urban and rural
sectors with the latter gaining and the former losing. But within-sector
distributions are also altered because of differences in the amount received
(paid by) the various income groups within each sector. Plan II alters
both types of distributions.

The effect of the secondary changes depends on factor ownership and
sectoral location of the various income groups. The changes in sectoral
output resulting from the direct transfer lead to changes in factor use
and thereby personal incomes according to the distribution of factor
ownership across households and the sector in which those factors are
utilized. The effect of the sum of these two changes on the distribution of income is shown in Table 14 for Experiments 4-6 (the basic
run when changes in non-monetary consumption is excluded). Changes in
the total incomes of each bracket for urban, rural and estate sectors
are also calculated for each experiment but the post-redistribution
pattern is not shown. A clear picture of this pattern can be obtained
by comparing the absolute changes of income in these experiments to that
in the basic run. The results of these other experiments are shown in
Tables 15-17.

The final impact depends on the type of redistribution plan and the amount of income transferred. In redistributive Plan I (experiment 7), the transfer is limited to within each sector so that the net loss or gain of each sector is zero. However, there is a net leakage of about 2 million from the urban sector while the rural and estate sectors register a net gain of {8 and {4.5 million respectively. These effects are entirely due to the secondary forces generated by the initial income transfer. Within-sector distribution remains unaffected.

Under Plan II (experiment 5), about {23 million are transferred from the urban to the rural sector. The latter gains an additional 9 through increases in the demand for agricultural products. The estate sector also gains {4 million while urban households lose {5 million. The former gains because it shares in the increases in the demand for agriculture products; the latter loses because the consumption of urban goods falls as a result of the transfer. With the urban and rural sectors as net losers and gainers of income respectively, overall distribution of income becomes more equal. This reinforces the improvement brought about by the exogenous transfer.

The improvement in the distribution of income is most marked under Plan III (experiment 6) where the entire cost of the transfer to the rural poor is born by the urban rich. Rural gains would be even higher if non-monetary consumption is included (see Table 15, experiment 3), so that the leakages to the urban and estate sectors are minimized.

The reason why most of the secondary change in income favors the rural and estate sectors is that most of the increases in demand are for agricultural goods while that for sectors like electricity and water,

commerce, transportation and communication, and business and personal
services declines (see Tables 11 & 12). The latter are located in the
urban sector. Thus the urban loses and the rural and estate sectors
(producers of agricultural goods) gain as a result of redistribution.

Most of the secondary gains accrue to the rural sector because
rural households, who gain most by the transfer, consume more rural- than
estate-produced items.

Redistribution of factor income in favor of labor (experiments
13-15) leaves total income as well as its distribution in the urban and
estate sectors unaffected. Rural income is, however, substantially reduced (see Table 16, experiments 7-9; and Table 15, experiments 4-6),
while the relative distribution is slightly improved. This is because
lower groups supplement their farm incomes by performing various rural
jobs and thus there is a higher proportion of them in wage employment,
as compared to higher income groups. Increased labor share favors these
groups. But the income of all groups fall and so poverty in the rural
area is worsened by factoral redistribution. (Overall relative distribution
of income is thus worsened.) This implies that there is little relationship between the functional and personal distribution of income in the
urban and estate sectors and that while such a relationship exists in
the rural sector, it is in the direction opposite to that usually envisioned.
It is usually argued that increasing labor share at the expense of non-
wage share improves the size distribution of income. This argument is
based on the assumption that wage incomes are more evenly distributed
than non-wage incomes. In most LDCs, including Kenya, however, the
majority of poorest segments of the population -- rural and informal-urban

households -- are self-employed and so are the recipients of non-wage income. Many are even outside the wage economy, so redistribution in favor of wages would hurt the poor and so worsen rather than improve the size distribution of income.

Increases in rural incomes, by 50%, through increases in rural productivity, raises the income of the rural and estate sectors through the secondary changes generated therefrom (see experiments 10-12, Table 16). The increase is highest under experiment 21 (transfer plan II). The income of the urban sector is hardly affected suggesting that the consumption of urban goods by rural households is extremely low.

The relative distribution remains unaffected. A policy of asset redistribution, coupled with increased productivity of the rural sector, would most help the poor of the poorest.

A policy of import substitution[*] (experiments 13-15, Table 16) increases the absolute incomes of all sectors but the increases are greatest in the urban sector because the marginal propensity to import is highest in this sector. Also, a high proportion of foodstuffs are imported and so the food-producing sectors (estate and rural) would also gain if the additional demand can be met domestically. The relative distribution of income within each sector remains unaffected.

Changes in parametric values (experiments 22-27, Table 17) leave the absolute sectoral income as well as the distribution within and between sectors relatively unchanged. This implies that whatever the validity of the assumptions made in estimating these parameters, their

---

[*]It is assumed that the increases in consumption can be met domestically. The objective of this experiment is to investigate the magnitude of the leakage, through import, and so the extent of the reduction in the results obtained.

values, within the specified range, make little difference for the results. An even wider implication is that these results could be applicable to other countries in the same stage of development insofar as the parametric values reflect the general characteristics of the economy. It should be noted, however, that the values of these parameters depend on the assumptions about the size distribution of rental income.

In conclusion, Policy Packages involving both transfers and other policies aimed at changing the structure of the economy would have a greater, and possibly longer, impact than mere transfers of income. The latter is important but its impact is limited to the duration of its application. Once the transfer is terminated so does its impact. But even during the period when it is in force, the impact is much weaker than policies that directly raise the income of the target groups, possibly through increased productivity, rather than transferring it from another. The greatest improvement in the relative distribution of income and the highest increases in the absolute incomes of the poorest segment of the population occurs under experiments 10-12, i.e., when rural productivity is raised.

Another major conclusion is that redistribution of factoral income does not improve the relative distribution of income nor does it improve the absolute income of the poor. In fact, a "trickle-up" toward formal sector wage earners and from the self-employed farmers and informal-urban households occurs. Wage employees in the formal sector are in the upper income brackets while those self-employed in rural and informal-urban activities are at the bottom of the distribution "pyramid." Redistribution in favor of the former would obviously worsen the size distribution of income. However, the top 1% or so of the population (7.3% of urban sector--Table 14, Chapter 5--which in turn is only 13% of the total population) are recipients of property or rental income and redistribution in favor of labor would obviously hurt these groups. The loss, however, would be mitigated since these same groups receive a high proportion of wage income (see Table, Chapter 5). But they would lose some income nevertheless. Their loss is the gain of wage earners, especially in the formal sector and size distribution of income would tend to improve in this sector. But this sector is very small compared to the whole economy (15% of total employment), and redistribution within this sector does not affect the bulk of the population. When the urban sector as a whole is considered, there is loss to the informal sector and thus little or no improvement in the size distribution of income within the urban sector.

TABLE 16

Size Distribution of Income Before and After
Transfers (Including Effects) in £000 (4)

SECTOR	Predistribution Pattern			Experiment 4			Experiment 5			Experiment 6			Final Group Incomes							
Income Groups	Group Income	% Inc.	% Income	Transfer	Sec. Changes	Total Income	Transfer	Sec. Changes	Total Income	Transfer	Sec. Changes	Total Income	Exp. 4	Exp. 5	Exp. 6	4	5	6		
1	£3,147	£3.1	.94	£10,431	£-15	£10,417	£10,000	£-76	£9,943	£0	£0	£-4	£13,564	£13,090	£3,143	4.07%	4.95%	1.3		
2	5,40	9.5	1.68	11,799	-21	11,778	11,000	-102	10,898	0	0	-3	17,421	16,541	5,640	5.22	6.25	2.5		
3	5,57	7.7	1.45	5,817	-22	5,795	6,000	-64	5,936	0	0	-40	10,592	10,833	4,957	3.29	4.13	2.1		
4	5,557	25.0	8.76	5,700	-38	5,662	6,000	-303	5,692	0	0	-214	34,419	34,449	28,543	9.72	13.02	12.5		
5	41,997	2.9	12.30	0	-71	-71	0	-361	-361	0	0	-276	41,226	40,936	41,021	12.36	15.43	18.1		
6	28,595	8.9	3.52	0	-118	-118	0	-382	-382	0	0	-334	28,477	28,234	23,261	3.54	10.57	12.3		
7	24,206	5.9	7.21	0	-275	-275	0	-684	-584	0	0	-651	23,931	23,522	23,555	7.17	8.83	10.		
8	31,180	5.4	8.29	0	65	66	-7,000	-772	-7,772	-7,030	-1,365	-8,365	31,247	24,181	22,816	9.37	9.14	10.		
9	5,925	2.8	6.83	-5,300	-523	-5,823	-8,000	-800	-8,800	-9,030	-300	-8,700	14,102	13,928	14,225	4.23	5.26	6.3		
10	32,053	2.2	11.63	-10,440	758	-9,682	-16,000	-980	-16,849	-16,000	-1,906	-17,905	29,374	23,056	21,150	3.31	3.72	9.		
11		2.1	18.08	-18,027	625	-17,382	-25,000	-1,405	-26,405	-25,000	-3,205	-28,205	43,228	35,710	32,593	12.39	13.59	14.		
	333,536			0			-23,030	-4,781	-27,781	57,000			331,556	264,507	225,716					
1	£1,020	49.9%	11.2%	£28,660	£112	£28,872	£28,600	£194	£28,794	£32,000	£240	£32,240	£60,853	£60,822	£64,266	20.42%	18.60%	18.08%		
2		13.8	8.9	-	479	479	0	515	515	25,000	1,114	26,114	25,134	33,140	51,733	8.84	10.14	14.55		
3	43,170	11.7	10.5	0	661	661	0	717	717	0	847	847	30,763	30,819	30,949	10.42	9.43	8.70		
4		13.6	16.8	0	1,483	1,483	0	1,650	1,650	0	1,917	1,917	49,683	49,850	50,117	15.83	15.25	14.13		
5		3.0	14.3	-8,024	1,157	-6,867	0	1,276	1,276	0	1,521	1,521	34,197	42,340	42,365	11.59	12.95	11.05		
		12.0	33.4	-20,640	-4,233	-16,417	-5,000	4,721	-279	0	5,512	5,512	93,347	103,995	115,773	31.79	33.64	32.57		
				0			23,600	9,067	32,673	57,000	11,151	68,151	295,177	326,954	353,432					
1	9,949	£41.3	£19.56	£6,030	£1,114	£7,144	£6,000	£1,270	£7,270	£0	£1,474	£1,474	£15,993	£16,119	£13,323	31.60%	32.90%	23.33%		
2		36.1	16.72	1,530	1,149	2,578	1,500	1,319	2,819	0	1,531	1,531	10,243	13,384	9,096	20.24	21.14	13.44		
3		7.4	5.15	0	298	298	0	342	342	0	397	397	2,630	2,674	2,729	5.20	5.64	5.53		
4		2.3	3.81	0	510	510	0	596	596	0	680	680	4,494	4,664	3,304	9.88	9.52	2.70		
5		1.2	3.70	0	298	298	0	342	342	0	397	397	4,020	4,052	4,119	7.94	8.29	8.35		
6		.5	2.61	0	170	170	0	195	195	0	227	227	2,337	2,362	2,332	4.62	4.82	4.85		
7	1,9.4	.6	4.31	0	85	85	-500	98	-402	0	113	113	1,264	772	1,292	2.50	1.57	2.62		
8		.37	6.00	0	170	170	-1,200	195	-1,005	0	227	227	2,174	953	2,191	4.72	1.46	4.44		
9	2,312	.41	9.71	-1,500	128	-1,372	-1,800	147	-1,653	0	170	170	1,341	1,609	2,433	1.46	3.26	5.9		
10	6,356	.3	14.07	-2,539	213	-2,355	-2,600	246	-2,356	0	283	283	3,037	2,035	4,675	5.03	4.16	9.43		
11				-3,500	255	-3,245	-3,500	293	-3,207	0	340	340	3,121	6,706	2,322	5.17	13.59	4.85		
				0			-2,100	5,031	2,931	0	5,839	5,839	50,614	48,994	47,715					

NOTES: (1) Tables 6 & 12, Ch. 5, (2) Table 2, Ch. 5, (3) Table 17, Ch. 5, (4) Rest: Tables 1, 15, Ch. 8.

Table 16 (cont)

	7	8	9	10	11	12	13	14	15
Urban									
1	10415.1	9940.93	-5.47764	10421.4	9947.7	2.55675	10474.8	9911.37	-33.685
2	11774.8	10894.8	-6.39159	11787	10907.8	8.99414	11890.3	10839.7	-58.172
3	5793.84	5935.66	-40.5744	5797.23	5939.15	-36.6531	5834.53	5889.69	-76.7465
4	5657.98	5693.55	-211.526	5679.4	5711.97	-190.209	6024.31	5471.72	-274.082
5	-75.6261	-361.915	-276.185	-53.8663	-341.623	-253.257	229.724	-629.917	-473.64
6	-122.618	-383.738	-335.178	-105.404	-367.298	-316.996	72.1603	-656.067	-595.037
7	-279.713	-635.835	-651.283	-260.053	-667.713	-631.943	-81.5619	-1139.95	-1121.65
8	-53.5402	-7624.37	-7915.75	88.0349	-7696.77	-8335.31	470.696	-8285.35	-8903.36
9	-7000.22	-12112.3	-13359.2	-8715.59	-16068	-17810.2	-6562.87	-17897.1	-19912.3
10	-9906.13	-16650.6	-17137.2	-9643.37	-16835.9	-17853.5	-8923.47	-17578.8	-18527.5
11	-17768.7	-26032.5	-26920	-17314.1	-26328	-28114.5	-16083	-27551.1	-29236
Rural									
1	20067.5	20072.8	7481.56	20168.3	20181.3	7598.82	20104.5	20086.8	7498.06
2	8774.06	8696.06	24740.1	8973.66	8874.13	24957.9	8883.56	8683.8	24733
3	281.674	293.687	23.864	1084.23	1174.82	26896.5	661.733	527.524	26148.1
4	336.119	351.011	431.838	1495.09	1632.3	1924.42	906.65	742.334	901.546
5	741.528	810.563	959.705	3344.47	3734.82	4340.26	1985.71	1749.75	2078.07
6	7447.52	614.391	759.083	5400.24	2907.43	3453.5	-6457.5	1333.24	1624.96
7	-18267.4	-2801.88	2627.03	-11099.6	5679.75	12481.9	-14991.9	-3.67053	5964.87
Estate									
1	7091.09	7209.78	1404.06	7286.24	7433.84	1664.05	7476.39	7377.13	1619.6
2	2623.6	2756.31	1458.07	2826.25	2988.99	1728.05	3023.72	2930.09	1681.89
3	283.525	325.711	378.017	336.065	386.034	448.013	387.26	370.765	436.046
4	486.044	558.361	648.03	576.1 12	661.773	768.022	663.874	635.598	747.507
5	283.525	325.711	378.012	336.065	386.034	448.013	387.26	370.765	436.046
6	162.015	186.12	216.01	192.037	220.591	256.007	221.291	211.866	249.169
7	81.0073	-406.94	108.005	96.0186	-389.705	128.004	110.646	-394.067	124.585
8	162.015	-1013.88	216.01	192.038	-979.408	256.007	221.293	-988.134	249.168
9	-1378.49	-1660.41	162.007	-1355.97	-1634.56	192.004	-1334.03	-1641.1	186.876
10	-2365.48	-2367.35	270.01	-2327.95	-2324.26	320.005	-2291.38	-2335.16	311.457
11	-3256.97	-3220.82	324.012	-3221.93	-3169.11	384.005	-3168.05	-3182.2	323.746

Table 16 (cont)

	19	20	21	22	23	24
Urban						
1	9948.12	1148.14	1154.78	9964.07	9885.85	9941.69
2	10908.6	10908.6	10929	10941.5	10786.9	10896.5
3	5939.52	5939.52	5943.68	5984.51	5916.91	5936.64
4	5727.33	5727.17	5572.72	6053.94	5521.4	5709.42
5	-441.527	-448.08	-375.888	-110.117	-827.99	-471.386
6	-442.333	-381.796	-381.969	-82.1455	-656.8	-399.657
7	-799.382	-577.545	-754.398	-146.175	-878.418	-600.078
8	-7711.06	-7604.91	-7653.02	-7228.08	-7878.56	-7631.2
9	-8489.95	-8406.33	-8428.36	-8141.84	-8604.76	-8425.25
10	-16670.7	-16869	-16586.7	-16360.7	-17706.8	-16916.2
11	-26122.1	-26470.7	-25980.2	-25512.9	-27932	-26565.4
Rural						
1	20181.4	20181.4	20181.6	20178.1	20005.1	20084.4
2	8874.97	8875.03	8883.28	8924.37	8534.98	8720.07
3	1175.71	1175.89	1200.58	1240.19	-24.4085	537.978
4	1633.42	1633.67	1667.25	1709.35	-18.2605	749.052
5	3736.54	3737.08	3810.5	3853.81	41.8413	1721.24
6	2909.08	2909.49	2969.46	2057.78	-17.111	1333.93
7	5684.51	5686.01	5897.75	6062.48	-4896.68	-81.8756
Estate						
1	7434.21	7434.39	7961.92	7975.02	6084.88	7324.72
2	2989.37	2989.56	3535.37	3550.99	1588.14	2875.68
3	386.133	386.181	528.208	531.737	22.8521	356.657
4	661.942	662.025	905.5	911.55	39.175	611.411
5	386.133	386.101	528.208	531.737	22.8521	356.657
6	220.647	220.675	301.833	303.85	13.0583	203.804
7	-389.676	-389.663	-349.083	-343.075	-493.471	-398.098
8	-979.352	-979.324	-898.167	-896.15	-1186.94	-996.195
9	-1634.51	-1634.49	-1573.63	-1572.11	-1790.21	-1647.15
10	-2324.19	-2324.15	-2222.71	-2220.19	-2583.67	-2345.24
11	-3169.02	-3168.98	-3047.25	-3044.23	-3480.41	-3194.29

CONCLUSIONS

The effect on output, factor requirements, imports, and savings as well as the final pattern of income distribution of alternative income transfer schemes were investigated. The sensitivity of the results to alternative assumption about parametric values was also investigated. The transfer schemes were subsequently coupled with other redistributive policies, like directly increasing rural productivity and import substitution, and the same process repeated.

In general, it has been observed that:

1. Policies involving transfers have small secondary effects compared to other policies. Most of the changes in the variables that have been estimated result from the transfer itself and very little from secondary changes started by the transfer.

2. The distribution of income improves as a result of the transfers but subsequent changes sometimes work in the opposite direction.

3. The impact of the transfers might be limited to the duration of its application. So, unless the transfers are permanently maintained, their initial impact would dissipate.

4. As an implication of #3 above, only policies that change the structure of the economy would have lasting impact.

5. There is little connection between personal (or size) and functional (or factoral) distribution of income and whatever connection there is in a direction opposite to that envisioned by many economists. Redistribution of income in favor of labor actually worsens the personal distribution of income.

6. Functional redistribution would have a greater impact on the size distribution within particular ranges than on its overall distribution. The size distribution would improve within the upper income strata because most of the recipients of property or rental income in the formal sector are concentrated in the highest 1% or so of the population.

7. Income transfer coupled with other policies like increased productivity of the rural sector leads to the most marked results as compared to single policies (transfers only). Such policies might also have an effect that lasts beyond the period of their application.

8. Changes in parametric values (e.g., the share of each income in sectoral rental income) leave the results unchanged. The importance of this conclusion lies in the fact that some of the parameters were estimated using alternative assumptions because of data unavailability. This does not imply that changes in parameter values are relatively inconsequential, only that the assumptions made were such that similar distributions resulted.

9. Aggregate savings fall and capital requirements rise for all experiments. This would tend to imply that economic growth would fall as a result of income redistribution and so support the existence of a tradeoff between equality and economic growth. But these results should be interpreted cautiously. First, while the total amount of capital required rises, the capital

output ratio falls as demand shifts in favor of relatively labor-intensive products. Second, the estimates on capital-output ratios are very tentative. The values used were estimated by James Tobin from official statistics. The latter mostly concentrate on the formal sector, and any sectoral ICORs thus derived would tend to be upwardly biased. These estimates were used only because they were the best of the available ones. Third, it has been assumed that the additional income that accrues to rural households is spent on purchased products. Thus, the non-monetary sector is excluded. If the contrary assumption is taken, i.e., that part of the transferred income is used to purchase own-products (consumed more and sell less of the items produced), then capital requirements would be appreciably lower. In fact, it would be negative under transfer plan 3 (see Table 15).

10. The decline in aggregate savings indicates that the MPS of the rich is higher than that of the poor. Investible funds would therefore fall, implying the existence of growth-equity tradeoff. However, while the direction of the fall in aggregate savings might be correct, the magnitude is not. Savings, according to this study, are composed of personal, government, and business savings. Personal and government savings register a substantial decline while that of business rises a little. Most of the decline in the government component results from the fall in direct tax revenues as income is transferred from upper to lower tax brackets. This, however, is based on the assumption that

current public expenditures remain unchanged, and that all the
reductions in tax revenues translate themselves into reductions
in public savings (or investment). It is possible that as government revenues fall some current expenditures would be cut back or
the deficit corrected in other ways, e.g., foreign aid. So public
savings need not fall by the amount indicated in the tables.

Business savings is defined as retained earnings which is
composed of depreciation allowance and undistributed profits.
It has been assumed that both are constant functions of sectoral
output. While this might be true for depreciation, there is no
reason to believe that retained earnings would depend on sectoral
output. It is possible that as capital requirements increase and
other sources of funds become limited, businesses would plough
back more of their profits, thus increasing its component of
savings. Aggregate savings would, therefore, probably not fall
by as much, if at all, as indicated by Tables 3-13.

Many of these conclusions conform to the findings of others [see
Adelman-Robinson (6), for example] and thus contain no new revelations.
But the study is nevertheless important in that it augments the pool of
empirical evidence relating distribution and growth.

CHAPTER 9

SUMMARY AND CONCLUSIONS

The main purpose of this study has been to investigate the potential effects of various income redistribution policies on selected growth-related variables. The policies chosen were three transfer schemes used by themselves and in conjunction with other policies like redistribution of factoral income, import substitution, and increased rural productivity. The selected variables affected by these policies were: output (total and sectoral), demand composition, employment (broken down into four skill-categories), capital requirements, imports (final, intermediate, and capital), savings (personal, business, and government), and the final pattern of size distribution of income. As a result of about forty simulation experiments it has been found that:

1. Total employment increases under all experiments but there is a slight decline for skill-level 2 (technical and clerical). The increases in employment are directly related to the magnitude of the transfer and the amount of net gain by the rural sector.

2. Capital requirements rise for all experiments (except one) but by less than the increase in output. Therefore, overall

capital-output ratios decline as consumption moves in favor of relatively labor-intensive products. Total capital requirements fall when non-monetary consumption by rural households is considered and the transfer is from urban to rural (Exp. 3). This would imply excess capacity.

3. Aggregate savings decline under all experiments. The greatest declines are in personal and government savings while that by business registers a small increase. The increase in the latter results from the assumption that retained earnings are positively related to sectoral profits which in turn is directly related to output. The decline in personal savings is due to the different saving propensities by the higher and lower income groups. The decline in government is a result of declines in income tax revenues as income is transferred from households in higher tax brackets.

4. Total imports rise under most experiments. When broken down into components, imports of final and intermediate goods rise while that of capital goods decline. The greatest increase is in final goods. This is partly due to the fact that a large amount of foodstuffs are imported.

5. The consumption of foodstuffs increases substantially for all experiments. Foodstuffs are broken down into two broad categories: "unprocessed" food produced by the agricultural sector, and "processed" food which is produced by the sector labeled "manufacture of food and food preparations." The increase in the consumption of the former is much higher than that of the latter.

6. Aggregate output rises but the output of half of the sixteen major sectors considered decline. The declining sectors include transportation and communication, business and financial services, personal services, construction, and housing. The sectors that register the greatest increase are agriculture and the manufacture of food.

7. Aggregate and sectoral output are higher when the consumption and production multipliers are combined than when only the latter (a la Leontief) is included (see cf $\Delta X_1, \Delta X_2$, Table 13, Chp. 8). The consumption-production multiplier considers not only the relationship between sectors through the input-output table, but also the effect of increases in personal consumption as sectoral output and thus employment and income rise.

8. The final pattern of income distribution indicates an increase in the income of lower groups and a decline for the upper groups. The impact on personal income is the sum of the transfer and the subsequent endogenous changes started by the initial transfer. In general, the secondary changes are relatively very small probably indicating the weak internal linkages of the Kenyan economy. An implication of the weak secondary effects is that the effect of the transfers might not last much beyond the duration of the policy unless complemented by other policies that affect the structure of the economy. Moreover, the secondary changes sometimes work in a direction opposite to that of the transfer leading to a "trickle-up".

9. Among the complimentary (to the transfer that is) redistributive policies considered, the least "effective" (i.e., having the

least impact) in changing the size distribution of income was factoral
redistribution and the most effective was raising rural productivity
with import substitution falling in between.

These results are generally in accord with other studies [Chinn
(21), Cline (22), Paukert-Skolka-Maton (79), for example] and
reveal no new startling evidence. This despite the fact that the model
used in this study is much more disaggregated and contains more interactions than most of those previous models (see first-genre models).
For example, the integration of the consumption, production,
and distribution matrices for the urban, rural, and estate sector and
the inclusion of the extended (consumption-production) multipliers
which these first-genre models do not consider, makes little difference
for the results obtained. Later models developed mostly under the
auspices of the World Bank [Adelman-Robinson (6), Sengupta-
Thorbecke (84)] and the ILO [Pyatt-Thorbecke (86), for example]
allow for such interactions but the results are not very much different.
This may imply that some of these interactions are weak or that some
of the linkages are unimportant. Whether this is due to dualism and
the low level of linkages within many LDC economies or due to some
other factors cannot be ascertained. Further research on more developed economies could provide a clue.

Although no new evidence was unearthed by this study, several
important accomplishments were made:

1. The pool of empirical evidence on income redistribution
has been augmented. Previous studies were mostly on Asian or Latin
American countries and this is the first one on an African country.

Insofar as the results depend on parametric values which in turn depend on the underlying socioeconomic structure, an increase in the number of countries covered would be valuable.

2. Although the model was developed to investigate the effect of income redistribution it is flexible enough to be used for other purposes. It is highly disaggregated and policy changes in any one sector of the economy can be traced throughout the economy. As such, it could be used as part of a multi-sector planning model.

3. A wealth of data has been constructed on income distribution in the urban, rural, and estate sectors (Chapter 5), the sectoral location and source of income for each income group (Chapter 6), and the consumption characteristics of each group and the production relationship within and between sectors (Chapter 7). These data have been constructed by piecing together information from various sources and with the help of simplifying assumptions. Some of these assumptions are arbitrary, though by no means unrealistic. However, the data subsequently derived are cross-checked with other data sets where available, e.g., national accounts.

4. A method for mapping sectoral to personal income has been formulated so that changes in sectoral output and income can be distributed across households. As personal income changes, the consumption and subsequently the output of different goods changes. Thus the production, income-formation, and consumption matrices are integrated. This in turn increases the size of the multiplier. Sectoral output changes by a multiple not only of the changes in exogenous (transfer-induced) consumption (via inter-industry relations)

but also through endogenous changes in consumption resulting from the income generation process. Thus the size of the multiplier is enlarged. The extent to which the enlarged (consumption-production) multiplier is greater than the simple production (or Leontief-type) multiplier will partly depend on the leakages of consumption expenditures through imports and the extent of internal linkages.

The "mapping" method was formulated by estimating the share in sectoral wage and non-wage income of the various groups in the urban, rural, and estate sectors. Assuming that mobility across sectors is limited during the period of analysis, each group maintains its relative share of income within the relevant sector.

5. In formulating the "mapping" method, the composition and characteristics of the various income groups, sectoral location and main sources of income, and linkages with other groups have been discussed. This would help suggest some "appropriate" redistributive policies or at least exclude them from being considered. For example, it has been observed that most of the poor are self-employed on small farms or in the informal-urban sector and thus do not receive wage incomes. Redistribution of factoral income in favor of wages would therefore be of little help to the poorest segments of the population. On the other hand, policies aimed at raising rural productivity, possibly through redirection of government investment to small-scale agriculture, the extension of credit facilities to poor farmers and the creation of extension services would help alleviate poverty.

In spite of these positive effects of the study, both the model and the data are deficient in several respects. The shortcomings of the model and its formulation include the following:

1. It is short-run and does not consider such factors as migration, skill-upgrading, household asset accumulation, and capacity expansion. Nor are the effects of redistribution on such qualitative factors as entrepreneurial incentives, worker motivation, or possible flight of capital considered.

2. It is limited to a single time period (1974) and all values are in 1974 prices. Thus these values would have to be inflated or deflated to obtain the corresponding values of another period.

3. It is assumed that excess capacity exists and that increases in demand lead to increased output in the same year. If there is no excess capacity, then adjustment may occur through price increases.

4. Changes in capital requirements and savings in the current year affect output only in next time periods. Thus the effect of declines in aggregate savings on capacity creation is not considered.

5. Only the effect of redistribution on selected growth-related variables is investigated. The effect on growth itself is not estimated.

6. Many of parameter values estimated reflect the existing socioeconomic structure and so might not be applicable to another country or even to Kenya in the future.

In spite of these shortcomings, the model is based on generally-accepted theory. It would have been preferable to validate it by testing it with actual values. The latter however is not available.

The data used are also deficient in several respects:

1. The data obtained from different sources are inconsistent and sometimes outright contradictory and whatever data exist are riddled with gaps which have to be carefully filled. In filling these gaps or piecing together information from the various sources, several key assumptions were made among which are:

    a. the number of secondary workers in urban and estate households.

    b. the distribution of non-wage income across households.

    c. that each group maintains its relative share in sectoral non-wage income as output changes.

    d. that factors are immobile across sectors during the period of analysis.

    e. That households maintain their pre-redistribution consumption patterns, i.e., that redistribution in itself does not alter expenditure patterns.

An attempt was made to justify these assumptions but nevertheless an element of arbitrariness remains. The major limitation of the study is therefore data. The values of many parameters depend on the assumptions made in estimating them and in the absence of independent information there is no way of checking the reliability of the estimates obtained. However, when various parametric values were used (in the distribution of non-wage income and urban consumption patterns, for example), results did not change by much. This would imply that even though some elements of error may be introduced by these assumptions, the data so compiled could still be trusted. The fact that the results obtained conform to those by others further strengthens this belief. Nevertheless, it should be emphasized that the conclusions will remain tentative and their acceptance, especially for policy purposes, would have to wait for improvements in the data base.

Among the data that need to be collected are (not exhaustive):

a. The number of secondary workers by income group.

b. The distribution of asset ownership across households.

c. The portion of formal sector operating surplus that accrues to individuals.

d. A more detailed survey of the informal-urban sector.

e. The expenditure patterns of urban and estate households.

f. The characteristics and income of the landless and pastoralists. Very little information is available on these groups and they may be the ones to whom any policy aimed at alleviating poverty should be directed.

g. The distribution of government expenditure, including hidden subsidies, by sector and income group.

h. Sectoral ICORs.

Once such data become available, many development and distributional issues can be analyzed more in detail and the results could form the basis for policy formulation. A better data base could also contribute to improvements in model-building. The latter is influenced by the available data and data collection in turn is affected by its intended end-use. Since interest in distributional issues is of relative recency the stock of distribution data is very limited.

The model developed in this study can also be improved by relaxing the time frame, extending it to a multi-period model and introducing some more changes. This could be done by allowing for:

1. Household asset accumulation through personal savings.

2. Capacity-creation resulting from changes in aggregate savings and capital requirements.

3. Changes in household composition of sectors as migration takes place.

4. Relaxing the fixed coefficient assumption and allowing for substitution between factor inputs.

5. As a corollary of (4), allowing for price changes.

6. Changing the first impact of income redistribution. In this model, the initial impact of the income transfer is on consumption. For other policies, however, it could be anywhere in the model. For example, the first impact of asset redistribution would be on the distribution of factor income across households with consumption affected only indirectly.

7. Allowing for changes in other components of demand like government expenditures, investment, and exports.

These and other improvements in models such as this one would go a long way in rendering them more realistic and thus the basis for policy decisions. However, the issue of achieving greater equality would be decided on the political rather than economic plane whether by concern or concession. The adoption of any policy and the feasibility of its implementation would depend on the relative strengths of the affected groups and the commitment of the government, and especially the implementing agencies, to its success. But unless some measures are taken to alleviate some of the acute features of poverty in the proximity of oasis of affluence, the chances of "gradualist" policies (i.e. redistribution of income without changing the socioeconomic structure) would become even more difficult. As the plight of the poor worsens, and their perception of it sharpens they are bound to become more politicized and realize that their relative position is not ordained, but is the result of the existing social structure. Gradual-ist policies such as those proposed might then be too late.

STATISTICAL APPENDICES

TABLE 1

GROSS NATIONAL PRODUCT, 1954, 1958-1973

Kf million

	1964	1968	1969	1970	1971	1972	1973
FACTOR INCOMES							
A. Outside the Monetary Economy	89.00	109.07	114.74	119.63	125.95	142.20	148.96
B. Monetary Economy							
1. Remuneration of Employees							
Enterprises	86.15	123.04	129.70	141.36	152.62	175.45	198.60
Private households	2.94	3.56	3.87	4.14	4.84	5.12	6.15
General Government	42.47	63.83	71.01	76.48	94.49	105.34	114.24
Total Remuneration of Employees	131.56	190.45	204.58	221.98	251.95	285.91	318.99
2. Rental Surplus (including depreciation)	13.34	15.86	18.42	21.57	24.61	28.12	31.16
3. Other Operating Surplus (including depreciation)	96.20	127.52	138.58	155.76	167.55	192.31	225.75
Total Monetary Economy	241.10	333.83	361.59	399.31	444.11	506.32	575.89
TOTAL FACTOR INCOMES--GROSS DOMESTIC PRODUCT	330.10	442.90	476.33	518.94	570.06	648.52	724.85
Add: Indirect Taxes	26.91	43.06	46.62	54.88	66.12	64.60	92.28
Deduct: Subsidies	0.35	2.64	2.10	1.16	1.04	1.30	2.26
GROSS DOMESTIC PRODUCT AT MARKET PRICES	356.66	483.32	520.85	572.66	635.14	711.82	814.87
Add: Factor Incomes Received from Abroad	4.95	8.43	12.43	16.87	12.34	12.92	10.22
Deduct: Factor Incomes Paid Abroad	15.54	31.09	30.84	37.85	31.43	34.60	54.20
GROSS NATIONAL PRODUCT	346.08	460.66	502.43	551.67	616.05	693.14	770.89

SOURCE: Central Bureau of Statistics, Statistical Abstract, 1976, p. 47.

TABLE 1 (Cont'd.)

Kf million

	1972	1973	1974	1975*
FACTOR INCOMES				
A. Outside Monetary Economy	146.57	156.48	175.69	220.86
B. Monetary Economy				
1. Remuneration of Employees				
Enterprises	187.91	208.92	251.40	273.38
Private Households	5.12	6.15	7.27	8.86
General Government	107.18	113.57	136.00	153.61
Total Remuneration of Employees	300.21	328.54	394.67	440.85
2. Rental Surplus (including depreciation)	27.22	30.23	35.39	46.01
3. Other Operating Surplus (including depreciation)	188.07	228.41	295.05	319.08
Total Monetary Economy	515.50	587.28	725.11	805.94
TOTAL FACTOR INCOMES--GROSS DOMESTIC PRODUCT	662.07	743.76	900.80	1026.80
Add: Indirect Taxes	65.06	91.11	123.66	138.64
Deduct: Subsidies	1.30	2.26	1.83	0.89
GROSS DOMESTIC PRODUCT AT MARKET PRICES	725.83	832.61	1022.63	1164.55
Add: Factor Incomes Received from Abroad	12.92	10.22	15.23	14.07
Deduct: Factor Incomes Paid Abroad	34.61	54.20	58.76	57.05
GROSS NATIONAL PRODUCT	704.14	788.53	979.10	1121.57

* Provisional.

SOURCE: Central Bureau of Statistics, Statistical Abstract, 1976, p. 47.

TABLE 2

GROSS DOMESTIC PRODUCT BY INDUSTRIAL ORIGIN,
1972-1975
At Current Prices

	Kfmillion			
	1972	1973	1974	1975
GROSS PRODUCT AT FACTOR COST				
A. Outside Monetary Economy				
Agriculture	110.75	115.49	131.30	173.41
Forestry	4.91	5.28	5.56	5.91
Fishing	0.15	0.16	0.18	0.21
Building and Construction	11.65	13.65	14.69	15.59
Water	5.00	5.16	5.28	5.51
Ownership of Dwellings	14.11	16.74	18.68	20.23
Total Product Outside Monetary				
Economy	146.57	156.48	175.69	220.86
B. Monetary Economy				
1. Enterprises and non-profit				
Institutions:				
Agriculture	94.36	107.43	123.08	128.90
Forestry	3.55	4.27	5.42	5.72
Fishing	1.26	1.34	1.45	1.69
Mining and Quarrying	2.23	3.20	3.14	3.47
Manufacturing	77.94	94.60	119.07	134.01
Electricity and Water	8.93	9.34	10.43	12.24
Building and Construction	35.73	38.70	43.39	43.50
Wholesale, Retail Trade,				
Restaurants and Hotels	66.26	80.48	115.88	120.34
Transport, Storage and				
Communications	39.61	46.13	55.65	60.59
Finance, Insurance, Real				
Estate, & Business Services	31.42	34.54	46.80	55.03
Ownership of Dwellings	27.22	30.23	35.39	46.01
Other Services	14.69	17.30	22.14	24.97
Total	403.20	467.56	581.84	638.47
2. Private Households (Domestic				
Services)	5.12	6.15	7.27	8.86
3. Producers of Government Services:				
Public Administration	29.32	29.68	34.24	--
Defense	5.36	5.67	7.43	--
Education	39.24	43.64	55.00	--
Health	11.68	12.04	13.93	--
Agricultural Services	8.47	8.76	9.73	--
Other Services	13.11	13.78	15.67	--
Total	107.18	113.57	136.00	158.61
TOTAL PRODUCT MONETARY ECONOMY	515.50	587.28	725.11	805.94
TOTAL GROSS PRODUCT AT FACTOR COST				
(Monetary and Non-Monetary)	662.07	743.76	900.80	1026.80
GROSS DOMESTIC PRODUCT PER CAPITA Kf	54.87	59.58	69.76	76.63

SOURCE: Statistical Abstract, p. 44.

TABLE 3

IMPORTS AS A PROPORTION OF SECTORAL
GROSS OUTPUT, 1974

Sector *	M^i	M^c	M^k	D
1	0	0	0	0
2	.066	.146	.049	.121
3	.087	0	0	.476
4	.095	.144	0	.237
5	.360	.555	0	.168
6	.343	.472	.248	.109
7	.554	.609	0	.220
8	.166	.437	1.000	.241
9	.441	.565	.843	.199
10	.100	.012	0	.178
11	.145	0	.006	.069
12	.064	.037	.002	.157
13	.154	.252	.910	.218
14	.071	.000	0	.239
15	0	.010	0	.187
16	.077	.055	0	.111

KEY: M^i = intermediate imports

M^c = consumer imports

M^k = imports of capital goods

SOURCE: I-O Tables from Kenya, 1977.

*See Table VIII.

TABLE 4

EMPLOYMENT AND EARNINGS IN KENYA
MODERN SECTOR 1969-1974

Employ 000's
Earnings K£ 000's

	1969		1972		1974	
Agriculture, forestry & fishing	195.0	14,400	247.0	26,746	261.0	30,483
Mining & quarrying	2.6	833	3.2	928	3.9	1,411
Manufacturing	72.7	24,950	85.0	32,302	101.0	44,259
Electricity & water	5.2	8,227	5.1	2,253	5.7	2,788
Construction	28.9	2,258	37.6	12,447	44.4	15,539
Wholesale & retail trade Rest. & hotels	44.2	21,851	47.6	22,306	57.0	28,782
Transportation &* communication	51.8	22,111	45.3	21,393	46.3	27,677
Finance, Insurance, real estate**, and bus. services	--	--	17.5	15,287	21.9	19,112
Community, social & personal ser.	226.8	58,964	231.8	73,192	284.6	104,253
Total	627.2	153,593	719.8	206,854	826.3	274,305

SOURCE: Statistical Abstract, 1975, Tables 220 and 223.
Statistical Abstract, 1972, Tables 222 and 230.

* Has been declined to 44.4 in 1973.

** After 1971 this item is included in services.

TABLE 5

HIGH AND MIDDLE LEVEL MANPOWER BY MAJOR OCCUPATIONAL GROUPS AND BY ECONOMIC ACTIVITY

Major Occupational Group	Activity*								Number
	Agriculture, Forestry, Hunting and Fishing	Mining and Quarrying	Manufacturing and Repair	Building and Construction	Electricity and Water	Commerce	Transport and Communications	Services	Total
Managerial	4,750	96	2,893	346	3	5,602	680	1,333	15,708
Professional	378	41	651	395	100	706	193	3,283	5,747
Semi-professional or technical	1,091	19	1,643	439	520	1,795	1,270	24,533	31,310
Skilled office and clerical	602	20	3,136	352	421	7,097	4,512	9,515	25,625
Skilled manual	713	122	11,743	3,323	243	2,270	1,196	1,821	21,431
TOTAL	7,534	298	20,041	4,855	1,287	17,470	7,851	40,485	99,821

SOURCE: Manpower Survey 1972 Central Bureau of Statistics.

* Based on the old United Nations' 3-digit International Standard Industrial Classification.

SOURCE: Statistical Abstracts, 1976, p. 281.

TABLE 5 (Cont'd.)

ESTIMATES OF EMPLOYMENT BY SECTOR, 1969 AND 1971

(thousand)

Sector	1969				1971			
	Formal Wage Employment	INFORMAL EMPLOYMENT		Total	Formal Wage Employment	INFORMAL EMPLOYMENT		Total
		Rural	Urban			Rural	Urban	
Agriculture, forestry, and fishing	196	4,168	-	4,364	211	4,436	-	4,647
Mining and quarrying	3	1	-	4	3	1	-	4
Manufacturing	75	30	15	120	93	32	16	141
Building and construction	29	1	11	41	35	1	12	48
Electricity and water	5	-	-	5	5	-	-	5
Transport, storage, and communication	48	3	1	52	46	3	1	50
Wholesale and retail trade	44	96	30	170	47	102	32	181
Services	227	19	39	285	240	20	41	301
Total	627	4,318	95	5,041	680	4,595	102	5,377

SOURCE: Mission estimates. IBRB, Kenya: Into the Second Trends, p. 146.

TABLE 6

SIZE DISTRIBUTION OF ESTABLISHMENT:
NUMBER OF ESTABLISHMENTS BY SIZE AND EMPLOYMENT, 1975

Industry	0	1-49	50+	Total
1. Agriculture, forestry & fishing	756	1,859	765	3,380
2. Mining and quarrying	113	44	18	175
3. Manufacturing:				
3.1 Food, bev. & tobacco	287	183	106	576
3.2 Textile, Apparel & leather products	685	218	65	968
3.3 Wood products & furniture	585	348	92	1,025
3.4 Chemical, petroleum, rubber & plastic	67		49	207
3.5 Non-metalic mineral products	41	91	21	86
3.6 Basic metal, machinery; equip., and other mfc.	392	364	102	858
Sub-total	2,063	1,277	425	3,765
4. Electricity & water	6	25	14	45
5. Construction	1,023	385	118	1,526
6. Trade, restaurants & hotels	11,828	4,623	186	16,837
7. Transport & communications	750	575	115	1,440
8. Financial & bus. services	1,500	956	104	2,560
9. Community, social & personal services:				
9.1 Public Adm., defense & soc. ser.*	749	1,356	229	2,334
9.2 Personal & household services**	2,623	692	50	3,365
Sub-total	3,366	2,055	279	5,700
Total	21,405	12,450	2,024	35,879

* includes religious & professional organizations.

** includes activities not adequately defined.

SOURCE: Statistical Abstracts, 1975, Table 78(a).

TABLE 7

DISTRIBUTION OF ESTABLISHMENTS:
NUMBER OF EMPLOYEES BY SIZE OF ESTABLISHMENTS, 1975

Industry*	1-49	50+	Total
1	31,767	177,628	209,395
2	626	2,917	3,543
3	17,188	82,982	100,170
3.1	2,363	22,063	24,426
3.2	2,735	17,069	19,804
3.3	4,907	13,586	18,493
3.4	1,134	5,423	6,557
3.5	465	3,876	4,341
3.6	5,285	21,265	26,550
4	112	4,161	4,473
5	5,110	25,260	30,370
6	30,580	23,110	53,690
7	7,287	37,724	44,011
8	8,948	14,879	23,827
9	19,449	133,266	152,715
9.1	13,567	125,832	139,399
9.2	5,882	7,434	13,316
Total	120,267	501,927	622,194

SOURCE: Statistical Abstracts, 1975, Table 73(b).

TABLE 8

Distribution of Wage Employment by Industry and Income Groups*1972-1974

1974

Number

	Sh. Under 100	Sh. 100-149	Sh. 150-199	Sh. 200-399	Sh. 400-599	Sh. 600-799	Sh. 800-999	Sh. 1,000-1,499	Sh. 1,500-1,999	Sh. 2,000-2,999	3,000 and Over	Total
Agriculture, and Forestry												
Agriculture and hunting	35,921	82,422	19,580	18,543	6,639	2,749	1,282	1,403	866	953	750	171,108
Forestry and logging	1,221	8,820	518	1,479	490	323	71	75	79	67	11	13,154
Fishing	1	12	6	7	2	2	-	-	-	1	2	33
Total	37,143	91,254	20,104	20,029	7,131	3,074	1,353	1,478	945	1,021	763	184,295
Mining and Quarrying												
Crude petroleum and natural gas	-	-	-	1	-	-	-	4	1	-	-	6
Metal Ore mining	6	14	71	163	81	17	4	10	4	6	32	408
Other mining	5	127	132	914	420	194	95	137	47	51	82	2,204
Total	11	141	203	1,078	501	211	99	151	52	57	114	2,618
Manufacturing												
Manufacturing of food, beverage and tobacco	184	1,249	1,636	5,295	3,939	2,421	1,376	1,614	661	603	661	19,639
Textiles, wearing apparel and leather industries	51	194	1,399	12,316	2,435	551	195	327	194	216	284	18,162
Manufacture of wood and wood products including furniture	135	1,049	1,759	3,311	863	266	108	199	86	97	151	8,024
Manufacture of paper and paper products printing and publishing	3	42	28	1,188	1,736	826	502	692	461	326	395	6,199
Manufacture of chemicals, petroleum, rubber and plastic products	6	24	112	1,777	1,982	672	378	501	330	386	621	6,789
Manufacture of non-metallic mineral products except products or petroleum	108	83	59	1,032	850	339	101	115	55	107	182	3,031
Basic metal industries	-	-	-	318	364	92	33	39	28	25	39	938
Manufacture of fabricated metal products, machinery and equipment	4	13	262	10,565	5,549	2,405	1,533	1,244	731	679	751	23,736
Other manufacturing industries	61	171	191	456	225	64	47	57	40	30	37	1,379
Total	522	2,825	5,446	36,258	17,943	7,636	4,273	4,788	2,586	2,469	3,121	87,897
Electricity and Water												
Electric light and power	14	2	1	324	1,139	425	345	456	182	244	196	3,328
Water works and supply	-	-	4	21	5	1	-	-	1	-	3	35
Total	14	2	5	345	1,144	426	345	456	133	244	199	3,363
Construction												
Special trade contractors	2	15	63	1,126	951	486	233	227	93	110	174	3,530
General trade contractors	259	254	1,793	11,094	6,107	2,240	1,323	1,420	760	643	685	26,578
Total	261	269	1,856	12,220	7,053	2,726	1,606	1,647	853	753	859	30,180
Trade, Restaurants and Hotels												
Joint wholesale and retail trade	2	11	42	1,458	1,564	1,145	753	875	512	602	839	7,803
Wholesale trade	184	346	466	4,177	2,787	1,330	918	1,305	805	1,015	1,307	14,640
Retail trade	366	587	1,047	6,103	1,695	913	392	547	274	369	378	12,691
Restaurants and hotels	622	759	1,682	9,312	2,418	1,197	410	448	222	191	292	17,553
Total	1,174	1,703	3,237	21,050	8,464	4,585	2,473	3,175	1,813	2,177	2,815	52,667
Transport and Communication												
Transport and storage	77	99	3,410	8,951	7,073	5,690	8,396	3,681	1,688	1,360	1,184	41,609
Communications	-	-	-	659	65	512	290	484	142	107	55	2,906
Total	77	99	3,410	9,610	7,730	6,202	8,686	4,165	1,830	1,467	1,239	44,515
Finance, Insurance, etc.												
Financial institutions	19	6	11	310	993	427	1,801	1,752	760	663	803	7,550
Insurance	-	3	13	195	233	283	311	437	228	219	278	2,200
Real estate and business service	16	121	415	4,955	1,279	539	408	669	510	763	1,372	11,057
Total	35	130	439	5,470	2,510	1,249	2,520	2,858	1,498	1,645	2,453	20,807
Community, Social and Personal Services												
Public administration and defense	3,334	838	2,065	22,006	29,697	7,172	2,887	4,106	3,415	2,365	943	78,828
Social and related community services	2,510	1,376	2,149	36,685	36,626	24,776	13,593	12,178	5,356	2,383	1,243	138,873
Recreation and cultural services	33	78	210	1,918	573	205	78	132	90	93	154	3,564
Personal and household services	1,915	3,903	27,594	13,020	2,448	1,553	792	955	441	401	321	53,343
International and other extra-territorial bodies	2	-	-	80	100	52	24	78	84	99	71	590
Activities not adequately defined	8	13	23	23	4	2	2	-	4	3	1	83
Total	7,802	6,208	32,041	73,730	69,448	33,760	17,376	17,449	9,390	5,344	2,733	275,281
TOTAL	47,069	102,631	66,741	179,790	121,929	59,869	38,731	36,167	19,150	15,177	14,297	701,551

SOURCE: Statistical Abstract, 1976, p. 298.

TABLE 9

Distribution of Wage Employment by Major Towns** and Income Groups 1972-1975

(c) 1974

Number

	Under 100	100-149	150-199	200-399	400-599	600-799	800-999	1,000-1,499	1,500-1,999	2,000-2,999	3,000 and Over	Total
	Sh.	Sh.	Sh.	Sh.	Sh.	Sh.	Sh.	Sh.	Sh.	Sh.	Sh.	
Nairobi	3,003	3,984	24,876	58,585	38,526	18,851	12,373	15,621	10,217	9,781	10,315	206,132
Central Province												
Thika	43	81	222	5,099	1,374	344	234	319	153	119	128	8,115
Nyeri	90	193	378	1,450	991	302	664	262	149	86	49	4,614
Murang'a	53	56	166	336	560	105	67	59	39	26	9	1,476
Nyahururu	40	75	163	605	332	139	293	102	45	58	12	1,864
Total	226	405	929	7,490	3,257	890	1,258	742	386	289	198	16,070
Coast Province												
Malindi	30	167	182	882	462	123	54	60	28	22	17	2,027
Mombasa	243	302	6,017	20,459	12,040	7,485	5,124	4,905	2,136	1,672	1,493	61,876
Voi	12	17	65	162	156	33	100	31	16	9	1	602
Total	285	486	6,264	21,503	12,658	7,641	5,278	4,996	2,180	1,703	1,511	64,505
Eastern Province												
Embu	55	70	124	501	299	130	54	82	45	36	15	1,411
Machakos	64	54	182	606	236	78	311	147	47	26	21	1,772
Athi River	4	22	16	201	729	66	259	216	43	78	46	1,680
Meru	67	139	195	782	791	296	684	142	97	37	19	3,249
Total	190	285	517	2,090	2,055	570	1,308	587	232	177	101	8,112
Nyanza Province												
Kisii	82	62	177	793	530	225	128	140	60	31	20	2,248
Kisumu	129	229	573	4,634	1,799	756	1,472	688	404	308	193	11,185
Total	211	291	750	5,427	2,329	981	1,600	826	464	339	213	13,433
Rift Valley Province												
Kericho	42	171	374	781	269	105	300	135	42	31	25	2,275
Nanyuki	20	99	211	832	282	121	159	77	41	25	22	1,889
Nakuru	148	338	1,042	5,735	1,971	958	661	749	365	283	281	12,531
Naivasha	58	187	249	705	590	120	61	49	34	27	15	2,101
Kitale	92	143	186	1,150	581	239	341	139	64	57	50	3,042
Eldoret	63	212	613	3,197	960	386	729	354	172	139	105	6,930
Total	423	1,150	2,675	12,400	4,659	1,929	2,251	1,503	718	562	498	28,768
Western Province												
Kakamega	162	105	273	709	422	176	95	132	58	39	20	2,191
Total	4,500	6,706	36,284	108,204	63,906	31,038	24,163	24,409	14,255	12,890	12,856	339,211

* Excluding casual employees, unpaid family workers and unpaid directors.

** Towns with 1,000 or more persons engaged since 1972.

SOURCE: Statistical Abstracts, 1976.

TABLE 9 (cont)

(d) 1975

Number

	Under 100 Sh.	100-149 Sh.	150-199 Sh.	200-399 Sh.	400-599 Sh.	600-799 Sh.	800-999 Sh.	1,000-1,499 Sh.	1,500-1,999 Sh.	2,000-2,999 Sh.	3,000 and Over Sh.	Total
Nairobi	2,514	17,517	15,858	37,182	35,935	19,502	15,996	20,382	11,623	12,086	12,906	201,501
Central Province												
Thika	37	159	96	5,470	1,723	492	348	463	175	128	195	9,286
Nyeri	45	1,065	136	1,548	774	231	296	343	202	126	71	4,837
Murang'a	19	182	66	559	257	77	85	78	34	41	12	1,410
Nyahururu	44	520	59	343	122	81	124	121	68	57	31	1,570
Total	145	1,926	357	7,920	2,876	881	853	1,005	479	352	309	17,103
Coast Province												
Malindi	18	446	30	1,732	350	114	106	93	42	33	19	2,983
Mombasa	748	3,267	9,751	14,579	11,389	6,875	4,894	6,231	3,529	2,099	1,095	65,267
Voi	2	161	32	170	87	26	33	29	22	9	1	572
Total	768	3,874	9,813	16,481	11,826	7,015	5,033	6,353	3,593	2,141	1,925	68,822
Eastern Province												
Embu	48	380	72	355	162	113	93	120	74	51	28	1,496
Machakos	8	133	52	771	375	135	89	133	78	46	31	1,851
Athi River	5	125	9	156	774	205	122	148	89	101	39	1,773
Meru	99	1,036	68	478	530	250	242	269	108	81	31	3,192
Total	160	1,674	201	1,760	1,841	703	546	670	349	279	129	8,312
Nyanza Province												
Kisii	89	627	148	806	191	151	195	206	95	62	38	2,608
Kisumu	91	1,168	917	5,102	2,124	780	661	845	448	425	256	12,817
Total	180	1,795	1,065	5,908	2,315	931	856	1,051	543	487	294	15,425
Rift Valley Province												
Kericho	42	179	198	1,031	461	134	92	123	61	55	23	2,399
Nanyuki	9	129	53	408	209	121	71	77	30	31	27	1,165
Nakuru	65	651	610	4,560	2,527	1,007	837	983	504	369	386	12,499
Naivasha	30	564	95	1,370	197	68	76	73	29	39	19	2,560
Kitale	32	363	65	1,840	567	234	185	199	79	90	54	3,708
Eldoret	33	399	131	3,734	1,084	504	375	458	236	153	162	7,269
Total	211	2,285	1,152	12,943	5,045	2,068	1,636	1,913	939	737	671	29,600
Western Province												
Kakamega	83	659	64	534	150	103	169	168	126	74	29	2,159
Total	4,061	29,730	28,510	82,728	59,988	31,203	25,089	31,542	17,652	16,156	16,263	342,922

* Excluding casual employees, unpaid family workers and unpaid directors.

** Towns with 1,000 or more persons engaged since 1972.

SOURCE: Statistical Abstracts, 1976.

TABLE 10

SELF EMPLOYED AND FAMILY WORKERS BY SEX
AND AGE IN SMALL NON-AGRICULTURAL RURAL
ENTERPRISES 1969 (000's)

Category of Workers	Men	Women	Juniors	Total
Self-employed	63	4	1	68
Family Workers	9	15	14	38
Total	72	19	15	106

SOURCE: ILO, p. 37

WAGE EMPLOYMENT AND ANNUAL EARNINGS BY
SMALL NON-AGRICULTURAL RURAL ENTERPRISES, 1969

	Employed 000's	Av. Earnings £	Total Earnings/Yr. £000
Regular	48	64	3,200
Casual	34	50	1,500
	82		4,700

SOURCE: ILO, p. 39, Table 6.

Wage Employment by Industry and Major Towns* 1972-1975

(c) 1974

	Agriculture and Forestry	Mining and Quarrying	Manufacturing	Electricity and Water	Construction	Whole-sale and Retail Trade, Restaurants and Hotels	Transport and Communications	Finance Insurance, Real Estate and Business Services	Community Social and Personal Services	Total
Nairobi	6,933	1,230	44,598	2,420	24,916	27,604	18,612	15,381	85,265	226,959
Central Province										
Thika	9	--	6,073	121	476	488	95	513	1,550	9,325
Murang'a	17	--	144	149	2	706	70	53	694	1,835
Nyahururu	186	--	397	6	37	221	268	44	937	2,096
Nyeri	210	--	321	116	678	875	676	182	2,352	5,410
Total	422	--	6,935	392	1,193	2,290	1,109	792	5,533	18,666
Coast Province										
Malindi	60	--	56	23	95	633	136	89	1,174	2,266
Mombasa	950	575	14,813	1,490	4,687	8,559	16,913	2,470	16,691	69,148
Voi	26	--	28	--	--	179	131	13	264	641
Total	1,036	575	14,897	1,513	4,782	9,371	19,180	2,572	18,129	72,055
Eastern Province										
Embu	39	19	34	11	59	511	32	49	824	1,578
Machakos	--	--	108	--	4	398	477	85	759	1,831
Athi River	35	14	1,452	--	--	40	23	12	165	1,741
Meru	590	--	121	14	31	392	575	104	1,752	3,579
Total	664	33	1,715	25	94	1,341	1,107	250	3,500	8,729
Nyanza Province										
Kisii	208	--	50	23	52	470	43	168	1,349	2,363
Kisumu	109	98	2,390	133	526	1,712	2,684	668	3,614	11,934
Total	317	98	2,440	156	578	2,182	2,727	836	4,963	14,297
Rift Valley Province										
Kericho	15	21	339	25	222	372	292	135	986	2,407
Nanyuki	17	77	79	11	259	655	180	53	812	2,143
Nakuru	58	5	3,741	147	2,320	2,211	843	384	4,048	13,757
Naivasha	15	--	509	9	18	416	52	27	1,312	2,358
Kitale	25	--	244	27	333	711	428	129	1,458	3,355
Eldoret	203	--	2,527	43	342	921	986	307	2,309	7,438
Total	333	103	7,439	262	3,294	5,286	2,781	1,035	10,925	31,658
Western Province										
Kakamega	51	--	245	4	188	273	25	72	1,442	2,300
Total	51	--	245	4	188	273	25	72	1,442	2,300
Total	9,756	2,039	78,269	4,772	35,045	48,347	45,541	29,938	129,757	374,464

* Towns with 1,000 or more persons engaged since 1972.

SOURCE: Statistical Abstracts, 1976, p. 274.

TABLE 12

PERCENTAGE DISTRIBUTION OF HOLDINGS BY HOUSEHOLD GROUP AND HOLDING SIZE GROUP

	Below 0.5 hectares	0.5-0.9 hectares	1.0-1.9 hectares	2.0-2.9 hectares	3.0-3.9 hectares	4.0-4.9 hectares	5.0-7.9 hectares	8.0 hectares & over	Percent Total
Less than 0. K shs.	6.71	4.40	6.64	8.68	7.32	4.47	12.06	2.59	6.67
0000-999 K shs.	20.87	15.48	10.89	10.37	11.48	0.86	3.03	9.73	11.80
1,000-1,999 K shs.	18.50	30.19	25.87	21.45	14.07	23.20	10.99	16.52	22.44
2,000-2,999 K shs.	15.39	12.53	12.35	12.62	19.92	14.31	9.95	17.34	13.82
3,000-3,999 K shs.	13.27	9.46	12.87	16.36	8.42	12.19	6.05	6.44	11.73
4,000-5,999 K shs.	10.93	15.07	13.46	13.94	12.02	8.64	23.95	8.71	13.52
6,000-7,999 K shs.	6.10	2.91	7.04	5.05	14.17	16.95	15.13	12.96	7.95
8,000 K. Shs. & over	7.08	9.95	10.89	11.52	12.60	19.38	13.85	25.63	12.08
Total	100.00	100.00	100.00	100.00	100.00	100.00	100.00	100.00	100.00
Number of holdings	206,366	265,816	400,371	224,072	131,916	107,031	96,386	51,464	1,483,422

SOURCE: IRS, p. 53.

TABLE 13

HOUSEHOLD INCOME DISTRIBUTION BY ECONOMIC GROUP AND INCOME SIZE, 1968-70

Economic Group	Annual Income (f)	Number of households (thousands)
Owners of medium-sized to large non-agricultural enterprises in the formal sector of commerce, industry and services; rentiers; big farmers; self-employed professional people; holders of high-level jobs in the formal sector.	1000 and over	30
Intermediate-level employees in the formal sector; owners of medium-sized non-agricultural enterprises in the formal sector; less prosperous big farmers.	600-1000	50
Semi-skilled employees in the formal sector; prosperous smallholders; better-off owners of non-agricultural rural enterprises; a small proportion of owners of enterprises in the formal sector.	200-600	220
Unskilled employees in the formal non-agricultural sector; significant proportion of smallholders; most of the owners of non-agricultural rural enterprises.	120-200	240
Employees in formal-sector agriculture; a small proportion of unskilled employees in the formal sector; better-off wage earners and self-employed persons in the informal urban sector; a small proportion of owners of non-agricultural rural enterprises.	60-120	330
Workers employed on small holdings and in rural non-agricultural enterprises; a significant proportion of employed and self-employed persons in the informal urban sector; sizeable number of smallholders.	20-60	1,140
Smallholders; pastoralists in semi-arid and arid zones; unemployed and landless persons in both rural and urban areas.	20 and less	330
Total		2,340

SOURCE: ILO, pp. 74.

TABLE 14

URBAN HOUSEHOLD INCOME DISTRIBUTION BEFORE AND AFTER TAX, 1968-69

Income Bracket (sh. per month before tax)	Households Absolute number (thousands)	Percentages	Share of Total Urban Household Income (percentages) Before Tax	After Tax
0-199	15.3	8.5	1.1	1.1
200-299	31.9	16.6	4.8	4.8
300-399	25.5	13.3	5.2	5.3
400-499	17.4	9.1	4.6	4.6
500-699	26.0	13.5	9.2	9.3
700-999	19.0	9.9	9.6	9.5
1,000-1,399	18.9	9.9	13.4	14.3
1,400-1,999	17.8	9.3	17.9	17.8
2,000 and over	19.1	9.9	34.1	33.3
Total	191.8	100	100	100

SOURCE: ILO, p. 75.

BIBLIOGRAPHY

1. Abramovitz, M. "Resource and output trends in the U.S. since 1870." AER, May 1956, pp. 5-23.

2. Abramovitz, M. and David. "Reinterpreting economic growth: Parables and realities." AER, 1973, pp. 428-439.

3. Adelman, I. "Development economies: A reassessment of goals." AER, 1975, pp. 302-309.

4. Adelman, I. and C. Morris. Economic growth and social equity in developing countries. Stanford, California: Stanford University Press, 1973.

5. Adelman, I. and S. Robinson. "Poverty, inequality and structural change." Paper presented at a conference on income distribution and economic development sponsored by Centre de Estudios Sobre Desarrollo Economico, Bogota, Columbia, June 1977.

6. Adelman, I. and S. Robinson. Income distribution policy in developing countries: A case study of Korea. New York: Oxford University Press, 1978.

7. Ahluwalia, M. "Inequality, poverty and development." Journal of Development Economics, December 1976, pp. 307-342.

8. Ahluwalia, M. "Income distribution and development: Some stylized facts." AER, May 1976, pp. 128-136.

9. Almon, C. Matrix methods in economics. Massachusetts: Addison-Wesley Publishing Co., 1974.

10. Almon, C., et al. Interindustry forecasts of the American economy. Lexington, Mass.: Lexington Books, 1974.

11. Arrow, K., H. Chenery, B. Minhas, and Solow. "Capital-labor substitution and economic efficiency." Review of Economics and Statistics, August 1961, pp. 225-250.

12. Atkins, A. "On the measurement of inequality." Journal of Economic Theory, 2, 1970.

13. Balassa, B. "Growth strategies in semi-industrial countries." Quarterly Journal of Economics, pp. 24-47.

14. Baran, P. The political economy of growth. New York, Monthly Review, 1957.

15. Baranson, J. Industrial technologies for developing countries. New York: Praeger, 1969.

16. Bardhan, P. Planning models and income distribution with special reference to India. Mimeo, New Delhi, Indian Statistical Institute, 1973.

17. Best, M. "Uneven development and dependent market economies." AER, May 1976, pp. 136-142.

18. Cairucross, A. and M. Puri (eds.). Employment, income distribution, and development strategy. New York: Holmes and Meier, 1976.

19. Chenery, H. and M. Bruno. "Development alternatives in an open economy: The case of Israel." Economic Journal, March 1962, pp. 79-103.

20. Chenery, H., et al. Redistribution with growth: An approach to policy. London: Oxford University Press, 1974.

21. Chinn, D. "Distributional equality and economic growth: The case of Taiwan." Economic Development and Cultural Change, October 1977, pp. 65-79.

22. Cline, W. Potential effects of income redistribution on economic growth: Latin American case. New York: Praeger, 1972.

23. Cline, W. "Income distribution and development: A survey." Journal of Development Economics, February 1975.

24. Denison, E. Sources of growth in the U.S. and the alternatives before U.S. New York: Committee for Economic Development, 1962.

25. Eckaus, R. "The factor proportions problem in LDCs." AER, September 1955, pp. 539-565.

26. Fei, J. and G. Ranis. Development of labor surplus economy: Theory and practice. Homewood, Illinois: Richard D. Irwin, 1964.

27. Fei, J. and G. Ranis. "Technological transfer, employment and development." In Economic development and planning. Essays in honor of Jan Tinbergen (North-Holland, Amsterdam), 1975, pp. 75-102.

28. Fishlow, A. "Brazilian size distribution of income." AER, May 1972, pp. 391-402.

29. Foxley, A. Income distribution in Latin America. Cambridge University Press, 1976.

30. Frank, A.G. Capitalism and underdevelopment in Latin America. New York: Monthly Review Press, 1967.

31. Friend, I. and I. Kravis. "Entrepreneurial income, savings and investment." AER, June 1957, pp. 269-301.

32. Furtado, C. "Development and stagnation in Latin America: A structuralist approach." Studies in Comparative International Development, 1965, pp. 59-175.

33. Galenson and H. Leibenstein. "Investment criteria, productivity and economic development." QJE, August 1955, pp. 343-370.

34. Gupta, S. "Income distribution, employment and growth: A case study of Indonesia." World Bank Staff Working Paper No. 212, August 1975.

35. Hendrick, John. Economic accounts and their uses. New York: McGraw-Hill, 1972.

36. Hodd, M. "Income distribution in Kenya (1963-1972)." Journal of Development Studies, April 1976, pp. 221-228.

37. Hopkins, M., G. Rodgers, and R. Wery. "A structural overview of Bachue-Philippines." ILO, World Employment Program, Working Paper No. 20, May 1975.

38. Houthaaker, H. "An international comparison of personal savings." Bulletin de L'institut International de Statistique, XXXVIII, 1961, pp. 55-69.

39. International Labor Office. Toward full employment: A program for Columbia, Geneva, 1970.

40. International Labor Office. Employment, incomes and equalities: A strategy for increasing productive employment in Kenya, Geneva, 1972.

40a. Jain, Shail. The size distribution of Income in selected countries, World Bank, 1972.

41. Johnson, H. Economic policies toward less developed countries. Washington, DC: Brookings Institutions, 1967.

42. Johnson, L. "Problems of import substitution: The Chilean automobile industry." EDCC, January 1967.

43. Kaldor, N. "Alternative theories of distribution." RES, May 1956, pp. 83-100.

44. Kelly, A., et al. Dualistic economic development. Chicago: University of Chicago Press, 1972.

45. Kenya, Government of. Census of distribution. Ministry of Finance and Planning, Central Bureau of Statistics, 1973.

46. Kenya, Government of. Census of the population. Ministry of Finance and Planning, Central Bureau of Statistics, 1970.

47. Kenya, Government of. Census of manufacturing. Ministry of Finance and Planning, Central Bureau of Statistics, 1973.

48. Kenya, Government of. Consumer price indices for Nairobi. Ministry of Finance, Central Bureau of Statistics, 1977.

49. Kenya, Government of. Demographic baseline survey report (collaborated with Pop Labs at UNC-CH), Ministry of Finance and Planning, Central Bureau of Statistics, 1973.

50. Kenya, Government of. Development plan for the period 1970-1974. Ministry of Finance and Planning, Central Bureau of Statistics.

51. Kenya, Government of. Economic survey, annual. Ministry of Finance and Planning, Central Bureau of Statistics.

52. Kenya, Government of. Employment and earnings in the modern sector Ministry of Finance and Planning, Central Bureau of Statistics, 1974.

53. Kenya, Government of. Input-output tables. Ministry of Finance and Planning, Central Bureau of Statistics, 1976.

54. Kenya, Government of. Integrated rural survey. Ministry of Finance and Planning, Central Bureau of Statistics, 1977.

55. Kenya, Government of. Social perspectives, quarterly. Ministry of Finance and Planning, Central Bureau of Statistics.

56. Kenya, Government of. Statistical abstract, annual. Ministry of Finance and Planning, Central Bureau of Statistics.

57. Kenya, Government of. Survey of the high and middle level manpower. Ministry of Finance and Planning, Central Bureau of Statistics, 1972.

58. Kenya, Government of. The pattern of income, expenditures and consumption of African middle-class income earners in Nairobi, 1964.

59. Krueger, A. "Exchange control, liberalization and development: Turkey." Mimeo, University of Minnesota, Minneapolis, 1972.

60. Kuznets, S. "Economic growth and income inequality." AER, 1955, pp. 1-28.

61. Kuznets, S. "Quantitative aspects of the economic growth of nations: Distribution of income by size." Economic Development and Cultural Change, 1963.

62. Kuznets, S. "Demographic aspects of the size distribution of income: An explanatory essay." EDCC, October 1976, pp. 1-94.

63. Leontief, W. Input-output economics. New York: Oxford University Press, 1966.

64. Lewis, W.A. Economic development with unlimited supplies of labor. Manchester School, 1954.

65. Lewis, W.A. The theory of economic growth. London: Allen & Unwin, 1955.

66. Lubell, H. "Effects of redistribution of income on consumers' expenditures." Readings in Macroeconomics, edited by M.G. Muller. New York: Holt, Rinehart and Winston, 1966, pp. 49-60.

67. Meier, G. Leading issues in economic development: Studies in international poverty. New York: Oxford University Press, 1970.

68. Miyazawa. Input-output analysis and the structure of income distribution. New York: Springer-Verlag, 1976.

69. Morawetz, D. "Employment implications of industrialization in developing countries: A survey." EJ, September 1974.

70. Morgan, T. "The distribution of income in Ceylon, Puerto Rico, the United States, and the United Kingdom." EJ, March 1953, pp. 821-834.

71. Morley, S. and G. Smith. "The effects of changes in the distribution of income on labor, foreign investment and growth in Brazil." In Authoritarian Brazil - Origins, Policies and Future (A. Stepan, ed.), New Haven, Conn.: Yale University Press, 1973.

72. Myrdal, G. Asian drama: An inquiry into the poverty of nations. New York: Pantheon, 1968.

73. Oshima, H. "Labor force 'explosion' and the labor-intensive sector in Asian growth." EDCC, January 1971.

74. Paukert, F. and J. Skolka. Redistribution of income, patterns of consumption and employment: A framework for analysis. Geneva, September 1972.

75. Robinson, S. "Towards an adequate long-run model on income distribution and economic development." AER, May 1976, pp. 122-128.

76. Schumacher. Small is beautiful: Economics as if people mattered. New York: Harper and Row, 1976.

77. Seers, D. "What are we trying to measure." In special issue of development indicators of Journal of Development Studies, April 1973.

78. Singh, P. "Input-output analysis: An appraisal in the context of as yet an unconfirmed experiment in Kenya." Review of Income and Wealth, Series 18, No. 4, December 1972, pp. 393-399.

79. Slater, C., G. Walsham, and M. Shah. A systems simulation of the developing Kenyan economy, 1970-1978. Boulder, Colorado: Westview Press, 1977.

80. Soligo, R. "Factor intensity of consumption patterns, income distribution and employment growth in Pakistan." (Program for development studies, Paper No. 46). Texas: Rice University, 1973.

81. Sunman, T. "Short-run effects of income distribution on some macro-economic variables: The case of Turkey." (Program for development studies, Paper No. 46). Texas: Rice University, 1973.

82. Szaal, Richard. "Methodology for the evaluation and adjustment of income distribution data." (Research program in economic development, Discussion Paper No. 54). Princeton University, 1975.

83. Tobin, James. "Capital-output ratios for Kenya." Institute of Development Studies, Discussion Paper, Nairobi, 1972.

84. Thorbecke, E. and J. Sengupta. A consistency framework for employment, output and income distribution applied to Columbia. Paper prepared for the Development Research Center of the World Bank, January 1972.

85. Thorbecke, E. "The employment problem: A critical evaluation of four ILO comprehensive country reports." International Labor Review, 107, No. 5, pp. 393-423.

86. Thorbecke, E. and G. Pyatt. Planning techniques for a better future. Geneva, ILO, 1976.

87. Tinbergen, J. "The impact of education on income distribution." Review of Income and Wealth, Series 18, No. 3, September 1972, pp. 255-267.

88. Tokman, V.E. "Income distribution, technology and employment in developing countries: An application to Equador." JDE, March 1975.

89. Weiskoff, R. "Income distribution and economic growth in Puerto Rico, Argentina, and Mexico." Review of Income and Wealth, December 1970.

90. Whitelaw, W. and G. Johnson. "Rural-urban income transfers in Kenya." EDCC, April 1974, pp. 473-480.

91. World Bank. Into the second decade: A report of a World Bank mission to Kenya. Johns Hopkins University Press, 1975.

92. Yotopoulos, P. and J. Nugent. Economics of development: Empirical investigations. New York: Harper and Row, 1976.